Spatial Cognition and Computation
An Interdisciplinary Journal

Volume 3, Number 2 & 3, 2003

Special Issue:
Spatial Vagueness, Uncertainty and Granularity

Psychology Press
Taylor & Francis Group

New York   London

Editorial

Within computer programs, spatial information is normally represented in terms of idealised mathematical structures, typically some kind of coordinate geometry. But from the human perspective, coordinate representations are for many purposes inappropriate. Perhaps the main reason for this is that we rarely posses definite and completely accurate information about spatial situations. A further important factor is ease of communication: spelling out all spatial concepts in precise geometrical detail would make language cumbersome and long-winded.

The concepts ordinarily employed in natural language seem tailored to overcome these problems. Our vocabulary enables us to describe spatial properties and relationships in a way that avoids unknown and superfluous detail, while at the same time conveying those aspects of spatial information that are relevant to human activity. So, when we describe a mountain as 'very tall' or a pub as 'within walking distance', the usefulness of our communication is not greatly impaired by its lack of precision. But the mechanism by which human language achieves this capability is poorly understood and it is doubtful whether it is adequately captured by any existing formal analysis. This is a serious problem, since for many computational applications we would like to map between informal descriptions of spatial information and the digital representations employed to store and manipulate data.

Intrinsic to natural language is the presence of *vagueness* in the terminology employed and the use of *granular* abstractions that avoid commitment to irrelevant details. Both these phenomena lead to *uncertainty* in the relationship between natural descriptions and precise models of reality. But equally, vagueness and granularity also serve to facilitate communication despite ignorance of precise details. Hence, an analysis of vagueness and granularity and their relationship to uncertainty is essential to any theoretical treatment of natural forms of spatial description.

In computer science as a whole, the dominant approach to handling vagueness is *fuzzy logic* (Zadeh, 1975), which associates degrees of vagueness with numerical quantities akin to probabilities. A less well-known approach is that of *supervaluationism* (Fine, 1975, Williamson, 1994) according to which the semantics of vague terms is analysed in terms of multiple precise interpretations. It is as yet unclear whether there is a single uniform approach which can handle all manifestations of vagueness, uncertainty and granularity or whether a multiplicity of distinct semantic mechanisms are involved. Moreover, there is relatively little published literature that applies established general theories to the specific domain of spatial information.

The advent of computerised geographic information systems (GIS) has given rise to a practical need to represent spatial data in a way that: a) is able to consistently and robustly take account of possible uncertainty and errors in spatial data, and b) is directly accessible to computer users. The first of these requirements has received the most attention, and been met with the most success. There is a large literature on error handling in spatial information systems (e.g., Heuvelink, 1998, Worboys, 1998). But the need for accessibility to human users has exposed deep problems in relating formal spatial representations to informal concepts and modes of expression. The difficulties have been recognised and investigated by a number of researchers in geographic information science (Goodchild, 1993, Burrough and Frank, 1996) and also by certain philosophers (cf. Varzi, 2001). However, especially in the treatment vague and granular spatial information, many unresolved issues remain.

This special issue of *Spatial Cognition and Computation* collects enhanced and extended versions of papers that were presented at the Symposium on Spatial Vagueness, Uncertainty and Granularity, which was held at Ogunquit, Maine, in October 2001 (in conjunction with the FOIS-01 conference on Formal Ontology in Information Systems).[1] In fact for a while the time and place of the symposium were themselves very uncertain. Originally the event was to be held in conjunction with COSIT-01 on September 17th 2001, but was cancelled and rescheduled due to the events of September 11th.

The papers examine fundamental problems in the analysis of spatial vagueness, uncertainty and granularity from a variety of theoretical and methodological perspectives:

Galton (2003) looks at the ways in which spatial attributes of regions vary according to the level of granularity at which they are represented. Stell (2003) gives a qualitative classification of the extents of spatio-temporal regions relative to the cells of a granular representation. This is used to characterise the effects of further coarsening of a granular representation.

Bittner and Smith (2003) propose that a supervaluationistic theory of 'granular partitions' can be used to provide an analysis of spatial judgements that involve the

---

[1]The organisation of this event was partially supported by the EPSRC under grant GR/M56807.

use of vague singular terms, such as 'Mount Everest', whose spatial extension is not precisely definable. Kulik (2003) also employs a multiple valuation approach to describing spatial regions with vague extensions. This is applied in particular to the geographically important case where there is a vague transition between two types of land cover. This problem is also tackled by Kronenfeld (2003) using the framework of fuzzy sets.

Complementing the formal approaches of the previous papers, Montello, Goodchild, Gottsegen, and Fohl (2003) take an empirical approach to the analysis of vague concepts by surveying human interpretations of vague region descriptions. A similar methodology is employed by Zhan (2003), who looks at human judgements about degrees of spatial overlap.

Guesgen, Hertzberg, Lobb, and Mantler (2003) investigate the use of fuzzy buffering of raster maps to provide a flexible means of identifying locations in terms of their being near to or far from certain geographic features. The paper also presents a novel implementation method by showing how fuzzy buffering operations can be computed by means of the 'z-buffering' functionality supported by high-powered but widely available graphics chips.

We thank the editors of *Spatial Cognition and Computation* for the opportunity to publish this selection of papers, which we hope will catalise further investigations in this growing sub-field of the theory of spatial information.

Brandon Bennett, Leeds
Matteo Cristani, Verona

References

Bittner, T. and Smith, B. (2003). Vague reference and approximating judgments. *Spatial Cognition and Computation, 3,* 137–156.

Burrough, P. and Frank, A. (Eds.) (1996). *Geographical Objects with Undetermined Boundaries* (GISDATA). London: Taylor and Francis.

Fine, K. (1975). Vagueness, truth and logic. *Synthèse, 30,* 263–300.

Galton, A. (2003). Granularity-sensitive spatial attributes, *Spatial Cognition and Computation, 3,* 97–118.

Goodchild, M. F. (1993). Data models and data quality: problems and prospects. In M. F. Goodchild, B. O. Parks and L. T. Steyaert (Eds.), *Visualization in geographical information systems* (pp. 141–149). New York: John Wiley.

Guesgen, H. W., Hertzberg, J., Lobb, R. and Mantler, A. (2003). Buffering fuzzy maps in GIS. *Spatial Cognition and Computation, 3,* 205–220.

Heuvelink, G. B. (1998). *Error propagation in environmental modelling with GIS.* London: Taylor and Francis.

Kronenfeld, B. J. (2003). Implications of a data reduction framework to assignment of fuzzy membership values in continuous class maps. *Spatial Cognition and Computation, 3,* 221–237.

Kulik, L. (2003). Spatial vagueness and second-order vagueness. *Spatial Cognition and Computation, 3,* 157–183.

Montello, D. R., Goodchild, M. F., Gottsegen, J. and Fohl, P. (2003). Where's downtown?: Behavioral methods for determining referents of vague spatial queries. *Spatial Cognition and Computation, 3,* 185–204.

Stell, J. G. (2003). Qualitative extents for spatio-temporal granularity. *Spatial Cognition and Computation, 3,* 119–136.

Varzi, A. (ed.) (2001). *Topoi: special issue on the philosophy of geography, Vol. 20(2).* Kluwer.

Williamson, T. (1994). *Vagueness.* London: Routledge.

Worboys, M. F. (1998). Imprecision in finite resolution spatial data. *Geoinformatica, 2(3),* 257–280.

Zadeh, L. A. (1975). Fuzzy logic and approximate reasoning. *Synthese, 30,* 407–428.

Zhan, F. B. (2003). Cognitive evidence of vagueness associated with some linguistic terms in descriptions of spatial relations. *Spatial Cognition and Computation 3,* 239–255.

Granularity-sensitive Spatial Attributes

Antony Galton
University of Exeter

We investigate the effect of granulation on the spatial attributes of regions it is applied to. An informal illustrative treatment, using a single specific granulation and a variety of regions illustrating some key spatial attributes, is followed by a more rigorous theoretical development in which granulations are defined in terms of equivalence relations on the source space. It is found that many spatial attributes are *both-ways granularity-sensitive*, meaning that the attributes may be gained by some regions, but lost by others, under the same granulation.

Keywords: granulation, spatial attributes

1 Introduction

A *granulation*, in the sense that the term is used in this paper, is a mapping from a continuous source space into a discrete target space. Typically, this will be a many-to-one mapping, with the result that information present in the source space is lost under granulation. The particular concern of this paper is the behaviour of various spatial attributes under granulation. The attributes in question are qualitative properties and relations of regions in the source and target spaces. The formal theory will need to specify what is meant by a 'region' in each space, and what is meant by the 'same' property or relation for these two classes of regions.

A spatial attribute A may be *lost* under a given granulation g if there is a region R in the source space such that R possesses attribute A but its image $g(R)$ under the granulation does not. Likewise, A may be *gained* under g if there is a region R which does not possess A although its image $g(R)$ does. In the case of an attribute expressed by a binary relation, we must refer to two regions in the source space, but the essential idea is the same. We shall describe an attribute as *upward*

Correspondence concerning this article should be addressed to Antony Galton, School of Engineering and Computer Science, University of Exeter, Exeter EX4 4QF, UK email: A.P.Galton@exeter.ac.uk

granularity sensitive if it can be lost under granulation, and *downward granularity sensitive* if it can be gained. Some attributes may be both gained and lost under the same granulation, and these are referred to as *both-ways granularity-sensitive*.

Granularity-sensitivity matters because its presence is indicative of falsification: a granular representation is not veridical with respect to those attributes which are sensitive to the granulation which produced it. Granularity-sensitivity is a special case of the more general phenomenon of resolution-sensitivity, where by *resolution* is meant some measure of the level of discriminable detail present in an image or representation. The spatial attributes that an object is portrayed as having are heavily dependent on the resolution of the representation. A binary star may appear as a single point of light when looked at with the naked eye, but as two separate points of light when looked at through a telescope. From a distance a swarm of bees looks like a wisp of smoke, homogeneous in texture, but from closer up it resolves into many discrete individuals. These may be called *resolution effects*; they arise when one and the same object is ascribed contradictory attributes when represented at different resolutions. When the difference in resolution is attributable to granulation, we may refer to *granularity effects*.

The purpose of this paper is to investigate which spatial attributes are granularity-sensitive, i.e., susceptible to granularity effects. In Section 2, a range of spatial attributes is surveyed to investigate the extent of their granularity-sensitivity under one specific granulation. It turns out that surprisingly many spatial attributes are both-ways granularity-sensitive. The treatment here is discursive and informal. In Section 3, a more formal theory of granulations is developed, and the granularity-sensitivity of certain attributes is investigated in this more general setting. This will not be a comprehensive investigation, but is intended to establish a framework for further researches.

2 Some Examples of Granularity-sensitivity

This section systematically surveys the spatial attributes of regions, in each case giving examples where the value of the attribute is changed as a result of granulation. The list of attributes to be surveyed, which is based on that given in Galton (2000), is as follows:

1. Geometrical properties

    (a) Topological properties
        i. Dimension
        ii. Connectivity
    (b) Metrical properties
        i. Intrinsic properties
            A. Size

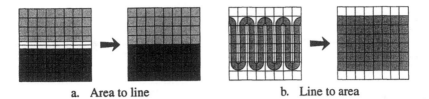

a. Area to line   b. Line to area

Figure 1. Change in dimension under granulation.

    B. Shape
ii. Extrinsic properties
    A. Location
    B. Orientation

2. Material properties

  (a) Texture

  (b) Gradation

  (c) Existence

'Material properties' is a miscellaneous residual category for all those attributes which cannot easily be characterised in purely spatial terms, requiring reference also to the material nature of the space-occupying entity.

The spatial regions whose attributes are to be considered are subsets of a fixed square planar region; they will be indicated by means of grey shading in the diagrams. The regions are assumed to be crisp in the sense that each space point is either in the region (including its boundary) or not. The granulation to be used is defined by the following discretisation procedure: the square area under consideration is divided into an 8 × 8 square grid, and a grid square is shaded if and only if *more than half* of its area is contained in the region (the ">50%" rule). The target space thus consists of 64 cells in an 8 × 8 array. The examples provided are simple, but they serve very effectively to illustrate the possible behaviour of the spatial attributes under granulation. Each sub-section below considers one spatial attribute.

2.1 Dimension

In Figure 1a the left-hand diagram shows two regions (differently shaded) with a narrow channel between them. This channel is a two-dimensional area, although its long thin form readily lends itself to conceptualisation as a one-dimensional line. This is reflected in the discretisation shown in the right-hand diagram, where the channel has been reduced to the strictly one-dimensional interface along which

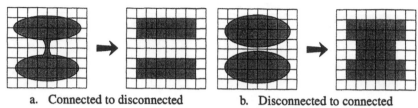

a. Connected to disconnected   b. Disconnected to connected

Figure 2. Change in connectivity under granulation.

the two regions now meet. Thus the number of dimensions of a feature has been modified from two to one as a result of granulation.

In Figure 1b, we have a feature which, though strictly two-dimensional (perhaps representing a meandering river with both length and breadth), is, like the channel in (a), readily conceptualised as linear. Under granulation, however, the meanders merge to produce a rectangular area that conspicuously resists such reconceptualisation. The number of dimensions (in this case the effective rather than strict dimensionality) is increased from one to two as a result of granulation.

2.2 Connectivity

In Figure 2a, the left-hand illustration shows a connected region consisting of two elliptical areas joined by a narrow isthmus. Under granulation, as shown in the right-hand illustration, the isthmus disappears from view, with the result that the region is now portrayed as disconnected.

Conversely, in Figure 2b, a disconnected region is portrayed as connected under granulation, the reason being that the channel separating the two components is too narrow to show up in the granular representation.

2.3 Size

The size of a region might be measured in various ways. An obvious choice for two-dimensional regions is area. It is easiest to illustrate a granulation effect on *relative* size. In Figure 3 are shown, in the left-hand illustration, two circular regions, one larger than the other. Under granulation, the size relationship is reversed.[1] Of course, this phenomenon is dependent on the way the circles are positioned in relation to the discretisation grid. But the point is that once we have decided where the grid to be placed, and what procedure is to be used for carrying out the discretisation, the consequences are inescapable. This has implications

---

[1]The smaller circle has a radius equal to four-fifths of the side of a grid square; the area of one quadrant is then 0.503 of a square — so each quadrant shows up as a complete square under the ">50%" granulation.

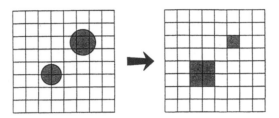

Figure 3. Change in relative size under granulation.

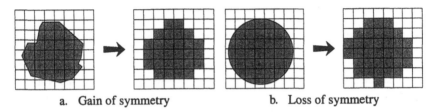

  a. Gain of symmetry   b. Loss of symmetry

Figure 4. Change in symmetry under granulation.

for any automated map-generalisation process: it will inevitably produce some results at variance with what the map-maker really wants to express. In such cases, there seems to be no alternative but to regard the automated process as merely a preliminary stage, with further adjustments to be performed manually.

2.4 Shape

Shape is notoriously difficult to characterise in terms of simple descriptors. This is because there are so many dimensions along which variation of shape is possible. This section will focus on just two aspects of shape which are comparatively straightforward to handle, namely symmetry and convexity.

There are many different types of symmetry, though in two dimensions the symmetry of a bounded figure can be characterised by the multiplicity of rotational symmetry and the presence or absence of reflectional symmetry. Both of these factors are granularity-sensitive, but here the different varieties of symmetry are ignored, and only the presence or absence of symmetry will be considered.

The shape in the left-hand illustration of Figure 4a lacks all symmetry. Under granulation it acquires a vertical axis of reflectional symmetry, as portrayed in the right-hand illustration. This kind of granularity-dependent symmetry gain is discussed by Clementini and di Felice (1997), under the description 'qualitative symmetry'.

Loss of symmetry is also possible, as shown in Figure 4b. Here a circular region (the most perfectly symmetrical of all plane figures!) is transformed under

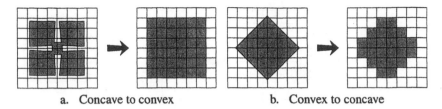

a. Concave to convex   b. Convex to concave

Figure 5. Change in convexity under granulation.

granulation to a figure lacking any symmetry. This loss of symmetry arises from the fact that the circle is asymmetrically situated with respect to the discretisation grid, and as such the loss of symmetry might be regarded as an artefact of the discretisation process. And of course it is! But this is really precisely what is at issue: all anomalous effects resulting from an algorithmic procedure for granulation can be regarded as 'artefacts' of that procedure. But some such effects might seem more grossly artificial than others, and one's intuitive feeling is that this kind of symmetry-loss is particularly bad in that respect. It is pertinent here to note that if the circle had been shifted slightly, so as to be situated symmetrically with respect to the grid, then the result of the discretisation would have retained some, though not all, of the original symmetry (namely just those symmetries which are shared by the grid itself: four-fold rotation and reflection).

The second element of shape to be considered is convexity. Figure 5 shows how it is possible, under granulation, both for a concave figure to become convex, and for a convex figure to become concave. The former case is more 'natural': we can say that the concavities are too small to show up under the coarser grain, and it is entirely reasonable to drop them. In the latter case we once again see a phenomenon which there is a strong temptation to dismiss as an artefact. The concavities which have appeared simply result from the fact that the edges of the grid elements all meet at right angles, so that it is impossible to duplicate accurately the 45° gradients found in the original figure. But this observation points to a deeper problem: how can the notion of convexity be defined in a discrete space? One obvious solution (Sklansky, Cordella & Levialdi, 1976) is to define a region of discrete space to be convex if and only if it is the image under discretisation of some genuinely convex region in continuous space (it will also, of course, be the image of countless non-convex regions as well). This definition is tailor-made to discredit the supposed loss of convexity in Figure 5b, since it has the consequence that *any* digital image of a convex region must count as convex. Here, then, is a case where, at least under one interpretation, a spatial attribute is granularity-sensitive in one direction only. Some of the other attributes considered in this section might be remodelled in a similar way by defining the discrete form

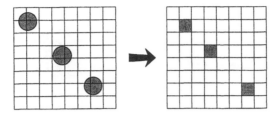

Figure 6. The relative distance of three regions changes under discretisation.

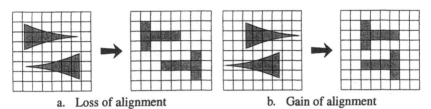

a. Loss of alignment   b. Gain of alignment

Figure 7. Change in north-south alignment under granulation.

of the attribute in terms of how the continuous form behaves under all possible discretisations.

2.5 Location

One aspect of location is *relative distance*. In the left-hand illustration of Figure 6 are seen three circular 'islands' aligned along a NW-SE axis so that the middle island is closer to the south-eastern island than to the north-western one. Under granulation, shown in the right-hand illustration, this relationship is reversed.

Another aspect of location is *alignment*. In the left-hand illustration of Figure 7a are shown two regions which are perfectly aligned with respect to the north-south axis: that is, their easternmost points have the same longitude, as do their westernmost points. Under granulation, as seen in the right-hand illustration, the two figures no longer appear to be aligned in this way. Conversely, in Figure 7b, we see that initially unaligned regions can appear perfectly aligned after granulation.

2.6 Orientation

By the orientation of a figure is meant that property which is preserved under translation and scaling but altered under rotation. Strictly speaking, the orientation of two figures can only be compared if the figures are geometrically similar. Since our granulation procedure usually results in a figure that is not similar to the

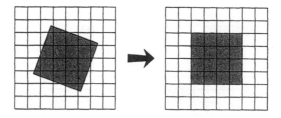

Figure 8. Rotation as a result of granulation.

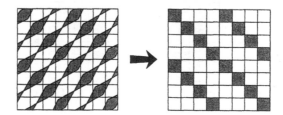

Figure 9. Direction of stripes changes under granulation.

original, the scope for illustrating orientation change under granulation is limited. However, Figure 8 shows a case in which the image of a square under granulation is rotated through 20° relative to its original position — a curious result, to be sure, though perhaps not one of great practical significance.

2.7 Texture

Texture is concerned with the pattern of distribution of repeated units over an area of space. In Figure 9 we can see how under granulation a texture in the form of parallel stripes running from north-east to south-west becomes remodelled in the form of stripes running from north-west to south-east. Of course, how one describes a texture is to some extent dependent on the rather fickle nature of our perceptions, and it is certainly possible to perceive the north-west to south-east stripes as already present in the left-hand diagram. But the fact remains that the *connections* between the repeating units support the descriptions originally given above. (As a matter of fact, it is easiest to see the north-west to south-east stripes in the left-hand picture by viewing it from a distance, or with the eyes screwed up, thereby inducing a natural granularity effect.)

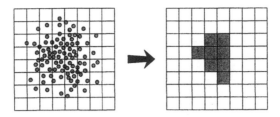

Figure 10. Gradation of population density is sharpened under granulation.

2.8 Gradation

This section considers spatial entities which in some sense lack clear-cut boundaries, so that the presence or absence of the entity over spatial locations exhibits some form of gradation. The various forms that such gradation can take have been analysed in some detail by Plewe (1997), who in particular draws attention to the fact that, in our terminology, gradedness is a granularity-sensitive phenomenon. This is illustrated here (Figure 10) by means of an *agglomeration* (Smith, 1999), consisting of a large number of small units, represented in our diagram as circles (these could be, for example, trees — the entity in question being a portion of woodland grading into the untreed surrounding area). Under discretisation, the gradation in population density is sharpened to an all-or-nothing crisp boundary between 'densely' and 'sparsely' populated areas.

2.9 Existence

Philosophers may look askance at our including existence in the catalogue of spatial attributes. A non-existent thing is not, after all, a thing. None the less, when it comes to *representations* of things, it is an important issue. A feature which exists in one representation may not exist in another. The world is full of islands too small to show up on most maps, but of course, the non-existence of a representation is not the same as a representation of non-existence. (On the other hand, the fact that an atlas does not show a land-mass twice the size of Great Britain in the middle of the Atlantic Ocean may be indicative of the map-makers' intention to inform us that no such land-mass exists.)

Figure 11 shows how an entire archipelago can vanish under our granulation process. Not one of the grid squares is more than half filled with land, and hence no land is shown. The reverse transformation, from non-existence to existence, does not occur, unless we include under this description, for example, the appearance of a mythical land-bridge joining the two islands in Figure 2b.

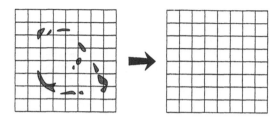

Figure 11. An archipelago disappears under discretisation.

3 Towards a Formal Theory of Granularity

The granulation considered in the previous section used a specific way of dividing up the source space (as an 8×8 grid), and also a specific procedure for selecting cells of the target space to form part of the image (the ">50%" rule). Either or both of these specific details can be varied. To take them in reverse order, it is obvious that different results might be obtained if we replaced the ">50%" condition by other conditions having the form ">P%" or "$\geq P$%". At the extremes, we have the rule ">0%", which includes in the granulation any cell which overlaps the region, by however small an amount, and the rule "$\geq$100%", which only includes in the granulation those cells entirely contained in the region. These two extremes are closely related to the inner and outer approximations familiar from the theory of rough sets (Pawlak, 1991). As to the division of the source space, one can obviously choose a coarser or finer square grid, or one could move to a different form of tessellation, e.g., hexagonal or triangular, or beyond that one could choose any number of more or less irregular ways of dividing up the area of interest. At the most general, we can say that granulation involves selecting an equivalence relation E on the source space (universe) U and taking the equivalence classes as the units of the granulation grid. This approach will be followed below.

3.1 Region-based Granularity

First, though, the notion of granulation is introduced in a still more general setting in which, since the objects of interest are regions, we do not consider the space to be made up of indivisible units at all, but rather take regions as primitive entities. We postulate a set $\mathcal{R}$ of regions, including amongst its members a *null region* $\perp$ and a *universal region* $\top \neq \perp$, with a reflexive, antisymmetric and transitive *parthood* relation $\leq$ such that for all $R \in \mathcal{R}$, $\perp \leq R \leq \top$. Thus in full, we have a structure $(\mathcal{R}, \perp, \top, \leq)$.

In this setting, we define a *granulation* on $\mathcal{R}$ to be a surjective mapping g :

$\mathcal{R} \to \mathcal{R}'$ (where $\mathcal{R}'$ is also a set of regions) such that for all $R_1, R_2 \in \mathcal{R}$,

$$R_1 \leq R_2 \implies g(R_1) \leq g(R_2).$$

Note that this means that $g(\perp) = \perp'$ and $g(\top) = \top'$ are the bottom and top elements of $\mathcal{R}'$. Let $G_{\mathcal{R}}$ be the set of all granulations on $\mathcal{R}$.

We define a partial order $\preceq$ on $G_{\mathcal{R}}$ as follows:

$$g_1 \preceq g_2 =_{\text{def}} \forall R, R' \in \mathcal{R}(g_2(R) = g_2(R') \to g_1(R) = g_1(R')).$$

In other words, regions that are indistinguishable under g_2 are also indistinguishable under g_1. Thus $g_1 \preceq g_2$ means that g_1 has lower resolution (or higher granularity) than g_2.

The top of the resolution scale is the *identity granulation* $g_{id} : \mathcal{R} \to \mathcal{R}$ defined by $\forall R \in \mathcal{R}(g_{id}(R) = R)$.

Since $\top \neq \perp$ we cannot have $g(\top) = g(\perp)$ (otherwise the target set $\mathcal{R}'$ would not, after all, be a set of regions), so there is no unique bottom element in the resolution scale. Instead, we single out for attention the granulations $g_{\perp}$ and $g_{\top}$ defined as follows:

$$g_{\perp}(R) = \left\{ \begin{array}{ll} \top & \text{(if } R = \top) \\ \perp & \text{(otherwise)} \end{array} \right.$$

$$g_{\top}(R) = \left\{ \begin{array}{ll} \perp & \text{(if } R = \perp) \\ \top & \text{(otherwise)} \end{array} \right.$$

In general the class of granulations mapping $\mathcal{R}$ to $\{\perp, \top\}$ is equivalent to the class of *upward hereditary* attributes on $\mathcal{R}$, that is, attributes which apply to a region whenever they apply to any of its subregions.

3.2   Point-based Granularity

In the previous subsection regions and granulations were characterised in an extremely general way. To progress further, it is convenient to focus on a more specific model in which, while regions remain the main focus of interest, they are no longer regarded as primitives, being instead identified with sets of points. Let U be the universe of points; then a region is identified with a set of points $R \subseteq U$. We do not necessarily wish to regard every subset of U as a region, so we let $\mathcal{R} \subseteq 2^U$.

3.3   Granulations from Equivalence Classes

Following Stell (1999), granulations will be generated using equivalence relations on U. Let $E \subseteq U \times U$ be an equivalence relation, and let U_E be the corresponding set of equivalence classes. Then E gives rise to a class of granulations G_E as follows:

- The *outer granulation* $g_E{\uparrow} : \mathcal{R} \to 2^{U_E}$ is defined by

$$g_E{\uparrow}(R) = \{X \in U_E \mid X \cap R \neq \emptyset\}.$$

- The *inner granulation* $g_E{\downarrow} : \mathcal{R} \to 2^{U_E}$ is defined by

$$g_E{\downarrow}(R) = \{X \in U_E \mid X \subseteq R\}.$$

These are standard definitions in the theory of rough sets. Note that we always have $g_E{\downarrow}(R) \subseteq g_E{\uparrow}(R)$, and also $\bigcup g_E{\downarrow}(R) \subseteq R \subseteq \bigcup g_E{\uparrow}(R)$.

An E-granulation is then any function $g : \mathcal{R} \to 2^{U_E}$ with the properties

1. $\forall R \in \mathcal{R}(g_E{\downarrow}(R) \subseteq g(R) \subseteq g_E{\uparrow}(R))$

2. $\forall R, R' \in \mathcal{R}(R \subseteq R' \to g(R) \subseteq g(R'))$

The E-granulations include the "$>P\%$" granulations $g_E^{>P\%}$ defined by

$$g_E^{>P\%}(R) = \left\{ X \in U_E \ \middle| \ \frac{|X \cap R|}{|X|} > \frac{P}{100} \right\},$$

where $|X|$ is some suitable measure of the "size" of X — for the case $U = \mathbb{R}^2$, this will be area. In this case, if we assume that regions are regular open sets, then $g_E{\uparrow} = g_E^{>0\%}$, and in general we have

$$P > Q \to g_E{\downarrow} \subseteq g_E^{>P\%} \subseteq g_E^{>Q\%} \subseteq g_E{\uparrow}.$$

The granulation used for illustrative purposes in §2 was $g_E^{>50\%}$, where E is an equivalence relation which partitions the unit square into the 8×8 chessboard pattern (the allocation of points along the cell boundaries is irrelevant since we are working with regular regions here).

Slightly different are the "$\geq P\%$" granulations $g_E^{\geq P\%}$ defined in the obvious way, giving $g_E{\downarrow} = g_E^{\geq 100\%}$ when the regions are regular.

Note that with this model of granulation, the granular region $g_E(R) \subseteq U_E$ can be "projected back" into the source space as the region $\bigcup g_E(R) \subseteq U$, and thus becomes subject to the possibility of further granulation (in effect, this is the way the granulations were portrayed in the diagrams of Section 2). Although it is not considered further in this paper, this observation could become important if the investigation were to be extended to a consideration of the behaviour of sequential compositions of granulations.

3.4 Resolution

We can define a resolution order on equivalence relations by

$$E_1 \sqsubseteq E_2 =_{\text{def}} \forall p, q \in U(pE_2q \to pE_1q).$$

This says that E_2 partitions U at least as finely as E_1 does.

Theorem 1 *If $E_1 \sqsubseteq E_2$ then each element of U_{E_1} is a union of elements of U_{E_2}.*

Proof. Let $X \in U_{E_1}$, let $p \in X$, and choose $Y \in U_{E_2}$ so that $p \in Y$ (this must be possible since E_2 partitions U). Then for any $q \in Y$ we have pE_2q and therefore (since $E_1 \sqsubseteq E_2$) pE_1q. Hence $q \in X$. Therefore $Y \subseteq X$. We now have

$$\bigcup \{Y \in U_{E_2} \mid X \cap Y \neq \emptyset\} \subseteq X.$$

For the reverse inclusion, we note that for any $p \in X$, with Y chosen as above, we have $p \in X \cap Y$. □

We single out for special mention two particular equivalence relations on U. Define $E_\perp$ so that $pE_\perp q$ for all pairs $p, q \in U$, so $U_{E_\perp} = \{U\}$; and define $E_\top$ so that $pE_\top q$ if and only if $p = q$, so $U_{E_\top} = \{\{x\} \mid x \in U\}$. We introduce the notation

$$\hat{X} =_{\text{def}} \{\{x\} \mid x \in X\}.$$

Note there is a natural bijection between X and $\hat{X}$: for many purposes they could be regarded as the same set.[2] We now have $U_{E_\top} = \hat{U}$.

What are the granulations generated by these relations like? We have

$$g_{E_\perp}\!\uparrow(R) = \begin{cases} \emptyset & \text{(if } R = \emptyset) \\ \{U\} & \text{(otherwise)} \end{cases}$$

so $g_{E_\perp}\!\uparrow$ is essentially $g_\top$ of the region-based system (with $\emptyset$ and $\{U\}$ playing the roles of $\perp$ and $\top$ respectively).

$$g_{E_\perp}\!\downarrow(R) = \begin{cases} \{U\} & \text{(if } R = U) \\ \emptyset & \text{(otherwise)} \end{cases}$$

so $g_{E_\perp}\!\downarrow$ is essentially $g_\perp$ of the region-based system.

$$\begin{aligned} g_{E_\top}\!\uparrow(R) &= \{X \in U_{E_\top} \mid X \cap R \neq \emptyset\} \\ &= \{\{x\} \in \hat{U} \mid \{x\} \cap R \neq \emptyset\} \\ &= \{\{x\} \in \hat{U} \mid x \in R\} \\ &= \hat{R} \end{aligned}$$

so that $g_{E_\top}\!\uparrow$ is essentially (via the equivalence of R and $\hat{R}$) the identity granulation g_{id}. Similarly

$$\begin{aligned} g_{E_\top}\!\downarrow(R) &= \{\{x\} \in \hat{U} \mid \{x\} \subseteq R\} \\ &= \{\{x\} \in \hat{U} \mid x \in R\} \\ &= \hat{R} \end{aligned}$$

so $g_{E_\top}\!\downarrow = g_{E_\top}\!\uparrow$.

We next prove that under both outer and inner granulations, the lattice of equivalence relations maps homomorphically onto the lattice of granulations.

---

[2] In fact U is the "back-projection" of $\hat{U}$ as defined in Section 3.3.

Theorem 2 *If $E_1 \sqsubseteq E_2$ then $g_{E_1}\!\downarrow \preceq g_{E_2}\!\downarrow$.*

Proof. Let $E_1 \sqsubseteq E_2$ and suppose $g_{E_2}\!\downarrow(R) = g_{E_2}\!\downarrow(R')$. We must show that $g_{E_1}\!\downarrow(R) = g_{E_1}\!\downarrow(R')$.

Let $X \in g_{E_1}\!\downarrow(R)$, so $X \in U_{E_1}$ and $X \subseteq R$. Since $X \in U_{E_1}$ and $E_1 \sqsubseteq E_2$, $X \subseteq \bigcup W$ for some $W \subseteq U_{E_2}$, by Theorem 1. We shall show that each element of W is in $g_{E_2}\!\downarrow(R)$. Let $Y \in W$, so also $Y \subseteq X$ and $Y \in U_{E_2}$. Then since $X \subseteq R$, we have $Y \subseteq R$. Hence $Y \in g_{E_2}\!\downarrow(R)$ and therefore $Y \in g_{E_2}\!\downarrow(R')$ (since these sets are equal by hypothesis). We must now show that $X \in g_{E_1}\!\downarrow(R')$. Since $Y \in g_{E_2}\!\downarrow(R')$, $Y \subseteq R'$. Since this holds for all $Y \in W$, $\bigcup W \subseteq R'$, so $X \subseteq R'$. Now $X \in U_{E_1}$, so $X \in g_{E_1}\!\downarrow(R')$ and we have shown that $g_{E_1}\!\downarrow(R) \subseteq g_{E_1}\!\downarrow(R')$. The reverse inclusion follows by an exactly similar argument, so $g_{E_1}\!\downarrow(R) = g_{E_1}\!\downarrow(R')$. Hence $g_{E_1}\!\downarrow \preceq g_{E_2}\!\downarrow$. $\square$

Theorem 3 *If $E_1 \sqsubseteq E_2$ then $g_{E_1}\!\uparrow \preceq g_{E_2}\!\uparrow$.*

Proof. Let $E_1 \sqsubseteq E_2$ and suppose $g_{E_2}\!\uparrow(R) = g_{E_2}\!\uparrow(R')$. We must show that $g_{E_1}\!\uparrow(R) = g_{E_1}\!\uparrow(R')$.

Let $X \in g_{E_1}\!\uparrow(R)$, so $X \in U_{E_1}$ and $X \cap R \neq \emptyset$. Since $X \in U_{E_1}$, $X = \bigcup W$ for some $W \subseteq U_{E_2}$, by Theorem 1. We need some element of W to be in $g_{E_2}\!\uparrow(R)$. Since $X \cap R \neq \emptyset$, and $X = \bigcup W$, there must be a $Y \in W$ such that $Y \cap R \neq \emptyset$. Also, since $Y \in W$, $Y \in U_{E_2}$, so $Y \in g_{E_2}\!\uparrow(R)$, and hence $Y \in g_{E_2}\!\uparrow(R')$. We must show that $X \in g_{E_1}\!\uparrow(R')$. Since $Y \in g_{E_2}\!\uparrow(R')$, $Y \cap R' \neq \emptyset$, and since $Y \in W$, $\bigcup W \cap R' \neq \emptyset$, so $X \cap R' \neq \emptyset$. Moreover, since $X \in U_{E_1}$ it follows that $X \in g_{E_1}\!\uparrow(R')$. Thus $g_{E_1}\!\uparrow(R) \subseteq g_{E_1}\!\uparrow(R')$, and likewise conversely. Hence $g_{E_1}\!\uparrow(R) = g_{E_1}\!\uparrow(R')$, and $g_{E_1}\!\uparrow \preceq g_{E_2}\!\uparrow$. $\square$

4 Qualitative Properties and Relations

The goal of this section is to investigate the granularity-sensitivity of spatial attributes. A simple attribute of regions in U is just a subset of $\mathcal{R}$; likewise a relational attribute of regions in U is a subset of $\mathcal{R} \times \mathcal{R}$. We want to investigate how attributes behave under granulation. The problem is how to define the *same* attribute across all the universes U_E. We consider whether an attribute can be gained, lost, both, or neither as a result of granulation.

Before proceeding, we must make some definite decisions about regions. Whatever a region is, it is not an arbitrary set of points. It could be an open set of points, or a regular open set (that is, a set which is equal to the interior of its closure), or a regular closed set (equal to the closure of its interior), or an element of a more restricted class such as a polygon. All these possibilities have been suggested in the literature. Here we do not have space to explore all of these possibilities, and from now on we shall identify regions in U with *regular closed subsets* of U. This presupposes, of course, that U is endowed with a topology; later it will be necessary to place further restrictions on the kind of topology U should be assumed to have.

In keeping with this decision, we stipulate that the partition cells (elements of U_E) are *regular open subsets* of U. This means that the partition is not, in fact, exhaustive, since boundary points are now not assigned to any cell.[3] This does not matter, however, since any region (i.e., regular closed set) which contains a boundary point of a partition cell must also overlap at least one of the cells on whose boundary that point lies, and thus the boundary points can be ignored without affecting the essential overlap and containment relations between regions and partition cells.[4] The inclusions $\bigcup g_E{\downarrow}(R) \subseteq R \subseteq \bigcup g_E{\uparrow}(R)$ no longer hold as written; the former may be strengthened, and the latter must be weakened, giving

$$\mathrm{cl}(\textstyle\bigcup g_E{\downarrow}(R)) \subseteq R \subseteq \mathrm{cl}(\textstyle\bigcup g_E{\uparrow}(R)),$$

the closure operations restoring the 'missing' boundary points.

Finally, a region in U_E will be any collection of partition cells.

4.1 Parthood

Since regions are represented as sets, we can express the 'part of' relation by $R \subseteq R'$. By the definition of a granulation, $R \subseteq R'$ implies $g(R) \subseteq g(R')$, so parthood cannot be lost. But it can be gained.

Under outer granulation, it is clearly possible, even if $R \not\subseteq R'$, for every partition cell (i.e., element of U_E) overlapped by R to be overlapped by R', and in this case we have $g_E{\downarrow}(R) \subseteq g_E{\downarrow}(R')$, so parthood is gained. Under inner granulation, we can likewise have every partition cell contained in R also contained in R', even though R is not part of R'. Again, parthood is gained. More generally, it is possible for every partition cell of which more than $P\%$ is in R to have more than $P\%$ in R', even though R is not part of R'. Thus parthood can be gained under $>P\%$ granulation, for any P.

In contrast to parthood *tout court*, proper parthood, represented by $R \subset R'$, can be lost as well as gained. Suppose $R' = R \cup R''$, where $R \cap R'' = \emptyset$. Suppose further that R'' does not contain any complete partition cells, whereas R is (the closure of) a union of partition cells. Then $R \subset R'$; but under inner granulation we have, $g_E{\downarrow}(R) = g_E{\downarrow}(R') = R$. Hence proper parthood is lost. Similarly, if $R' = R \setminus R''$, where R consists of complete partition cells and R'' contains no complete partition cells, then $R' \subset R$, but under outer granulation we

---

[3]Note that this constraint means that many equivalence relations on U are now disqualified from forming the basis of a granulation partition; in particular, the identity relation E_T can no longer be used for this purpose.

[4]In fact the partition is "quasi-exhaustive" in the sense that U is the *regular union* of U_E, i.e., the interior of the closure of the set-theoretic union.

have $g_E\uparrow(R) = g_E\uparrow(R') = R'$. Again proper parthood is lost. Notice that since parthood cannot be lost, loss of proper parthood implies gain of another attribute, namely equality.

4.2 Overlap

Two regions overlap so long as they contain a common subregion, i.e., for $R, R' \in \mathcal{R}$,

$$O(R, R') =_{\text{def}} \exists R'' \in \mathcal{R}(R'' \subseteq R \cap R').$$

Note that in U, set-theoretic overlap, $R \cap R' \neq \emptyset$, is a necessary but not sufficient condition for region overlap. On the other hand, a region in U_E is identified with any set of partition cells, so that in this case the condition $R \cap R' \neq \emptyset$ is both necessary and sufficient — so overlap in U_E means having at least one partition cell in common.

Under outer granulation, overlap can be gained but not lost. If $R \cap R' = \emptyset$ (so $\neg O(R, R')$), but some partition cell overlaps both R and R', then that cell is in $g_E\uparrow(R) \cap g_E\uparrow(R')$, so overlap is gained. On the other hand, if $R'' \subseteq R \cap R'$, so $O(R, R')$, then any cell overlapping R'' is in $g_E\uparrow(R) \cap g_E\uparrow(R')$, so overlap cannot be lost.

Under inner granulation, overlap can be lost but not gained. If $R'' \subseteq R \cap R'$ consists of incomplete partition cells, then $g_E\downarrow(R) \cap g_E\downarrow(R') = \emptyset$, so overlap is lost. But since any partition cell in $g_E\downarrow(R) \cap g_E\downarrow(R')$ is contained in $R \cap R'$, overlap cannot be gained.

What happens with the $P\%$ granulations? In order to have $g_E^{\geq P\%}(R) \cap g_E^{\geq P\%}(R') \neq \emptyset$, some partition cell must be such that more than $P\%$ of it falls in R and more than $P\%$ of it falls in R'. So long as $P < 50$, this is possible without R and R' overlapping. Thus overlap can be gained under any granulation $g_E^{\geq P\%}$ where $0 \leq P < 50$; and likewise under any $g_E^{\geq P\%}$ where $0 < P \leq 50$.

For loss of overlap, we require $R'' \subseteq R \cap R'$ but $g_E^{\geq P\%}(R) \cap g_E^{\geq P\%}(R') = \emptyset$. This can happen for any value of P satisfying $0 < P < 100$. All we require is that any partition cell overlapped by R'' is such that either at most $P\%$ of it falls within R or at most $P\%$ of it falls within R'.

4.3 Connection

For the regular closed regions in U, the binary connection relation $C(R, R')$ may be defined as point overlap, i.e., for $R, R' \in \mathcal{R}$,

$$C(R, R') =_{\text{def}} R \cap R' \neq \emptyset.$$

Since regions are closed, this is equivalent to $\text{cl}(R) \cap \text{cl}(R') \neq \emptyset$. (Note that had we defined our regions to be open sets or in some other way, then we should have had to correspondingly alter our definition of connection — see Cohn and Varzi (1998) for a discussion of different connection relations.)

For regions in U_E, since they are collections of open subsets of U, connection must be defined somewhat differently, as follows: for $X, Y \in 2^{U_E}$,

$$C(X, Y) =_{\text{def}} \exists P \in X \exists Q \in Y (\text{cl}(P) \cap \text{cl}(Q) \neq \emptyset).$$

Thus two regions in U_E are connected so long as they either overlap (in which case we can put $P = Q$ in the above definition) or some element of one is adjacent to an element of the other (i.e., they contain neighbouring partition cells).

Under outer granulation, connection can be gained but not lost. To see that it cannot be lost, suppose we have $C(R, R')$, so $R \cap R' \neq \emptyset$. Let $x \in R \cap R'$. There are two possibilities. If x is in the interior of a partition cell, then R and R' must both overlap that cell, so $g_E\uparrow(R)$ and $g_E\uparrow(R')$ both contain it, so $C(g_E\uparrow(R), g_E\uparrow(R'))$. Otherwise x is on the boundary between adjacent partition cells. Hence R and R' must each overlap at least one of the cells on whose boundary x lies, which means that some cell in $g_E\uparrow(R)$ must be connected (i.e., equal or adjacent) to some cell of $g_E\uparrow(R')$, so again we have $C(g_E\uparrow(R), g_E\uparrow(R'))$. Thus connection cannot be lost under outer granulation. It is obvious that connection can be gained, since all that is needed is for R and R', while not themselves connected, to overlap cells X and X', respectively, which *are* connected.

Under inner granulation, connection can be lost but not gained. Loss would occur if $R \cap R'$ only overlaps cells which are completely contained in neither R nor R'. If $g_E\downarrow(R)$ and $g_E\downarrow(R')$ contain cells X and X' respectively, where X is connected to X', then R contains X and R' contains X', so $R \cap R' \neq \emptyset$ (since it includes $cl(X) \cap cl(X') \neq \emptyset$). Hence $C(R, R')$, so connection cannot be lost.

Turning now to the ">$P\%$" granulations, for $P > 0$, connection can be lost. All that is required is to have regions R and R' meeting at a single point, x say, such that each of R and R' overlaps at most $P\%$ of the partition cell containing x (we need $P > 0$ here since R and R' must both overlap that partition cell, since it contains $x \in R \cap R'$). Then this cell will be absent from both $g_E^{\geq P\%}(R)$ and $g_E^{\geq P\%}(R')$, and hence $g_E^{\geq P\%}(R)$ will be disconnected from $g_E^{\geq P\%}(R')$.

For any $P < 100$, connection can be gained. For this to happen all we need is that, with R disconnected from R', there are two adjacent partition cells, one of which has more than $P\%$ in R and the other more than $P\%$ in R'.

Note that the behaviour of connection with respect to these different kinds of granulations is very similar to that of overlap. This is because, conceptually, these two relations are extremely close, in that, first, overlap implies connection, and second, for regular regions, external (i.e., non-overlapping) connection arises as the limiting case of overlap as the size of the overlap region decreases to zero.

4.4 Connectedness

Connectedness is a unary relation $c(R)$. In point-set topology, a set X is connected so long as whenever $X \subseteq O_1 \cup O_2$, where O_1 and O_2 are open and $X \not\subseteq O_1$ and $X \not\subseteq O_2$, we have $O_1 \cap O_2 \neq \emptyset$. How is connectedness related to connection? This depends on the nature of the regions, and also on the topological characteristics of the space in which they are defined.

With the regular closed regions in $\mathbb{R}^2$, the relationship is quite simple: R is connected to R' if and only if $R \cup R'$ is connected. The reason for this is that in $\mathbb{R}^2$, any pair of disjoint closed sets are contained within a disjoint pair of open sets. More generally this holds for any *normal* (T_4) topological space, this topological property being defined precisely by the possibility of separating disjoint closed sets in this way.

We shall assume now that $U = \mathbb{R}^2$, so $\mathcal{R}$ is the set of regular closed subsets of $\mathbb{R}^2$. Then a region $R \in \mathcal{R}$ is connected so long as it is not the union of two disjoint (i.e., disconnected) regions, that is, for $R \in \mathcal{R}$

$$c(R) =_{\text{def}} \forall R_1, R_2 (R = R_1 \cup R_2 \wedge R_1 \neq \emptyset \wedge R_2 \neq \emptyset \rightarrow C(R_1, R_2)).$$

We still need a definition of connectedness in U_E, and in fact it is quite natural to use the above definition in this case too, with the connection relation C understood as it applies to U_E.

We now investigate how connectedness, thus understood, behaves under granulation.

Under inner granulation, connectedness can be lost. For example, let $R = R_1 \cup R_2 \cup R_3$, where R is connected, but R_1 is not connected to R_2. Therefore R_3 supplies the connection between R_1 and R_2. Assume further that both R_1 and R_2 are unions of closures of partition cells, whereas R_3 does not contain any complete partition cells. Then $g_E \downarrow (R_3) = \emptyset$, and $g_E \downarrow (R) = g_E \downarrow (R_1) \cup g_E \downarrow (R_2)$ is disconnected. (Compare Figure 2(a).)

Connectedness can also be *gained* under inner granulation, through the loss of entire componenents. Let $R = R_1 \cup R_2$, where R_2 is a proper subset of some partition cell disconnected from R_1, and R_1 is the regular union of a connected set of partition cells. Then R is not connected, but $g_E \downarrow (R) = g_E \downarrow (R_1)$ is.

Under outer granulation, connectedness can be gained. For example, suppose $R = R_1 \cup R_2$, where R_1 is not connected to R_2 (so R is disconnected). Suppose further that R_1 overlaps a partition cell that is connected to a partition cell overlapped by R_2. Then $g_E \uparrow (R_1)$ is connected to $g_E \uparrow (R_2)$, so $g_E \uparrow (R)$ is connected. (Compare Figure 2(b).)

Can connectedness be lost under outer granulation? Suppose R is connected, and let $g_E \uparrow (R) = X_1 \cup X_2$ where $X_1 \neq \emptyset$ and $X_2 \neq \emptyset$. To lose connectedness it must be possible for X_1 to be disconnected from X_2. We have

$$R \subseteq \text{cl} \bigcup (g_E \uparrow (R)) = \text{cl} \bigcup (X_1 \cup X_2) = \text{cl}(\bigcup X_1 \cup \bigcup X_2)$$
$$= \text{cl}(\bigcup X_1) \cup \text{cl}(\bigcup X_2),$$

and since R is connected this means that $\text{cl}(\bigcup X_1)$ is connected to $\text{cl}(\bigcup X_2)$ in U. Hence X_1 is connected to X_2 in E_U, so $g_E \uparrow (R)$ is connected. Thus connectedness cannot be lost under outer granulation.

Under ">$P\%$" granulation, connectedness can be gained in two ways. First, let R consist of two connected components R_1 and R_2 such that $R_1 = R_1' \cup R_1''$ and $R_2 = R_2' \cup R_2''$, where R_1' and R_2' are the closures of unions of partition cells, and R_1'' and R_2'' are both entirely contained in a single cell, more than $P\%$ of which is covered by $R_1'' \cup R_2''$. Then that cell will be included in $g_E^{>P\%}(R)$, making the latter region connected. This can clearly happen for any $P \geq 0$.

The other possibility is to gain connectedness by losing all but one component. For any $P < 100$, we can have a disconnected region R consisting of, first, a component R_1 which includes more than $P\%$ of at least one partition cell, and second, one or more components each including no more than $P\%$ of any one partition cell. So long as no two components overlap a common cell, all but the first will disappear under $g_E^{>P\%}$, so $g_E^{>P\%}(R) = g_E^{>P\%}(R_1)$ is connected.

For loss of connection, all we require is that the connected set R consists of $R_1 \cup R_2 \cup R_3$, where R_1 and R_2 are closures of unions of partition cells, with $R_1 \cup R_2$ disconnected, and R_3 (which forms the partition between them) covering no more than $P\%$ of any cell. Under $g_E^{>P\%}$, R_1 and R_2 are retained but R_3 disappears, leaving the other two regions as components of the now disconnected $g_E^{>P\%}(R)$.

4.5 Summary

The results of this section are summarised in Table 1. "Upward" indicates that the attribute can be lost but not gained under the given type of granulation, "downward" that it can be gained but not lost, and "both" that it can both gained and lost.

5 Conclusions and Further Work

Section 2 demonstrated that many familiar qualitative spatial attributes exhibit granularity sensitivity under the ">50%" granulation, and that in most cases it is "both-ways" sensitivity, i.e., the attribute in question can be either lost or gained under granulation, depending on the particular regions involved.

Section 3 then established a formal framework within which questions of granularity-sensitivity can be investigated in a more rigorous, systematic, and

Table 1

Summary of Results

	Outer	>P%	Inner
Part	Downward	Downward	Downward
Proper part	Both	Both	Both
Overlap	Downward	Both ($P < 50$) / Upward ($P \geq 50$)	Upward
Connection	Downward	Both	Upward
Connectedness	Both	Both	Both

general way. Using this framework, a number of different spatial attributes were investigated to determine the nature of their granularity-sensitivity.

The investigation is incomplete in a number of ways, suggesting directions for further research. First, the attributes handled in the informal section were not the same as the attributes handled in the formal section. The former were chosen for their vividness as exemplars to stimulate the intuition and give the reader a good grasp of the issues involved. The latter were chosen as being particularly fundamental attributes for qualitative theories of space, as well as being particularly amenable to treatment within the formal framework. An obvious continuation of this work would be to investigate formally more of the attributes that have here been handled only informally. Just as, in order to handle connection and connectedness, we had to make some assumptions regarding the topology of the spaces and regions involved, so too, if we wished to investigate, for example, convexity, we would need to make sufficient further assumptions about the space to enable us to define convexity; and similarly with the other attributes.

Thinking more generally, it would be desirable to develop a way of classifying arbitrary spatial attributes with respect to granularity-sensitivity. The informal examples suggest a conjecture along the following lines: "All qualitative spatial attributes satisfying such-and-such conditions exhibit both-ways granularity-sensitivity with respect to some granulation from a given class". That some conditions must be imposed is clear from the results of the formal investigation in which the attribute 'part' was revealed as *not* exhibiting both-ways sensitivity under any of the granulations under consideration.

Why does any of this matter? Granularity effects, and resolution effects more generally, are *prima facie* undesirable. It is therefore important to know the conditions under which they can occur; this is necessary for us to be able to interpret, for example, the anomalous effects sometimes arising as a result of changing the computer screen resolution, or performing cartographic generalisation. Although, in practice, the range of operations involved in cartographic generalisation greatly exceeds the simple forms of granulation studied in this paper, the methods we have adopted suggest a possible approach in those cases too: for each generalisation operator that is precisely defined (as opposed to cases where the detailed application relies on the judgment of the human cartographer), it should be possible to investigate systematically which qualitative attributes are reliably preserved by the operator, and which are not. Information of this kind would be of obvious utility to both map-makers and map users.

But are granularity effects always undesirable? After all, it is to resolution and granularity effects that we can attribute our capacity for viewing complex, composite objects as unities. This is what enables us to conceive of a wood as a single connected entity as distinct from its constituent trees — so that a person may be *in the wood* without being in any of the trees — and likewise, at a finer granularity, to conceive of a tree as a single entity of much simpler form than the complex tangle of branches and leaves that compose it — so that a bird may be *in the tree* without being in any of the leaves or branches. In view of examples such as these, it seems clear that the very act of *conceptualising* the world at all involves the selection of appropriate levels of detail at which to represent it, the world 'in itself' being far too complex to be brought within the scope of our finite memory and information-processing capacities. The properties that we then ascribe to the bits of the world we conceptualise will be dependent on the granularity of our representation. Whether these property-ascriptions should be called 'true' or 'false' has to be judged in terms of the appropriateness of the chosen level of detail for the task in hand.

In conclusion, then, we may say that granularity effects are important because (i) they arise as an unavoidable by-product of lowering the level of detail in a spatial representation, (ii) they affect many of the major qualitative spatial attributes that are of interest to users of spatial representations, and (iii) the desirability or otherwise of such effects depends on the use to which representations at different granularity levels are to be put. Although these points were illustrated in relation to a single type of granulation, the formal development indicates that similar effects will arise under a wider range of possible granulations.

References

Clementini, E., & di Felice, P. (1997). A global framework for qualitative shape description. *GeoInformatica*, *1*, 11–27.

Cohn, A. G., & Varzi, A. C. (1998). Connection relations in mereotopology. In H. Prade (Ed.), *Proceedings of the Thirteenth European Conference on Artificial Intelligence ECAI 1998* (pp. 150–54). Chichester: John Wiley.

Galton, A. P. (2000). *Qualitative spatial change.* Oxford: Oxford University Press.

Pawlak, Z. (1991). *Rough sets: Theoretical aspects of reasoning about data.* Dordrecht: Kluwer.

Plewe, B. (1997). A representation-oriented taxonomy of gradation. In S. C. Hirtle & A. U. Frank (Eds.), *Spatial information theory: A theoretical basis for GIS*, COSIT'97, Vol. 1329 Lecture Notes in Computer Science (pp. 121–135). Berlin: Springer-Verlag.

Sklansky, J., Cordella, L P., & Levialdi, S. (1976). Parallel detection of concavity in cellular blobs. *IEEE Transactions on Computers, 25*, 187–196.

Smith, B. (1999). Agglomerations. In C. Freksa & D. M. Mark (Eds.), *spatial information theory: Cognitive and computational foundations of geographic science*, COSIT'99, Vol. 1661 Lecture Notes in Computer Science (pp. 267–82). New York: Springer-Verlag.

Stell, J. G. (1999). Granulation for graphs. In Freksa, C., & Mark, D. M. (Eds.), *Spatial Information Theory: Cognitive and Computational Foundations of Geographic Science*, COSIT'99, Vol. 1661 Lecture Notes in Computer Science (pp. 417–32). New York: Springer-Verlag.

SPATIAL COGNITION AND COMPUTATION, 3(2&3), 119–136

Qualitative Extents for Spatio-Temporal Granularity

John G. Stell
University of Leeds

The concepts of everywhere and somewhere generate three spatial extents: (1) everywhere, (2) somewhere but not everywhere, and (3) nowhere. These three extents can be used for the granular description of spatial regions. When spatio-temporal regions are considered there are two additional concepts: always and sometimes. The interaction of the four concepts can be used to produce various systems of spatio-temporal extents. The paper shows that if we want to give granular descriptions of spatio-temporal regions, then the system of extents needs to be chosen carefully. A suitable system of eleven spatio-temporal extents is identified, and a simplified system of six extents is also described. The systems of extents presented here are important in that they will allow various structures and theories understood only in a purely spatial context to be generalized to the spatio-temporal case.

Keywords: qualitative reasoning, granularity, spatio-temporal reasoning

1 Introduction

> *Over the last few years there have been some places in the world where the latest advances in spatial information theory have always been the main topic of conversation, and other places where this has never been the case.*

The preceding sentence makes a qualitative statement about the spatio-temporal extent of a region consisting of those locations in space-time where the latest

---

Correspondence concerning this article should be addressed to John G. Stell, School of Computing, University of Leeds, Leeds LS2 9JT, UK

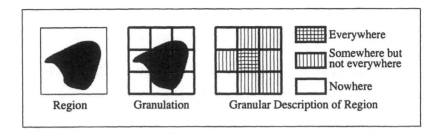

Figure 1. Qualitative spatial extents used for granular description.

advances in our subject are the main topic of conversation. As another example of such a statement, incompatible with the previous one, consider the following.

> *Over the last few years there have been some times when the latest advances in spatial information theory have been the main topic of conversation everywhere in the world, and other times when nowhere in the world has this happened.*

Simpler than these spatio-temporal extents are purely spatial ones appearing in statements like *The importance of spatial information is recognized everywhere*, and *Only some parts of the forest are affected by pollution*, and *None of the forest is affected by snow*. These spatial examples exemplify respectively the three qualitative spatial extents:

- *everywhere*

- *somewhere, but not everywhere*

- *nowhere*

These three qualitative spatial extents have been widely used in the approximate or granular description of regions. The general approach is well-known, but it is illustrated in Figure 1 since we need to recall the spatial case before we can describe the generalization to the spatio-temporal. Where a region is part of a space that has been subjected to a granulation (usually a partition of the space) we can describe the region in an approximate way by specifying, for each of the cells in the granulation, the extent to which the region occupies the cell. The three extents used in the simplest case arise from the two concepts *everywhere* and *somewhere*. It should be noted that *somewhere* as used here does not exclude the possibility of *everywhere*. The notations $\square$ and $\lozenge$ will be used for the concepts *everywhere* and *somewhere* respectively. Figure 2 illustrates how the three extents are generated by the two concepts. On the left of the figure we have the two

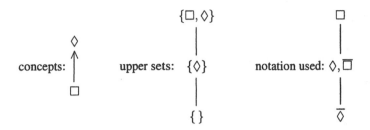

Figure 2. Basic system of three spatial extents.

concepts ordered by implication. The ordering expresses the fact that if a region is occupied everywhere then it is occupied somewhere. The ordering restricts the possible combinations of the two concepts which can hold. We can have (1) both $\square$ and $\lozenge$, (2) only $\lozenge$, or (3) neither. These three extents are the three upper sets[1] of the partially ordered set $\{\square, \lozenge\}$. The lattice of upper sets appears in the centre of figure 2. It is convenient to introduce a notation for extents which is not that of the upper sets and this is shown on the right of the figure. Here $\overline{\lozenge}$ should be read as the negation of *somewhere* i.e. nowhere, and $\lozenge, \overline{\square}$ as the conjunction somewhere and not everywhere.

This threefold classification has been used by Worboys (1998b) as the basis of a theory of finite resolution spatial data, and underlies all applications of rough set theory in the spatial context (Beaubouef & Petry, 2001; Bittner & Stell, 2001). The system of three extents is not the only one, and Bittner and Stell (1998) and Bittner (1997) have shown how it can be made more detailed by taking account of how the region being described interacts with the boundaries between each pair of cells in the granulation. There appears to have been little investigation of how a system of spatial extents might be generalized to deal with spatio-temporal regions. This, then, is the question addressed by the present paper: what systems of qualitative extents are there which can be used for the granular description of spatio-temporal regions?

1.1   Structure of the Paper

In Section 2 some related work is discussed. This is divided into two subsections: work on relations between regions, and work on change over time and spatio-temporal data. The relevance of systems of relations, such as RCC5, to the aims of the present paper is outlined in Section 2.1.2. The main technical content of the paper appears in Sections 3, 4, and 5. In Section 3 a first set of qualitative spatio-temporal extents is derived. The suitability of these for making granular

---

[1]An upper set X of a partially ordered set Y is a subset $X \subseteq Y$ such that $x \in X$ and $y \geq x$ imply $y \in X$.

descriptions is considered in the following section. It emerges that, while a useful set of extents for some purposes, they are unsuitable if we wish to take an already coarsened region and give it a still coarser description. A system of extents which does not suffer from this problem is presented in Section 4.2. A reduced set of only six extents is given in Section 5, and these should be useful when the full system provides a too detailed classification. Finally, conclusions and suggestions for further work are presented in Section 6.

2   Related Work

2.1   Relations Between Regions

Systems of extents for the granular description of regions are closely related to systems of relations between regions. Here we briefly review work on relations between regions before explaining how it is relevant to the present paper.

2.1.1   Work on Systems of Relations

Two spatial regions may relate to each other in a variety of ways, examples being that one region is a proper part of the other or that the two regions are equal. There are several well-known ways of systematizing the possible relations. One family of relations is that provided by the RCC work (Cohn, Bennett, et al., 1997). In this family the simplest classification is provided by the RCC5. More detailed classifications are the RCC8, which takes account of boundaries, and RCC23 which is sensitive to convexity.

Another approach to relationships between pairs of regions, is the work of Egenhofer and Franzosa. Given spatial regions A and B, we can measure how A relates to B by noting which of the intersections between interiors and boundaries of A and B are empty and which are non-empty. This way of describing the relationship of A to B is known as the "4-intersection model", and is studied in Egenhofer and Franzosa (1991). The 4-intersection model is relatively coarse. Finer distinctions between relationships of regions can be obtained by counting the number of connected components in the intersection of A with B, and in certain other regions determined by A and B. The investigation of this use of connected components is due to Galton (1998). Another way of describing the relationship of A to B, which provides for finer distinctions than in Galton's technique, is a refinement of the 4-intersection model also by Egenhofer and Franzosa (1995). Some recent work in this area includes the investigation of relations between three dimensional regions (Zlatanova, 1999). Since it is possible to regard time as the third dimension, this is likely to provide one way of treating relationships between two dimensional spatial regions which vary over a one dimensional time.

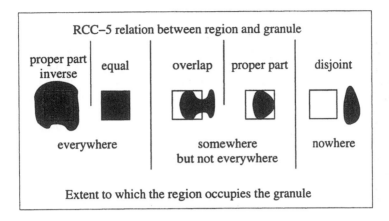

Figure 3. Relation between RCC5 and the 3 basic spatial extents.

2.1.2 Relevance of Systems of Relations to Granularity

To describe how systems of relations between regions are relevant to extents, let us assume a space S which has been subjected to a granulation G. We can take G to be a partition of S into cells, or granules, but in fact the basic idea does not depend critically on G being a partition. Given any region r of S, we can describe r with respect to the granulation by giving the relationship between each granule $g \in G$ and the region r. General systems for relations between arbitrary regions are not quite what we need here, because we are only interested in the part of r which intersects g. That is, we are interested in the relationship of the intersection $r \cap g$ to g. Thus the usual RCC-5 relations collapse to just three possibilities, as shown in figure 3. In the case that G forms a partition of S, we can recover the RCC-5 relation between r and g by examining the the extent to which r occupies g' for granules $g' \neq g$. For example, if r occupies everywhere in g, we can distinguish between the two possibilities that the RCC-5 relation is O or PP by determining whether the extent to which r occupies g is always *nowhere* when $g \neq g'$.

In a similar way we can obtain a system of boundary sensitive extents by starting from the RCC8 relations. This tie-up between the widely studied systems of relations, and the as yet less studied notion of extents for granularity, should be useful to the development of both notions. In particular the systems of extents derived later in this paper raise the question of whether they arise from systems of relations between spatio-temporal regions. Answering this question, which is beyond the scope of the present paper, should provide useful information about the possible relationships between spatial regions varying over time.

2.2 Spatio-temporal Granularity

From a conceptual viewpoint, space and time are very closely linked. The use of spatial metaphors in thinking about time has been stressed by Lakoff (1987), and the relevance of this to geographic information systems has been noted by Frank (1998). The collection (Egenhofer & Golledge, 1998) contains much further material on time and its interaction with space from the GIS perspective. Despite the close link between time and space, the qualitative description of spatio-temporal data in a unified way is still far from being understood. In fact there are many difficult issues concerning changes in any kind of data over time, without introducing problems which are specific to spatial data. A unifying model of temporal granularities, independent of spatial issues, is proposed by Bettini, Jajodia, and Wang (2000).

Hornsby and Egenhofer (1997, 2000) have proposed a change description language capable of modelling changes, over time. In other work (Hornsby & Egenhofer, 1999) they have addressed views at various levels of detail of objects which are subject to change. This uses a lattice of levels of detail in a similar way to the stratified map spaces of Stell and Worboys (1998).

Medak (1999) has proposed a formal approach to change over time in spatio-temporal databases. This uses four basic operations affecting object identity: create, destroy, suspend and resume. Algebraic rules for these operations are presented, and an implementation in the functional programming language Haskell is given.

In a theory of spatio-temporal granularity there must be an appropriate analogue of the notion of partition in the purely spatial sense. The work of Erwig and Schneider (1999) has provided a formal model of spatio-temporal partitions.

3 A First Set of Eleven Spatio-Temporal Extents

We have seen in Section 1 that the spatial concepts of *everywhere* and *somewhere* generate a system of three extents which can be used for the granular description of spatial data. In this section we show how to extend this by the addition of time to the purely spatial case.

In the spatio-temporal case there are four concepts which can be used to describe extents: *everywhere*, *always*, *somewhere* and *sometime*. The notation ■ will be used for *always* and ◆ for *sometimes*. Combinations of the four concepts can lead to complex situations, as evidenced by the examples at the very start of this paper. Figure 4 shows the possible compound concepts and the implications between them. Note the distinction between *somewhere always* and *always somewhere*. If we say an event occurs always somewhere, we mean that for each time there is a place where the event occurs, but different times may have different places. For example, the British Empire was once described as 'the empire on which the Sun never sets' because there was always somewhere in the empire where the Sun had not set. If we say an event occurs somewhere always, we mean that it happens in some fixed place for every time.

The possible combinations of the six compound concepts which may hold together are determined by the upper sets of the lattice in figure 4. This lattice of upper sets gives us a lattice of eleven spatio-temporal extents and these appear in figure 5. An explanation of the extents together with examples is given in Table 1.

In this table the top and bottom elements of the lattice are omitted as it should be clear what is meant by the extents everywhere always ($\square\blacksquare$) and never anywhere ($\lozenge\blacklozenge$). In the examples, which appear in the right hand column of the table, we have used a simple case of a space shown as a single rectangle at three moments in time. This is indicated by the text on the first example. Although the examples thus use a discrete time and a continuous space, this is merely for the ease of drawing simple examples. The concepts of somewhere and at some time are not tied to any particular kind of space or time and thus the notions of extent are quite general and are valid whether space or time is discrete or continuous. In reading the table it is important to bear in mind that 'everywhere is occupied at some time' can easily be mis-interpreted. It is used to mean that for every element of the space there is some time at which that element is occupied. It does not mean that there is a particular time at which the whole space is simultaneously occupied. The discussion in Section 4.1 may be helpful in interpreting the diagrams on the right hand side of the table.

4 Spatio-Temporal Granulation

4.1 First Coarsening

To illustrate the use of the extents obtained in the previous section, consider the diagram in figure 6. This figure shows one space at nine times, and for each time a region in the space is shown by a shaded area. Taken as a whole we have a single spatio-temporal region. A physical interpretation could be that we are looking at material on a conveyor belt (perhaps clay in a brick making factory). The nine times correspond to nine snapshots of the state of the conveyor. In such a manufacturing example, we might want to use spatio-temporal extents as part of the knowledge representation component of an automated monitoring system. To summarize the spatio-temporal situation we can impose a granulation, which is indicated by the bold lines in figure 7. The granulation has divided the space into nine granules or cells. In this paper it will be assumed that a spatio-temporal granulation is determined by two granulations: one of time and one of space. While more general spatio-temporal granulations are clearly important, this simple kind provides sufficient material for these initial investigations.

We can give a coarse description of the spatio-temporal region by specifying for each granule the extent to which the region occupies it. This is the extension

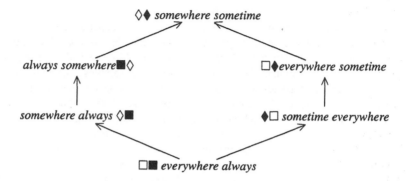

Figure 4. Implications between the six compound concepts.

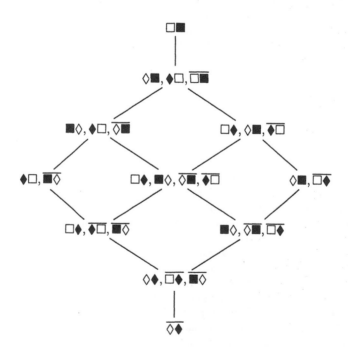

Figure 5.: The first system of spatio-temporal extents.

Table 1
Spatio-temporal Extents and their Interpretations

$\Diamond\blacksquare, \blacklozenge\square, \overline{\square\blacksquare}$	Somewhere is always occupied, and at some time everywhere is, but not everywhere is always occupied.	
$\blacksquare\Diamond, \blacklozenge\square, \overline{\Diamond\blacksquare}$	At every time some part of the space is occupied, and at some time all of the space is occupied, but there is no part of space which is always occupied	
$\square\blacklozenge, \Diamond\blacksquare, \overline{\blacklozenge\square}$	Everywhere in the space is occupied at some time, and some place is always occupied, but at no time is the entire space occupied.	
$\blacklozenge\square, \overline{\blacksquare\Diamond}$	At some time all the space is occupied, but at some time none of the space is occupied.	
$\square\blacklozenge, \blacksquare\Diamond, \overline{\Diamond\blacksquare}, \overline{\blacklozenge\square}$	Everywhere in space is occupied at some time, and at each time somewhere is occupied, but there is not time at which all of space is occupied nor anywhere in space which is always occupied.	
$\Diamond\blacksquare, \overline{\blacksquare\Diamond}$	Somewhere in space is occupied for all time, and for some time nowhere is occupied.	
$\square\blacklozenge, \overline{\blacklozenge\square}, \overline{\blacksquare\Diamond}$	Everywhere in space is occupied at some time, but there is no time at which all space is occupied, and at some time nowhere is occupied.	
$\blacksquare\Diamond, \overline{\Diamond\blacksquare}, \overline{\square\blacklozenge}$	At every time somewhere is occupied, but there is nowhere which is always occupied, and somewhere is never occupied.	
$\Diamond\blacklozenge, \overline{\square\blacklozenge}, \overline{\blacksquare\Diamond}$	At sometime somewhere is occupied, but somewhere is never occupied, and at sometime nowhere is occupied.	

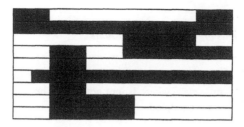

Figure 6.: Example, stage 1. One space at nine times.

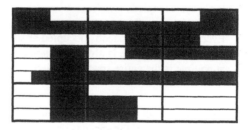

Figure 7. Example, stage 2. First spatio-temporal granulation.

to the spatio-temporal case of the simple example which appeared in figure 1. To achieve this for our example, we use the extents from figure 5 to obtain the diagram in figure 8.

4.2 Repeated Coarsening

Now, continuing with the same example, suppose a further granulation is performed. This is indicated by the bold lines in figure 9. Each of these four granules has to be assigned one of the extents. When we consider how to do this we find a difficulty with the interpretations given to some of the eleven extents. In particular consider the large granule in the upper right corner. This granule is made up of two cells. One of these cells is occupied to extent ◆□, ■◊̄, and the other to extent ■◊, ◆□, ◆□̄. If we were coarsening in one step from the space in figure 6, and using the extents in figure 5, the final extent would be ■◊, ◆□, ◊■̄. However, this cannot be the correct way to coarsen the two cells with extents ◆□, ■◊̄, and ■◊, ◆□, ◆□̄. This is because two such cells could equally well have arisen in an alternative way, as shown in figure 10. In the figure each of the arrows represents one coarsening step. In fact we can see that there is no way to fill in the question mark in figure 10 with one of the eleven values from figure 5. The problem arises

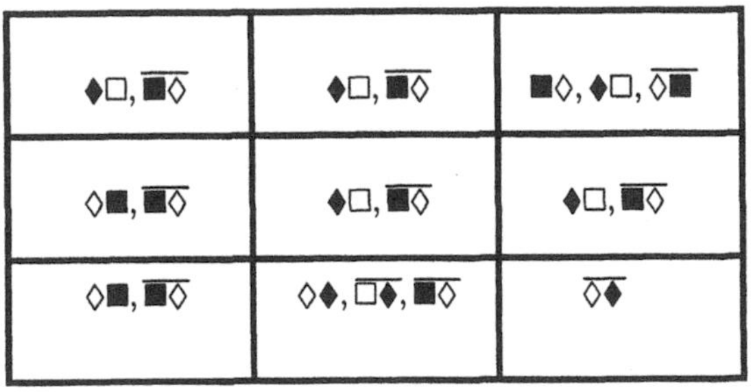

◆□, $\overline{■◊}$	◆□, $\overline{■◊}$	■◊, ◆□, $\overline{◊■}$
◊■, $\overline{■◊}$	◆□, $\overline{■◊}$	◆□, $\overline{■◊}$
◊■, $\overline{■◊}$	◊◆, $\overline{□◆}$, $\overline{■◊}$	$\overline{◊◆}$

Figure 8. Example, stage 3. Coarse spatio-temporal description.

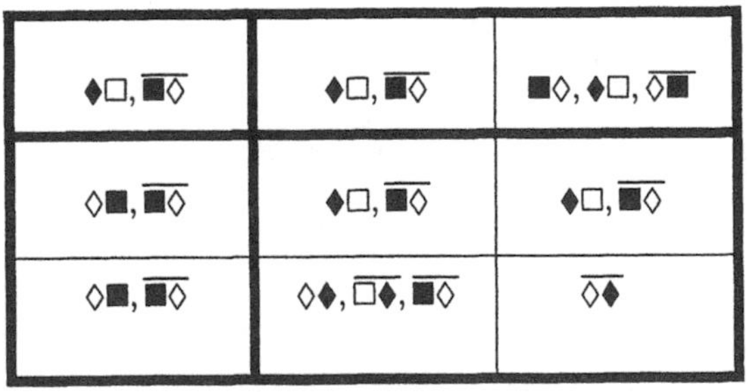

◆□, $\overline{■◊}$	◆□, $\overline{■◊}$	■◊, ◆□, $\overline{◊■}$
◊■, $\overline{■◊}$	◆□, $\overline{■◊}$	◆□, $\overline{■◊}$
◊■, $\overline{■◊}$	◊◆, $\overline{□◆}$, $\overline{■◊}$	$\overline{◊◆}$

Figure 9. Example, stage 4. Second spatio-temporal granulation.

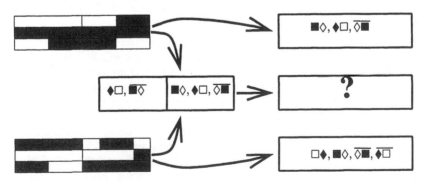

Figure 10. The problem of repeated coarsening.

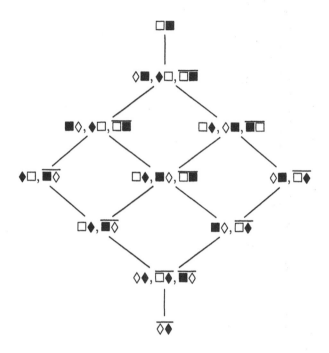

Figure 11. Extents suitable for repeated coarsening.

because the values refer to pairwise disjoint possibilities, and the solution is to weaken some of the eleven possibilities. This produces the lattice in figure 11, which differs from the previous one in five places.

The new system of extents no longer describes eleven pairwise disjoint possibilities. For example, if a granule is occupied to extent ◆□, ■◇̄, this implies it is also occupied to extent □◆, ■◇̄. These two extents are both needed because in certain circumstances we may have enough information to be sure the extent is ◆□, ■◇̄, but in other circumstances we may only be certain of □◆, ■◇̄ without being able to exclude the more informative ◆□, ■◇̄. These relationships provide a partial order, ⊑, on the extents with $e_1 ⊑ e_2$ being interpreted as e_1 is less informative than e_2. Among the relationships are □◆, ■◇̄ ⊑ ◆□, ■◇̄ and ■◇, □̄◆̄ ⊑ ◇■, □̄◆̄. The four elements ◇■, ◆□, □̄■̄, and ■◇, ◆□, □̄■̄, and □◆, ◇■, ■̄□̄, and □◆, ■◇, □̄■̄ are also related, in a way easily determined by the implications of figure 4. The remaining three elements are related only to themselves.

It is worth noting that the loss of detail when coarsening in two steps as opposed

Table 2
Rules for Determining Occupation Concepts Holding for g

$\mathcal{O}$	Condition for $\mathcal{O}(g)$ to hold
$\square\blacksquare$	$\forall i,j \;\square\blacksquare(g_{ij})$
$\Diamond\blacklozenge$	$\exists i,j \;\Diamond\blacklozenge(g_{ij})$
$\blacklozenge\square$	$\exists i,j \;\blacklozenge\square(g_{ij}) \wedge \forall k \; k \neq j \Rightarrow \square\blacksquare(g_{ik})$
$\Diamond\blacksquare$	$\exists i,j \;\Diamond\blacksquare(g_{ij}) \wedge \forall k \; k \neq i \Rightarrow \square\blacksquare(g_{kj})$
$\blacksquare\Diamond$	$\forall i \exists j \;\blacksquare\Diamond(g_{ij})$
$\square\blacklozenge$	$\forall j \exists i \;\square\blacklozenge(g_{ij})$

to one was anticipated in the equations proposed by Stell and Worboys (1998) but in that paper we had no explicit example of the phenomenon.

4.3 Rules of Coarsening

We now present the rules which specify how to coarsen a region labelled by the eleven values in figure 11. To describe the rules, we assume a matrix of cells is being condensed into a single granule.

$$\begin{bmatrix} g_{11} & g_{12} & \cdots & g_{1n} \\ g_{21} & g_{22} & \cdots & g_{2n} \\ \vdots & \vdots & \vdots & \vdots \\ g_{m1} & g_{m2} & \cdots & g_{mn} \end{bmatrix}$$

As in the example, each row in the matrix represents the same space; the m different rows corresponding to m different times. Each column represents a part of the space at m different times. In the matrix each g_{ij} is a cell and the notation $\square\blacksquare(g_{ij})$ will be used to denote that g_{ij} is occupied to the extent $\square\blacksquare$. The corresponding notation will be used for each of the other six basic concepts. In Table 2 we give the rules for determining when each of the six concepts holds for g. From these basic concepts we can determine which of the eleven extents holds for g, since each extent is a conjunction of these basic concepts and their negations. Using these rules it is now possible to provide the correct labels for the granulation in two stages of the space in figure 6; the result appears in figure 12.

5 Six-Valued Sub-system of Extents

In some applications, the system of eleven extents may be too detailed. Thus it is useful to have the subsystem shown on the right of figure 13. These six ex-

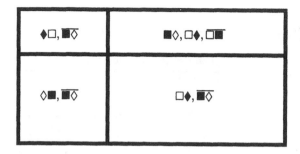

Figure 12. Example, stage 5. Final spatio-temporal granulation.

tents arise from the eleven by collapsing each connected component of the partial order ⊑ to its least element. This collapsing process is illustrated in figure 14. Alternatively, the sub-system can be generated from the four concepts shown on the left of figure 13. These four concepts generate a lattice of six jointly exhaustive and pairwise disjoint possibilities.

6 Conclusions and Further Work

This paper has shown how the three notions of spatial extent which arise from the concepts *everywhere* and *somewhere* can be generalized to the spatio-temporal case. This generalization arises from the four concepts *everywhere, somewhere, always* and *sometimes*. From these four concepts, eleven notions of extent are generated, but we have seen that the most obvious system of eleven extents is not in fact suitable for the granular description of spatio-temporal regions. The reason for this lack of suitability was the failure of the first set of eleven extents to handle the repeated coarsening of regions. A modified system of eleven extents, which are no longer pairwise disjoint, was obtained and the rules which allow these to be used in repeated coarsening were determined. The full system of eleven qualitative spatio-temporal extents may be too detailed for some applications, so a simpler system of only six extents was shown to be obtainable from the eleven. This set of six does have the property of being pairwise disjoint. Although there has been much work on the representation of spatio-temporal change, and some of this has been discussed in Section 2 above, the use of a system of extents which can be used for the granular description of spatio-temporal regions does not seem to have been investigated before.

The work in this paper has been directed towards the identification of a system of extents, and, having accomplished this, there is much further work for which it

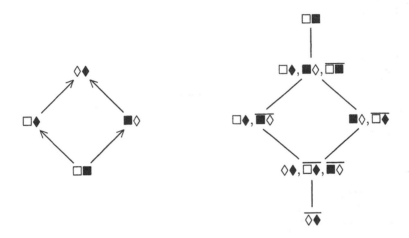

Figure 13. The six spatio-temporal extents.

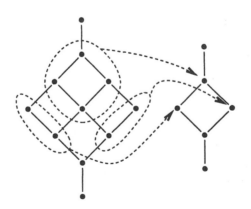

Figure 14. Collapsing the eleven extents to six.

provides a foundation. Since the system of extents is a generalization of the tripartite classification used in Worboys' work on finite resolution spatial data (1998b), it would be fruitful to investigate how far Worboys' results can be generalized to spatio-temporal data by using the extents derived in this paper.

It should be possible to extend the system of eleven spatio-temporal extents to a more detailed classification by taking into account the boundaries of the cells in the granulation. This would form a natural generalization to the spatio-temporal context of the researches of Bittner and Stell (Bittner, 1997; Bittner & Stell, 1998). A related question is how relations between granularly represented spatio-temporal regions can be described. What, for example, are the appropriate analogues of systems such as RCC5, RCC8, and the 4- and 9- intersection models? One direction to investigate this would be by using the systems of spatio-temporal extents to generalize the work in (Bittner & Stell, 2001) beyond the purely spatial case.

Time has been assumed to be one dimensional in generating the system of extents. However, models of time with two dimensions (event time and database time) are of practical significance (Worboys, 1998a). By taking time to have two dimensions we would have two notions of always and two notions of sometimes. When these are combined with the two spatial concepts of everywhere and somewhere the resulting system of extents would clearly be more elaborate just eleven cases, but further work would be needed to determine its exact form, and to find appropriate sub-systems for particular applications. Other work on granularity for a structured notion of time is reported in (Stell, 2003).

Acknowledgement

This work was supported by an EPSRC grant "Digital Topology and Geometry: An Axiomatic Approach with Applications to GIS and Spatial Reasoning".

References

Beaubouef, T., & Petry, F. (2001). Vagueness in spatial data: Rough set and egg-yolk approaches. In L. Monostori, J. Váncza, & M. Ali (Eds.), *Engineering of intelligent systems. 14th international conference on industrial and engineering applications of artificial intelligence and expert systems, IEA/AIE 2001*. Vol. 2070 Lecture Notes in Artificial Intelligence (pp. 367–373). Berlin: Springer-Verlag.

Bettini, C., Jajodia, S., & Wang, S. X. (2000). *Time granularities in databases, data mining, and temporal reasoning*. Berlin: Springer-Verlag.

Bittner, T. (1997). A qualitative coordinate language of location of figures within the ground. In S. C. Hirtle & A. U. Frank (Eds.), *Spatial information the-*

ory, COSIT'97, Vol. 1329 Lecture Notes in Computer Science (pp. 223–240). Berlin: Springer-Verlag.

Bittner, T., & Stell, J. G. (1998). A boundary-sensitive approach to qualitative location. *Annals of Mathematics and Artificial Intelligence*, *24*, 93–114.

Bittner, T., & Stell, J. G. (2001). Rough sets in approximate spatial reasoning. In W. Ziarko & Y. Yao (Eds.), *Proceedings of second international conference on rough sets and current trends in computing (RSCTC'2000)*. Vol. 2005 Lecture Notes in Computer Science (pp. 445–453). Berlin: Springer-Verlag.

Cohn, A. G., Bennett, B., et al.. (1997). Qualitative spatial representation and reasoning with the region connection calculus. *GeoInformatica*, *1*, 275–316.

Egenhofer, M. J., & Franzosa, R. (1991). Point-set topological spatial relations. *International Journal of Geographical Information Systems*, *5*, 161–174.

Egenhofer, M. J., & Franzosa, R. (1995). On the equivalence of topological relations. *International Journal of Geographical Information Systems*, *9*, 133–152.

Egenhofer, M. J., & Golledge, R. G. (1998). *Spatial and temporal reasoning in geographic information systems*. Oxford: Oxford University Press.

Erwig, M., & Schneider, M. (1999). The honeycomb model of spatio-temporal partitions. In M. H. Böhlen, C. S. Jensen, & M. O. Scholl (Eds.), *Spatio-temporal database management. international workshop (STDBM'99), Proceedings*. Vol. 1678 Lecture Notes in Computer Science (pp. 39–59). Berlin: Springer-Verlag.

Frank, A. U. (1998). Different types of "times" in GIS. In M. J. Egenhofer & R. G. Golledge (Eds.), *Spatial and temporal reasoning in geographic information systems*. Oxford: Oxford University Press.

Galton, A. (1998). Modes of overlap. *Journal of Visual Languages and Computing*, *9*, 61–79.

Hornsby, K., & Egenhofer, M. (1997). Qualitative representation of change. In S. C. Hirtle & A. U. Frank (Eds.), *Spatial information theory*, Vol. 1329 Lecture Notes in Computer Science (pp. 15–33). Berlin: Springer-Verlag.

Hornsby, K., & Egenhofer, M. (1999). Shifts in detail through temporal zooming. In A. Camelli, A. M. Tjoa, & R. R. Wagner (Eds.), *Tenth international workshop on database and expert systems applications (DEXA99)* (pp. 487–491). IEEE Computer Society.

Hornsby, K., & Egenhofer, M. (2000). Identity-based change: a foundation for spatio-temporal knowledge representation. *International Journal of Geographical Information Science*, *14*, 207–224.

Lakoff, G. (1987). *Women, fire, and dangerous things: What categories reveal about the mind*. Chicago: University of Chicago Press.

Medak, D. (1999). Lifestyles – An algebraic approach to change in identity. In M. H. Böhlen, C. S. Jensen, & M. O. Scholl (Eds.), *Spatio-temporal database management. international workshop STDBM'99* Vol. 1678 Lecture Notes in Computer Science (pp. 19–38). Berlin: Springer-Verlag.

Stell, J. G. (2003). Granularity in change over time. In M. Duckham, M. F. Goodchild, & M. F. Worboys (Eds.), *Foundations of geographic information science* (pp. 95–115). London: Taylor and Francis.

Stell, J. G., & Worboys, M. F. (1998). Stratified map spaces: A formal basis for multi-resolution spatial databases. In T. K. Poiker & N. Chrisman (Eds.), *SDH'98 proceedings 8th international symposium on spatial data handling* (pp. 180–189). International Geographical Union.

Worboys, M. F. (1998a). A generic model for spatio-bitemporal geographic information. In M. J. Egenhofer & R. G. Golledge (Eds.), *Spatial and temporal reasoning in geographic information systems.* Oxford: Oxford University Press.

Worboys, M. F. (1998b). Imprecision in finite resolution spatial data. *GeoInformatica, 2*, 257–279.

Zlatanova, S. (1999). On 3D topological relationships. In A. Camelli, A. M. Tjoa, & R. R. Wagner (Eds.), *Tenth international workshop on database and expert systems applications (DEXA99)* (pp. 913–919). IEEE Computer Society.

SPATIAL COGNITION AND COMPUTATION, 3(2&3), 137–156

Vague Reference and Approximating Judgments

Thomas Bittner
University of Leipzig

Barry Smith
University of Leipzig and
State University of New York at Buffalo

'Mount Everest' is a vague name. That is (on the account here defended) there are many portions of reality all of which have equal claims to serve as its referent. We propose a new account of such vagueness in terms of a theory of what we shall call *granular partitions*. We distinguish different kinds of crisp and non-crisp granular partitions and we describe the relations between them, concentrating especially on spatial examples. In addition, we describe the practice whereby subjects use systems of reference grids as a means for tempering the vagueness of their judgments, for example when they say that Libya straddles the Equator or that the meeting will take place between 2 and 3pm. We then demonstrate how the theory of reference partitions can yield a natural account of this practice, which is referred to in the literature as 'approximation'.

Keywords: ontology, granular partitions, vagueness, semantic partitions, partition theory, approximation

Consider the proper name 'Mount Everest'. This refers to a mereological whole, a certain giant formation of rock. A mereological whole is the sum of its parts, and Mount Everest certainly contains its *summit* as part. But it is not so clear which parts along the foothills of Mount Everest are parts of the mountain and which belong to its surroundings. Thus it is not clear which mereological sum of parts of reality actually constitutes Mount Everest. One option is to hold that there are multiple candidates, no one of which can claim exclusive rights to serve as the referent of this name. All of these candidates are involved, in some

Correspondence concerning this article should be addressed to Thomas Bittner, Institute for Formal Ontology and Medical Information Science, University of Leipzig; email thomas.bittner@ifomis.uni-leipzig.de.

sense, when we use the name 'Mount Everest.' We are however not conscious of this multiplicity of candidate referents, effectively because we simply do not care about the question where, precisely, the boundaries around Mount Everest are to be drawn.

Each of the many candidates has the summit, with its height of 29,028 feet, as part. Each is also a perfectly determinate portion of reality. The candidates differ only regarding which parts along the foothills are included and which are not.

Varzi (2001) refers to the above as a *de dicto* view of vagueness. It treats vagueness not as a property of objects but rather as a semantic property of names and predicates, a property captured formally in terms of a supervaluationistic semantics (Fraassen 1966), (Fine 1975). We shall concentrate our attentions in what follows on the case of *singular reference*, i.e., reference via names and definite descriptions to concrete portions of reality such as mountains and deserts. We shall also concentrate primarily on spatial examples. As will become clear, however, it is one advantage of the framework here defended that it can be generalized automatically beyond the spatial case.

In order to understand vague reference we use the theory of granular partitions we advanced in our earlier papers: (Bittner and Smith 2001a), (Bittner and Smith 2003), (Smith and Brogaard 2002). The fundamental idea is that every use of language to make a judgment about reality brings about a certain *granular partition*, a grid-like system of cells conceived as projecting onto reality in something like the way in which a bank of flashlights projects onto reality when it carves out cones of light in the darkness. Each judgment, J, can then be conceived as a pair consisting of a sentence, S, and an associated granular partition Pt.

We consider reference as a *two-step-process*. Language tokens are associated with cells in a grid-like structure, and these cells are projected onto reality in the way suggested by our flashlight metaphor. Granular partitions can then be conceived as the cognitive artifacts whereby language gains its foothold in reality. (They thus play a role somewhat similar to that of set-theoretical models in more standard treatments.) In our earlier papers, we showed how this two-step-process allows us to explain the features of selectivity and granularity of reference in judgments. In this paper, we show how the same machinery can help us to understand the phenomena of vagueness and approximation.

Crisp Granular Partitions

The theory of granular partitions has two parts: (A) a theory of the relations between cells and the structures they form, and (B) a theory of the relations between cells and objects in reality. Consider Figure 1. The left part shows a very simple cell structure, with cells labeled *Everest*, *Lhotse* and *The Himalayas*. The right part shows portions of reality onto which those cells project.

Figure 1. Left: a partition, with cells *Lhotse*, *Everest* and *The Himalayas*. Right: A part of the Himalayas seen from space, with admissible candidate referents for 'Mount Lhotse' (left) and 'Mount Everest' (right).

Language

In what follows, we use lower case roman letters o, o_1, o_2, ... to symbolize objects in reality; z, z_1, z_2, to symbolize cells of granular partitions; upper case roman letters from the beginning of the alphabet A, B, C, ... to symbolize sets of cells; upper case roman letters from the middle of the alphabet L, P, ... to symbolize sets of ordered tuples; and upper case Greek letters Δ, Δ_1, ... to symbolize sets of objects in reality.

Theory A

A granular partition Pt = $((A, \subseteq), (\Delta, \leq), P, L)$ is a quadtuple such that $(A, \subseteq)$ is a system of cells or a *cell-structure*, $(\Delta, \leq)$ is a *target domain*, $L \in Pow(\Delta \times A)$ is a *location* relation, and $P \in Pow(A \times \Delta)$ is a *projection* relation. The target domain $(\Delta, \leq)$, is hereby understood as a mereological structure with Δ a set of objects and $\leq$ a part-of relation defined on Δ which satisfies the axioms of general extensional mereology (GEM). A cell structure, $(A, \subseteq)$, is a finite set of cells, z_0, z_1, ... z_n with a binary *subcell* relation $\subseteq$. We say that z_1 is a subcell of z_2 in A if and only if the first is contained in the latter. We then impose four axioms (or 'master conditions') on cell structures as follows:

> MA1: The subcell relation $\subseteq$ is reflexive, transitive, and antisymmetric.
>
> MA2: The cell structure of a partition is always such that chains of nested cells are of finite length.
>
> MA3: If two cells have subcells in common, then one is a subcell of the other.
>
> MA4: Each partition contains a unique maximal cell.

These conditions, which are explored further in our earlier papers, together ensure that each cell structure can be represented as a tree (a directed graph with a root and no cycles).

Theory B

Theory (B) arises in reflection of the fact that partitions are more than just systems of cells. They are constructed in such a way as to project upon reality in the way names and other referring expressions in natural and scientific languages project onto entities in reality. Projection and location then are relations between cells in a cell structure on the one hand and objects in a target domain on the other. We write 'P(z, o)' as an abbreviation for: cell z is projected onto object o, and 'L(o, z)' as an abbreviation for: object o is located in cell z. The partitions of interest in this paper are *transparent*, which means that MB1 and MB2 hold:

$$\text{MB1} \quad L(o, z) \rightarrow P(z, o).$$
$$\text{MB2} \quad P(z, o) \rightarrow L(o, z).$$

(Here and in what follows initial universal quantifiers are taken as understood. We preserve L and P as distinct relations in order to hold open the possibility of dealing with certain sorts of breakdown in the relation between granular partitions and their targets.)

We demand further that projection and location be functional relations, i.e., that every cell projects onto just one object and every object is located in just one cell:

$$\text{MB3} \quad P(z, o_1) \text{ and } P(z, o_2) \rightarrow o_1 = o_2$$
$$\text{MB4} \quad L(o, z_1) \text{ and } L(o, z_2) \rightarrow z_1 = z_2$$

The partitions of interest in this paper are in addition *complete*, in the sense that every cell projects onto at least one object, i.e., they satisfy an axiom to the effect that they contain no empty cells (no cells projecting outwards into the void):

$$\text{MB5} \quad z \in A \rightarrow \exists o: L(o, z)$$

We require also that projection, considered as a function p: A $\rightarrow$ Δ between two partially ordered domains (A and Δ), be an order homomorphism:

$$\text{MB6:} \quad z_1 \subseteq z_2 \rightarrow p(z_1) \leq p(z_2)$$

The root or maximal cell in the cell structure is then the maximal object (the universal or total fusion) in Δ.

The resulting class of partitions is quite narrow. For a more general treatment, embracing also less well-behaved granular partitions, see (Bittner and Smith 2003). Note also that our axioms MB1-6 have been formulated for easy understandability and the system they form is not minimal. (Thus MB2 already follows from MB1, MB3 and MB5.) In order to simplify the notation in what follows, we write Pt = (A, P, L) as an abbreviation for Pt = ((A, $\subseteq$), (Δ, $\leq$), P, L). At the same time we assume a fixed target domain Δ, which the reader can think of as the whole of reality.

Vague Granular Partitions

The Theory

What, now, of vagueness? A *vague* granular partition $Pt^V = ((A, \subseteq), (\Delta, \leq), P^V,$ $L^V)$ is a quadtuple in which the cell structure and target domain are defined as above, and P^V and L^V are *classes* of projection and location relations (Bittner and Smith 2001b). Again, we will write $Pt^V = (A, P^V, L^V)$ in order to keep the notation simple.

Consider Figure 2, which depicts a vague partition $Pt^V = (A, P^V, L^V)$ of the Himalayas. This has a cell structure A, as shown in the left part of Figure 2, which is in fact identical to the corresponding part of Figure 1. In the right part of the figure, in contrast, there is a multiplicity of possible candidate projections for the cells in A, indicated by boundary regions depicted via cloudy ovoids. The boundaries of the actual candidates onto which the cells 'Lhotse' and 'Everest' are projected under the various P_i in P^V are continuous ovoids included somewhere within the cloudy regions depicted in the Figure.

The projection and location relations in these classes form pairs (P_i, L_j), which are such that each P_i has a corresponding unique L_j and vice versa, satisfying the following conditions (where the notation '$\exists!i$' abbreviates: 'there exists one and only one i'):

$$MB1^V \quad \forall j: L_j(o, z) \rightarrow \exists!i\, P_i(z, o)$$
$$MB2^V \quad \forall i: P_i(z, o) \rightarrow \exists!j: L_j(o, z)$$

We also demand that all P_i and all L_j are functional in the sense discussed in the crisp case:

$$MB3^V \quad P_i(z, o_1) \text{ and } P_i(z, o_2) \rightarrow o_1 = o_2$$
$$MB4^V \quad L_j(o, z_1) \text{ and } L_j(o, z_2) \rightarrow z_1 = z_2$$

Figure 2. A vague partition of the Himalayas.

We demand further that cells project onto some object (are non-empty) under every projection:

$$MB5^V: \quad Z(z, A) \rightarrow \forall j \, \exists o: L_j(o, z)$$

Again, every particular projection considered as a function from A to Δ is an order homomorphism:

$$MB6^V: \quad z_1 \subseteq z_2 \rightarrow p_i(z_1) \leq p_i(z_2)$$

We now add an axiom that governs the interrelations between projection relations with distinct indexes in the vague partition Pt^V. Recall that all projection relations operate on the same cell structure. We need to ensure that if the same object is targeted by two cells z_1 and z_2 under different projections P_i and P_j then the targeting cells must be identical:

$$MB7^V \quad P_i(z_1, o) \text{ and } P_j(z_2, o) \rightarrow z_1 = z_2$$

Equivalence of Candidate Referents

Given a vague partition as defined above, we can define an equivalence relation between entities in the target domain Δ as

$$D\approx \qquad o_1 \approx o_2 \equiv \exists z, i, j : P_i(z, o_1) \text{ and } P_j(z, o_2).$$

Clearly, $\approx$ is symmetric and reflexive. To see that $\approx$ is also transitive, assume $o_1 \approx o_2$ and $o_2 \approx o_3$. This means that there exist z_1, z_2, i, j, k, m such that $P_i(z_1, o_1)$, $P_j(z_1, o_2)$, $P_k(z_2, o_2)$ and $P_m(z_2, o_3)$. From $P_j(z_1, o_2)$ and $P_k(z_2, o_2)$ it follows by $MB7^V$ that $z_1 = z_2$, and hence for some cells z and some projections P_i and P_m it holds that $P_i(z, o_1)$ and $P_m(z, o_3)$, i.e., $o_1 \approx o_3$. In the remainder, we write $[o]_z$ to denote the set $\{o \mid \exists i : P_i(z, o) \}$.

Let $Pt^V = (A, P^V, L^V)$ be a vague granular partition. We call all partitions $Pt = (A, P_i, L_j)$ with $P_i \in P^V$ and $L_j \in L^V$ which satisfy the axioms MB1–MB6 *crispings* of the vague partition Pt^V. Consider a partition with cells labeled with vague proper names. Intuitively, each crisping (A, P_i, L_j) then recognizes exactly one candidate precisified referent for each such cell. The precise candidates carved out by the separate (A, P_i, L_j) are all slightly different. But each is perfectly crisp and thus it has all of the properties of crisp partitions discussed in the previous sections. All those different candidate referents are equivalent in the sense of our relation $\approx$. This captures the *de dicto* view of vagueness.

Semantic Partition

Given a vague partition $Pt^V = ((A^V, \subseteq), (\Delta, \leq), P^V, L^V)$, we can for each cell $z \in A^V$ classify corresponding portions of reality with respect to the vague projection of the cell z into three zones: the determinate zone, the indeterminate zone, and the exterior zone.

We say that x is part of the *determinate core* of the vague projection P^V of the cell z if and only if, under *all* projections $p_i(z)$ in P^V, x is a part of the targeted candidate referent:

$$\text{determinate}_V(x, z) \equiv \forall i: x \le p_i(z)$$

Thus the summit of Mount Everest is part of the determinate core of the vague projection of the name 'Everest' and its associated cell.

We say that x is a part of the *indeterminate* zone of the vague projection P^V of the cell z if and only if there are some projections p_i in P^V under which x is part of the targeted candidate referent and other projections $p_j(z)$ in P^V under which this is not the case:

$$\text{indeterminate}_V(x, z) \equiv \exists i: x \le p_i(z) \text{ and } \exists j: \neg(x \le p_j(z))$$

The dotted region in Figure 2 illustrates the indeterminate zone of the projection of the cell associated with the vague name 'Mount Everest'.

We say that x is a part of the zone *exterior* to the vague projection P^V of the cell z if and only if x is not reached by any projection $p_i(z)$ in P^V.

$$\text{exterior}_V(x, z) \equiv \forall i: \neg(x \le p_i(z))$$

There are parts of reality – such as Berlin – that are not reached by any projections of the cell 'Everest' in the partitions used by humans projecting in transparent fashion.

Reference via a vague name 'N' creates a partition of reality into determinate core, indeterminate zone, and exterior zone. Let $\sigma x \psi(x)$ denote the mereological sum of all x satisfying $\psi(x)$ and let z be the cell in the partition P^V which projects onto the candidate referents for 'N'. We then define determinate core, indeterminate zone, and exterior zone as the mereological sums of all determinate, indeterminate, and exterior parts of reality with respect to the vague projection of the cell z:

$$det_V(z) = \sigma x \text{ determinate}_V(x, z)$$
$$indet_V(z) = \sigma x \text{ indeterminate}_V(x, z)$$
$$ext_V(z) = \sigma x \text{ exterior}_V(x, z)$$

We define the *semantic partition* of reality with respect to the vague name N as a triple of determinate zone, indeterminate zone, and exterior zone. In general $det_V(z)$ is a partial function since there does not necessarily exist a portion of reality which is a part of all projections of the cell z.

Approximating Judgments

Approximation in Egg-yolk Partitions

Consider, again, Figure 1. The cells labeled 'Everest' and 'Lhotse' carve *mountain-candidates* out of a certain formation of rock. They do not do this physically, but rather by establishing fiat boundaries in reality, represented by the black lines in the right part of the figure (Smith 1995), (Smith 2001), (Bittner and Smith 2001a). But how are we to understand the phenomenon whereby judging subjects are able to impose spatial boundaries *vaguely*?

Suppose you are an expert mountain guide hiking through the Himalayas with your friends and you assert:

[A]: We will cross the boundary of Mount Everest within the next hour.

We shall assume that through your use of the phrase 'within the next hour' you successfully delimit a range of admissible candidates for the boundary of Mount Everest along the trajectory of your hike. Consider the left part of Figure 3. Here boundaries delimiting admissible candidates are imposed by specifying a time interval that translates to travel distance along a path; time serves here as *frame of reference*. The boundaries are defined by your current location (marked: 'now') and your location after the specified time has passed (marked: 'in one hour'). The boundary of each admissible candidate referent crosses the path at some point between these two boundaries, called the *exterior* and the *interior* boundaries, respectively.

The general case is illustrated in the right part of Figure 3, which is intended to depict how judging subjects project egg-yolk-like granular partitions onto reality involving three cells: an exterior, a core, and an intermediate region within which the boundary candidates lie. (See (Cohn and Gotts 1996) and (Roy and Stell 2001).) This granular partition serves as the frame of reference in terms of which the judging subject is able at the same time to both specify the range of admissible entities to which he (vaguely) refers and also to constrain this range.

Egg-yolk Partitions vs. Semantic Partition

Consider the egg-yolk partition in the right part of Figure 3. It is important to see that this is not a semantic partition in the sense discussed above. This is because it was created by a judging subject by imposing boundaries onto reality in order to constrain admissible candidate referents and at the same time to serve as a frame of reference.

A semantic partition on the other hand is induced by classifying portions of reality into determinate zone, indeterminate zone, and exterior zone with respect to the vague projection of a certain cell in a vague partition. Ideally, when corresponding to the same vague name, both partitions coincide but, as we

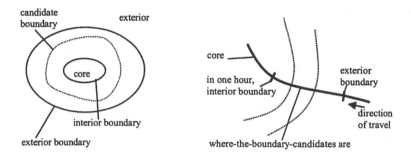

Figure 3. Egg-yolk like reference partitions.

shall see below, this is not the case in general. We will discuss the relationships between the two kinds of partitions in a later section. Until then we ignore the notion of semantic partition and focus on the kinds of partitions shown in the right part of Figure 3 and their use as frames of reference in approximations.

Approximation in Complex Partitions

In the case just discussed, new fiat boundaries are created by judging subjects in ad hoc fashion in order to delimit vagueness. But there are also cases where already existing systems of boundaries are *re-used* for this same purpose. There is one crisp granular partition of this sort with which we are all familiar. It has exactly 50 cells, which project onto the 50 United States of America. A fragment of this partition is presented in the left and right parts of Figure 4. In the foreground of the figure we see in addition an area of bad weather (also called 'Hurricane Walter'), represented by a dark dotted region that is subject to vagueness *de dicto* in the sense discussed above. Wherever the boundaries of this object might be located, they certainly lie skew to the boundaries of the relevant states. But the figure also indicates (with the help of suitable labeling) that:

> [B] Hurricane Walter extends over parts of Wyoming, parts of Montana, parts of Utah, and parts of Idaho.

In the sorts of contexts which we humans normally inhabit, it is impossible to refer to any *crisp* boundary when making judgments about the location of a region of bad weather of the sort described. However, it is possible to describe its (current) location relative to the grid of a map in the manner illustrated in judgment [B].

We, the judging subjects, then deliberately employ a corresponding partition as our frame of reference and we describe the *relationships* that hold between all admissible referents of the vague term 'Hurricane Walter' and the cells of this partition. In terms of spatial relations, this means in the given case that all admissible candidates partially overlap the states of Wyoming, Montana, Utah, and Idaho and that they do not overlap any other state. Consequently, if a judging subject can specify for every partition cell a unique relation – for example *part of* – that holds for all admissible candidate referents of a vague term, then this is a *determinate way to effect vague reference*. The technical name for this phenomenon is *approximation*. For details, see (Bittner and Stell 2002).

A meteorologist may achieve a finer approximation by employing a finer-grained partition as frame of reference in order to make a more specific judgment about the current location of the bad weather region. Thus she might use cells labeled Eastern Idaho, Southern Montana, Western Wyoming, and Northern Utah, and so on, yielding a fiat boundary of the sort depicted in the right part of Figure 4.

Notice that all these boundaries predate the judgments which use them as frames of reference in relation to this particular bad weather system. They are there to be used over and over again in formulating constraints on the possible locations of admissible candidate referents corresponding to vague referring terms. They represent a convenient and determinate way to make vague reference, which has even greater utility when the frame of reference is a commonly accepted one, as in the present case.

Approximation and Judgments

Approximating judgments are a special class of judgments that contain both vague names and a (relatively) crisp reference to boundaries that delimit this vagueness. [A], too, is an approximating judgment which contains the vague name 'Everest' and also a reference to boundaries delimiting the vagueness of

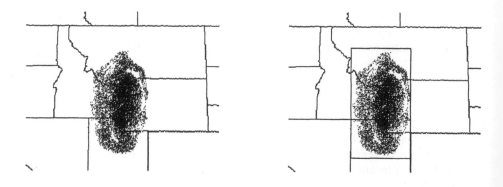

Figure 4. States of the United States with Hurricane Walter.

this term via the phrase '[crossable] within the next hour'. In this paper, we consider approximating judgments which contain a single vague name and a crisp reference frame. More complex cases are possible – including the case where the reference frame itself involves a certain degree of vagueness – but formal consideration of the latter is omitted here since its treatment follows the same basic pattern.

An approximating judgment J^A, if uttered successfully, imposes *two* partitions onto reality: a *vague* partition Pt^V and a *reference partition* Pt^R, along the lines above, whereby the latter serves to delimit the vagueness of the former. An approximating judgment J^A is thus a triple (S, Pt^V, Pt^R), consisting of a sentence, S, together with two granular partitions, Pt^V and Pt^R.

In the approximating judgment J^A = ([B], Pt^V, Pt^R), expressed by the sentence: 'Hurricane Walter extends over parts of Wyoming, Montana, Utah, and Idaho', the corresponding vague partition Pt^V contains a cell labeled 'Hurricane Walter', which projects onto a multiplicity of admissible candidates. At the same time this judgment reuses the partition depicted in the left part of Figure 4 as its reference partition Pt^R. The latter constrains the admissible projections of the cell labeled 'Hurricane Walter' in Pt^V in such a way that each candidate referent that is targeted by a projection P_i of Pt^V must extend over parts of reality targeted by the cells of Pt^R labeled 'Wyoming', 'Utah', 'Montana', and 'Idaho' respectively.

Partition Theory and Approximation

The idea underlying the partition-theoretic view of approximation is that a (crisp) granular partition can be used as a frame of reference (a generalized coordinate frame (Bittner 1997)), which allows us (a) to describe the *approximate location* of objects and thus (b) to project onto portions of reality in an approximate way. We call a granular partition which is used as a frame of reference in this manner a *reference partition*.

Consider a vague name such as 'Hurricane Walter' (hereafter: 'HW') and the corresponding multiplicity of admissible candidate referents for this name formed by crisp portions of reality in the domain of the northwestern United States at some given point in time. Consider some crisp partition structuring this same domain but without recognizing any of the candidates referred to by the name 'HW' directly. This might be the partition created by the boundaries of the separate States of the sort used in Figure 4, or it might be a partition formed by a raster of cells aligned to lines of latitude and longitude.

To understand the formal details of how the latter can serve as reference partition in relation to the former we introduce the three concepts of full overlap *(fo)*, partial overlap *(po)*, and non-overlap *(no)*, concepts which we shall now use to generalize the notions of projection and location, as follows. Consider a reference partition whose cells are projected onto regions of space on the surface of the Earth. Let o be a portion of reality that straddles the boundaries of the cells of this reference partition. The constants *fo, po, no* will now be used to measure the degree of mereological coverage of the object o by the corresponding regions of space.

We call the relation $L^R(o, z, \omega)$ the *rough location* of the portion of reality o with respect to the cell z and the relation $P^R(z, o, \omega)$ the *rough projection* of the cell z onto o. (We use the phrases 'rough location' and 'rough projection' in order to emphasize our indebtedness to the account of approximation in terms of rough sets advanced in (Pawlak 1982).) In both relations, ω stands for the degree of mereological overlap of the portion of reality targeted by the cell z with the actual portion of reality o, i.e., it takes one or other of the values *fo, po,* or *no*. Consider the left part of Figure 4. There the relation *po* holds between all admissible candidate referents HW_i and Montana, i.e., $\forall i: L^R(HW_i, \text{Montana}, po)$. The relation *no* holds between all the HW_i and Oregon, i.e., $\forall i: L^R(HW_i, \text{Oregon}, no)$.

We can characterize the relationships between exact and rough location and exact and rough projection in reference partitions as follows:

$$L^R(o, z, fo) \equiv \exists x \, (L(x, z) \text{ and } x \leq o)$$
$$P^R(z, o, fo) \equiv \exists x \, (P(z, x) \text{ and } x \leq o)$$
$$L^R(o, z, po) \equiv \exists x (\, L(x, z) \text{ and } \exists y \, (y \leq x \text{ and } y \leq o) \text{ and }$$
$$\exists y \, (y \leq x \text{ and } \neg(y \leq o)))$$
$$P^R(z, o, po) \equiv \exists x \, (P(z, x) \text{ and } \exists y \, (y \leq x \text{ and } y \leq o) \text{ and }$$
$$\exists y \, (y \leq x \text{ and } \neg(y \leq o)))$$
$$L^R(o, z, no) \equiv \exists x \, (L(x, z) \text{ and } \neg\exists y: y \leq x \text{ and } y \leq o)$$
$$P^R(z, o, no) \equiv \exists x \, (P(z, z) \text{ and } \neg\exists y: y \leq x \text{ and } y \leq o)$$

The notion of rough location gives rise to an equivalence relation in the domain of objects (portions of reality), with respect to a given reference partition Pt^R with rough location relation L^R, as follows:

$$D\sim \qquad o_1 \sim o_2 \equiv \forall z, \omega: L^R(o_1, z, \omega) \leftrightarrow L^R(o_2, z, \omega).$$

Thus two objects are equivalent with respect to the granular partition Pt^R if and only if they have an identical rough location with respect to all cells of this partition. The relation ~ can thus be interpreted as meaning: indiscernibility with respect to the frame of reference provided by Pt^R. In an approximating judgment $J^A = (S, Pt^V, Pt^R)$, the reference partition Pt^R will be chosen in such a way that the candidate referents targeted by a single cell in Pt^V are equivalent with respect to ~. Often there may be a number of possible choices for reference partitions, all of which have the feature that all candidate referents of the vague name in question are equivalent with respect to the indiscernibility relation ~ induced by the reference partition. For example in Figure 4 we could also have used a regular (raster-shaped) reference partition of some appropriate resolution. However, it is more appropriate in a weather forecast to use the reference partition defined by the boundaries of the separate States because of its familiarity. We will discuss different choices of reference partitions in later sections.

We define a *reference partition* as a quintuple, $Pt^R = ((A, \subseteq), (\Delta, \leq), P^R, L^R, \Omega)$ where $(A, \subseteq)$ and $(\Delta, \leq)$ are a cell structure and target domain as specified above, P^R and L^R are rough projection and location relations, and Ω is the set of values (*fo, po, no*) indicating degrees of overlap (coarser and finer distinctions are possible, as discussed in (Bittner and Stell 2003)). We then can prove that the following counterparts of MB1-3 hold for reference partitions:

TR1 $L^R(o, z, \omega) \rightarrow P^R(z, o, \omega)$

TR2 $P^R(z, o, \omega) \rightarrow L^R(o, z, \omega)$

TR3 $(\forall z, \omega: P^R(z, o_1, \omega) \leftrightarrow P^R(z, o_2, \omega)) \rightarrow o_1 \sim o_2$

TR1 follows from MB1. To see this assume $L^R(o, z, \omega)$ and let $\omega = fo$. We have $\exists x (L(x, z)$ and $x \leq o)$. By MB1 we have $\exists x (P(z, x)$ and $x \leq o)$, hence $P^R(z, o, fo)$ and similarly for $\omega = po$ and $\omega = no$. TR2 follows from MB2 in a similar manner. To see TR3 assume $\forall z, \omega (P^R(z, o_1, \omega) \leftrightarrow P^R(z, o_2, \omega))$. By TR1 and TR2 L^R and P^R are logically equivalent and can be substituted for each other. Therefore we have $L^R(o_1, z, \omega) \leftrightarrow L^R(o_2, z, \omega)$, i.e., $o_1 \sim o_2$.

Corresponding to MB4 we now demand that if all objects have the same relation $\omega \in \{fo, po, no\}$ with respect to the cells z_1 and z_2 then these two cells are identical:

R1 $(\forall o, \omega: L^R(o, z_1, \omega) \leftrightarrow L^R(o, z_2, \omega)) \rightarrow z_1 = z_2$.

Constraining Approximation

Well-Formed Approximations

If an approximating judgment like $([A], Pt^V, Pt^R)$ is to succeed, that is if a true judgment of this form is to have been made, then the reference partition needs to project onto reality in such a way that all admissible candidate referents are equivalent with respect to the indiscernibility relation imposed by Pt^R. Thus, in the hiker case, each value of p^V_i('Everest') must be such that its boundary can be crossed in one hour from the time when the judgment is made (Figure 3).

Let (S, Pt^V, Pt^R) be an approximating judgment and let Pt^V be a vague partition with a cell for each vague name in the sentence S. We then demand that in such an approximating judgment the reference partition Pt^R and the vague partition Pt^V be related to each other in such a way that candidate referents which are targeted by the same cell (i.e., are equivalent in the sense of $\approx$) have the same rough approximation in the underlying reference partition (i.e., are also equivalent in the sense of $\sim$):

EP $o_1 \approx o_2 \rightarrow o_1 \sim o_2$.

We call EP the *equivalence principle*. EP rules out many reference partitions Pt^R which cannot be used for constraining the vagueness of the vague partition Pt^V. Thus it rules out, for example, reference partitions with resolutions too fine for the degree of vagueness of the corresponding vague partition. Consider Figure 4. A raster-cell-partition with cell size of 1m^2 would violate the equivalence principle, since not all candidate referents of the vague name 'Hurricane Walter' would be indiscernible with respect to this reference partition. If the reference partition is too fine then equivalence in the sense of ≈ does not imply equivalence in the sense of ~.

Notice that the converse of the equivalence principle does not hold. This is because there might be portions of reality (x and y) that are equivalent with respect to the reference partition (x ~ y), but which are such that neither is a candidate referent targeted by the cell in question. Consider Figure 5. The approximation of the mereological sum of Yellowstone National Park and Zion National Park (YNP + ZNP) with respect to the Federal State reference partition (left) is identical to the approximation of the candidate referents of the name 'Hurricane Walter' (right) but surely (YNP + ZNP) is not a candidate referent for the name 'Hurricane Walter'.

Precise Approximation

In this section, we discuss the relationship between semantic partition and the kinds of reference partitions previously discussed.

Consider the approximating judgment J = ([A], Pt^V, Pt^R). The reference partition Pt^R shown in the left part of Figure 3 imposes two fiat boundaries onto reality: an interior boundary of the approximation and an exterior boundary of the approximation. As discussed above, this often results in a partition structure similar to the one depicted in the right part of the figure. The projection of this partition onto the path the judging subject takes on her journey towards the summit of Mount Everest results in the reference partition Pt^R.

Consider now the semantic partition imposed by the cell labeled 'Everest' in the vague partition Pt^V. We can see that the relationship between Pt^V and Pt^R satisfies the equivalence principle EP, which demands that all candidate

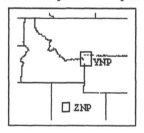 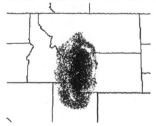

Figure 5. Left: Yellowstone National Park (YNP) and Zion National Park (ZNP). Right: Hurricane Walter.

referents of the vague name 'Everest' are equivalent under ~. Consider now the location of two pairs of boundaries: (a) the interior and exterior boundaries imposed by the judging subject as a frame of reference for her approximation; and (b) the boundaries imposed by the semantic partition into determinate zone, indeterminate zone, and exterior zone via the cells of Pt^V. We say that the approximating judgment is *precise* if and only if (1) the interior boundary of the approximation coincides with the boundary separating the determinate zone from the surrounding parts of the semantic partition; and (2) the exterior boundary of the approximation coincides with the boundary separating the exterior zone from the indeterminate zone of the semantic partition. This means that the semantic partition and the reference partition coincide.

In order to take more complex reference partitions into account, we now define upper and lower approximations of an object o with respect to such partitions. (Again, we use the notions of lower and upper approximation in order to emphasize the correspondence to rough set theory of Pawlak (1982).) The lower approximation of an object o with respect to a reference partition Pt^R is the mereological sum of all those portions of reality which are targeted by cells of Pt^R and which are contained in o:

$$\text{Lower(o)} = \sigma o'(\exists z(o' = p(z) \ \& \ P^R(z, o, fo))),$$

where $\sigma x\phi(x)$ is defined as above.

The upper approximation is the mereological sum of all those portions of reality which are targeted by cells of the reference partition and which overlap o:

$$\text{Upper(o)} = \sigma o'(\exists z(o' = p(z) \ \& \ (P^R(z, o, fo) \text{ or } P^R(z, o, po))))$$

Consider now the reference partitions shown in the left part of Figure 6, which is a refined version of the egg-yolk reference partition in the right part of Figure 6. The core cell of the latter is subdivided into eastern and western subcells (ec and wc for eastern part of the core region and western part of the core region, respectively). Moreover the region where the boundaries are is

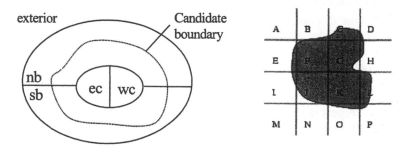

Figure 6. Approximation in complex partitions. Left: a refined egg-yolk partition. Right: a raster partition.

subdivided into a northern and southern region (nb and sb, respectively). The lower approximation of the candidate referent signified by its outer boundary is the mereological sum of those portions of reality which are targeted by the cells 'ec' and 'wc'. Its upper approximation has as parts in addition portions of reality targeted by the cells 'nb' and 'sb'.

For another example of lower and upper approximations, consider the right part of Figure 6. The upper approximation of the depicted region with respect to the raster-shaped partition is the mereological sum of the targets of the cells [B,..., L, O, P]. The lower approximation is identical to the target of the cell K.

Notice that upper approximations are always defined. Lower approximations, however, are only defined if the reference partition is sufficiently fine grained, so that $P^R(z, o, fo)$ holds for some cell z and some portion of reality o. This is because in mereology there is no counterpart to the empty set.

With respect to these more complex reference partitions we now say that an approximating judgment is precise if and only if (1) the boundary of the lower approximation of any candidate referent of 'N' coincides with the boundary separating the determinate zone from the surrounding parts of the semantic partition imposed by the vague projection of the cell associated with 'N'; and (2) the boundary of the upper approximation of any of the candidate referents coincides with the boundary separating the exterior zone from the indeterminate zone of the vague projection of the cell associated with 'N'.

In formal terms, we describe this as follows. Let $J = (N, Pt^V, Pt^R)$ be an approximating judgment with $Pt^V = ((A^V, \subseteq), (\Delta, \leq), P^V, L^V)$ and $Pt^R = ((A^R, \subseteq), (\Delta, \leq), P^R, L^R, \Omega)$. We then call J^A *precise* if and only if

$$\forall o \in [o]_z: \text{Lower}(o) = det^V(z) \text{ and } \text{Upper}(o) = (det^V(z) + indet^V(z)).$$

Here $z \in A^V$ is the cell in the vague partition corresponding to the vague name 'N', $[o]_z$ is the set of all objects targeted by the vague projection of z, and + is the mereological sum.

Constraining Approximation

We now discuss constraining approximations, defined as those approximations that do not have the property of being precise but still satisfy the equivalence principle.

Let z be the cell in the vague partition Pt^V which corresponds to the vague name 'N', and let $[o]_z$ be the set of all candidate referents of 'N', i.e., portions of reality targeted by z under P^V. The approximation of candidate referents $o \in [o]_z$ with respect to the approximating partition Pt^R is called *constraining* if and only if the following holds:

$$\forall o \in [o]_z:$$

either:

Lower(o) is defined and Lower(o) $\leq det_V(z) \leq (det_V(z) + indet_V(z)) \leq$ Upper(o)

or:

$det_V(z) \leq (det_V(z) + indet_V(z)) \leq$ Upper(o)

Consider Figure 4 and assume that the determinate zone of the vague reference of the name 'Hurricane Walter', $det_V(HW)$, is situated along the border between Idaho and Wyoming. It follows that the lower approximation is undefined for any of the candidate referents because the federal state partition is too coarse. The upper approximation however *is* defined, since any candidate referent is part of the mereological sum of Idaho, Montana, Wyoming, and Utah. Hence the resulting approximation is constraining.

Consider the class of constraining approximations. As already Aristotle repeatedly emphasized (at 1094b11 *sq.*, 1098a26, 1103b34 *sq.*, 1165a13), judging subjects will characteristically use those approximating judgments which are constraining but which are *as precise as necessary* in whatever is the context in hand. In (Bittner and Smith 2001b), we argue that this will imply that the limits imposed on vagueness by an approximation will normally be such that the resulting judgment is not subject to truth-value indeterminacy. The judgments we actually make in normal contexts (as contrasted with those types of artificial judgments invented by philosophers) are determinately either true or false even in spite of the vague terms which they contain.

Properties of Reference Partitions

Reference partitions are of central importance for approximating judgments. Examples of reference partitions include: any political subdivision, raster-shaped partitions adjusted to latitude and longitude, the block structure in American cities, the subdivision of Vienna into *Bezirke* and of France into *Départements*, etc. Other important groups of reference partitions are partitions imposed by quantity-scales of all kinds (Johansson 1989, chapter 4), including temporal partitions like calendars (Bittner 2002).

Consider again the judgment [B]: 'Hurricane Walter extends over parts of Wyoming, Montana, Utah, and Idaho' and the corresponding structure $J^A = ([B], Pt^V, Pt^R)$. The *skeleton* of the reference partition Pt^R is the partition Pt^S, which recognizes the United States (Figure 4) and thereby establishes the frame of reference for the approximation. Consider Figure 3. Here the skeleton Pt^S of the reference partitions is an egg-yolk structure containing the cells labeled 'core', 'exterior', and 'where the candidate boundaries are'.

Every reference partition $Pt^R = ((A, \subseteq), (\Delta, \leq), P^R, L^R, \Omega)$ has a crisp partition $Pt^S = ((A, \subseteq), (\Delta, \leq), P^S, L^S)$ called the skeleton of Pt^R. Both, Pt^S and Pt^R share the cell structure $(A, \subseteq)$ and the target domain $(\Delta, \leq)$. In order to ensure that the intuitions sketched in the previous paragraph (and implicitly assumed in our definitions of rough location L^R and rough projection P^R) are satisfied we demand that the skeleton has following properties:

    i. If $P^S(z, o)$ holds in Pt^S then so does $P^R(z, o, fo)$ in Pt^R. For all other cells z_1 in the shared cell structure A we have $P^R(z_1, o, no)$. That is:
$$P^S(z, o) \rightarrow (P^R(z, o, fo) \text{ and } (\forall z_1 \in A: z_1 \neq z \rightarrow P^R(z_1, o, no))).$$

    ii. If $L^S(o, z)$ holds in Pt^S then so does $L^R(o, z, fo)$ in Pt^R. For all other cells z_1 in A we have $L^R(o, z_1, no)$. That is:
$$L^S(o, z) \rightarrow (L^R(o, z, fo) \text{ and } (\forall z_1 \in A: z_1 \neq z \rightarrow L^R(o, z_1, no))).$$

    iii. Skeletons satisfy MB1–6.

Often skeletons are also full, exhaustive, and complete in the sense of (Bittner and Smith 2003), which means in effect that they create subdivisions of the targeted domain into jointly exhaustive and pairwise disjoint portions.

The skeletons of reference partitions which serve as frames of reference are often spatial or temporal in nature. They are relatively stable, i.e., they do not change over time. This implies in turn: (a) that the pertinent cell structure is fixed and (b) that the objects onto which the skeleton projects do not change (they are, for example, spatial regions tied to the surface of the Earth). Consider again the examples in Figure 4. The granular partition projecting onto the United States has existed for more than one hundred years without significant changes. (Hurricane Walter, in contrast, changes continuously throughout the course of its (brief) existence.) In fact, Figure 4 itself needs to be considered as a snapshot of reality at some determinate point in time (Smith and Brogaard, 2002, Bittner and Smith 2003a, Grenon 2003). It provides us with useful information when we are told that Hurricane Walter was located in parts of Montana, Idaho, Wyoming, and Utah at such and such a time. Every American child learns the corresponding reference partition in school, and uses it for all sorts of purposes thereafter (Stevens and Coupe 1978). Reference partitions are characteristically built out of boundaries with which human beings can become easily familiar, objects which facilitate easy learning.

Conclusions

We have proposed an application of the theory of granular partitions to the phenomenon of vagueness, a phenomenon which is itself seen in *de dicto* terms, i.e. as a semantic property of names and predicates. We defended a supervaluationistic theory of the underlying semantics and expressed it in terms of the theory of granular partitions. We showed that the use of frames of reference in making approximating judgments can be formulated very naturally in partition-theoretic terms, and that the framework of granular partitions then helps us to understand the relationships between vagueness and approximation. While the bulk of our examples were derived from the spatial domain, the generality of the theory of granular partitions allows an easy generalization to other sorts of cases.

Acknowledgments

The authors thank Wolfgang Heydrich and the reviewers for helpful comments. Part of this work was carried out under the auspices of the Wolfgang Paul Program of the Alexander von Humboldt Foundation. It was also supported by DARPA under the Command Post of the Future program, and by the National Science Foundation under its Research on Learning and Education program and also under NSF Research Grant BCS-9975557: "Geographic Categories: An Ontological Investigation".

References

Bittner, T. (1997). A qualitative coordinate language of location of figures within the ground. In S. Hirtle & A. U. Frank (Eds.), *Spatial information theory: A theoretical basis for GIS*, COSIT 99, 1329 Lecture Notes in Computer Science, Berlin: Springer, 223–240.

Bittner, T. (2002). "Approximate Temporal Reasoning." *Annals of Mathematics and Artificial Intelligenc,. 35*, 1-2

Bittner, T. and B. Smith (2001a). A taxonomy of granular partitions. In D. Montello (Ed.), *Spatial information theory: Foundations of geographic information science*, COSIT 01, Lecture Notes in Computer Science, 2205, Berlin: Springer, 28–43.

Bittner, T. and B. Smith (2001b). Vagueness and granular partitions. In C. Welty & B. Smith (Eds.), *Formal ontology and information systems*, New York: ACM Press, 309–321.

Bittner, T. and B. Smith (2003). A theory of granular partitions. In M. Duckham, M. F. Goodchild & M. F. Worboys (Eds.), *Foundations of geographic information science*, London: Taylor & Francis, 117–151.

Bittner, T. and B. Smith (2003a). Granular spatio-temporal ontologies. *AAAI Spring Symposium on Foundations and Applications of Spatio-Temporal Reasoning* (FASTR).

Bittner, T. and J. Stell (2002). Approximate qualitative spatial reasoning. *Spatial Cognition and Computation, 2*, 435–466.

Clementini, E. and P. D. Felice (1996). An algebraic model for spatial objects with undetermined boundaries. In P. Burrough and A. U. Frank (Eds.), *Geographic objects with indeterminate boundaries*. London: Taylor and Francis.

Cohn, A. G. and N. M. Gotts (1996). The egg-yolk representation of regions with indeterminate boundaries. In P. Burrough & A. U. Frank (Eds.), *Geographic objects with indeterminate boundaries*. London: Taylor and Francis.

Fine, K. (1975). Vagueness, truth and logic. *Synthese, 30*, 265–300.

Grenon, P. (2003) The spatio-temporal ontology of reality and its formalization. *AAAI Spring Symposium on Foundations and Applications of Spatio-Temporal Reasoning* (FASTR).

Johansson, I. (1989). *Ontological investigations: An inquiry into the categories of nature, man, and society.* New York: Routledge.

Pawlak, Z. (1982). Rough sets. *International Journal of Computation Information. 11*, 341–356.

Roy, A. J. and J. G. Stell (2001). Spatial relations between indeterminate regions. *Journal of Approximate Reasoning,* 27(3), 205-234.

Smith, B. (1995). On drawing lines on a map. In A. U. Frank & W. Kuhn (Eds.), *Spatial information theory: A theoretical basis for GIS,* COSIT 95, Lecture Notes in Computer Science 988 , Berlin: Springer, 475–484.

Smith, B. (2001). Fiat objects. *Topoi, 20(2),* 131–148.

Smith, B. and B. Brogaard (2002). Quantum mereotopology. *Annals of Mathematics and Artificial Intelligence, 35,* 1–2, 153–175.

Smith, B. and B. Brogaard (to appear). A unified theory of truth and reference. *Logique et Analyse.*

Stevens, A. and P. Coupe (1978). Distortions in judged spatial relations. *Cognitive Psychology, 10,* 422–437.

Varzi, A. (2001). Vagueness in Geography. *Philosophy and Geography, 4,* 49–65.

SPATIAL COGNITION AND COMPUTATION, *3*(2&3), 157–183
Copyright © 2003, Lawrence Erlbaum Associates, Inc.

Spatial Vagueness and Second-Order Vagueness

Lars Kulik
University of Maine

This paper presents a geometric characterization of geographic objects with vague boundaries. Since the framework is based on ordering geometry and does not rely on numerical concepts, it can be applied to qualitative spatial reasoning. The characterization describes vague regions and gradual transitions between two vague regions. This approach takes into account that the region of all points that definitely belong to an object is also vague, called *higher-order vagueness*. Higher-order vagueness is usually neglected by theories modeling spatial vagueness. The approach distinguishes first- and second-order vague regions and characterizes the gradual transitions of second-order vague regions. These gradual transitions allow transitions within transitions. In general, it is not possible to reduce higher-order vagueness to first-order vagueness. Using a spatial ordering structure the article shows when second-order vagueness is useful and examines the relationship between first- and second-order vagueness. An example shows how second-order vagueness can be used to represent geographic objects.

Keywords: Axiomatics, Geographic Information Science, Higher-Order Vagueness, Qualitative Spatial Representation, Spatial Vagueness

1 Introduction

Most modern geographic information systems model the spatial extensions of geographic objects as sharp regions that have a unique boundary. A sharp region enables a clear distinction between which points belong to the object region and which do not. However, almost every natural geographic object has a vague

---

Correspondence concerning this article should be addressed to Lars Kulik, National Center for Geographic Information and Analysis, Department of Spatial Information Science and Engineering, 348 Boardman Hall, University of Maine, USA; kulik@spatial.maine.edu

boundary (cf. Couclelis 1996). Meadows, habitats of animals, spheres of influence of cities, or climate zones do not have precisely defined regions. These objects are called *vague objects*, since there are points for which it is indeterminate if they belong to the object region. The points that definitely belong to a vague object region signify the *core* of the object region. A vague object has a *gradual boundary* if we can determine for two given points which of the two belongs to the object region to a higher degree.

Two vague regions can share a common gradual boundary like the transition of a desert and a prairie, of different soil strata, or of a hill and a valley. For a point of a gradual transition of two vague regions there is no criterion that determines to which of the two regions the point clearly belongs. Typically, there are no abrupt changes in gradual transitions, and Hadzilacos (1996) calls them *blend-in constellations*.

A theory taking into account that the core of a vague object or the spatial extension of a gradual boundary is vague, too, has to cope with second-order vagueness. We provide an example of second-order vagueness: the gradual transition between a forest and a snow region on a mountain (see Figure 1). Using first-order vagueness, the gradual transition between the forest and the snow region is given by a meadow with scattered trees. However, following a path from the interior of the forest to the meadow, there is no last point on the path that definitely belongs to the forest, or a first one that definitely belongs to the gradual transition of the forest and the meadow. The transition between the meadow with trees and the forest or the snow region is smooth as well. These smooth transitions can be considered as separate entities, called the *sparse forest* and the *region of stunted trees*. Within the sparse forest, the density of the trees decreases, and within the region of the stunted trees, their growth decreases. To capture the sparse forest and the region consisting of stunted trees as gradual transitions within the gradual transition of the forest and the snow region we have to employ a geometric description that captures second-order vagueness.

There are at least two perspectives in which way objects can be considered as spatially vague: the objects themselves are vague, or the concepts or representations of the objects are vague. The first view is called *ontic vagueness* (cf. for instance Tye 1990). The second view is called *semantic vagueness* and was established by Russell (1923) (for a recent view cf. Varzi 2001). Spatial vagueness is considered in this paper as a variant of semantic vagueness: A predicate like "forest" does not refer to a single (vague) object in the world but we can represent the spatial location of a forest by a vague region (for a similar idea cf. Morreau 2002). The idea is to describe a vague region by ordered sharp regions, which represent different ways to render a precise spatial location of a vague region. The goal of the paper is a qualitative, geometric description of vague regions with gradual boundaries and gradual transitions between them. The formal description supplies a relative description of vagueness in Section 3 that does not rely on numbers. It

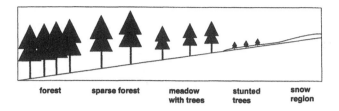

forest   sparse forest   meadow   stunted   snow
                           with trees   trees   region

Figure 1. The gradual transition of a forest and a snow region on a mountain is a meadow with trees. The transitions of the definite meadow region and the definite forest region or the definite snow region are also gradual transitions: the sparse forest and the region of stunted trees.

employs orders and pre-orders to compare points regarding their degree of membership to a vague region.

In Section 4 we propose an approach that is able to cope with second-order vagueness. It can also be employed to represent *higher-order indeterminacy* of vague objects. Higher-order indeterminacy occurs if we take into account that there are different interpretations of the vague regions of an spatial object depending on different experts opinions, different contexts, or different criteria determining the spatial extension of the object. For instance, in the case of the forest region we can associate different vague regions depending on the height of the trees, the density of the trees, the diameter of the trees, or the overall size of the forest region.

2 Current Work

The modeling and formal characterization of vague objects plays an increasingly important role in geography (cf. Burrough & Frank 1996) and in spatial databases (Erwig & Schneider 1997). We give a brief overview of approaches used currently in computer and geographic information science to represent spatial vagueness: fuzzy approaches, accounts based on rough set theory, and qualitative characterizations. Since the approach presented in this paper takes up central ideas of the theory of supervaluation (without actually using the technique of supervaluation), it is discussed in more detail at the end of this section.

Within geographic information science, spatial vagueness is often modeled by employing fuzzy methods. Fuzzy methods use the concept of different degrees of membership to describe vagueness. Burrough (1996) considers fuzzy sets as an appropriate method "to deal with ambiguity, vagueness and ambivalence in mathematical or conceptual models of empirical phenomena" (p. 18). Recently, Fisher (2000) remarked that many geographic phenomena are vulnerable to the

Sorites Paradox and reviewed applications in geography using fuzzy set theory. Guesgen & Albrecht (2000) uses fuzzy techniques to model imprecise and qualitative spatial relations between geographic objects. Brown (1998) applies fuzzy set theory to aggregate point data from a vegetation area like a forest to a continuous representation of the area, which incorporates the boundary vagueness of this area. Schneider (1999) introduced fuzzy points, fuzzy lines, and fuzzy regions and studies their algebraic and topological properties on a discrete geometric structure (Schneider 2003). Originally, the theory of fuzzy sets had been developed by Zadeh (1965) to provide a general representation of vagueness based on different degrees of membership. Later, Zadeh (1975) extended his work and introduced fuzzy logic to reason about vagueness. Dubois, Ostasiewicz & Prade (2000) give an overview about the fundamentals of fuzzy sets, their history, and their applications.

A different strategy is pursued by approaches based on rough set theory. Instead of using the concept of membership, the theory of rough sets generalizes the concept of classical mathematical sets by introducing a boundary region for a set. A rough set lies between its lower and upper approximations, i.e. the points that definitely belong to the set and the points that may belong to the set. Rough set theory has been introduced by the work of Pawlak (1982) and has been discussed in greater detail in Pawlak (1991). Worboys (1998b) uses rough set theory to represent imprecise spatial data that results from different finite resolutions. This theoretical foundation is further refined in Worboys (1998a) by including semantic components. Beaubouef & Petry (2001) employ the theory of rough sets to investigate mereotopological relations between spatial entities represented within a continuous structure. Ahlqvist, Keukelaar & Oukbir (2000) define measures based on rough sets to assess imprecision and uncertainty in classifications. Duckham, Mason, Stell & Worboys (2001) use rough set theory to model imprecise knowledge in geodemographic applications.

Since many tasks in spatial reasoning about geographic objects only require qualitative knowledge like topology (Egenhofer & Franzosa 1991) and ordering geometry (Kulik & Klippel 1999), a description is desirable that does not rely on a numerical representation like fuzzy theories. Cohn (1997) gives an overview of qualitative spatial reasoning theories. Recently, a few approaches have been developed, which formalize spatial reasoning about vague entities that involve topological or mereological relations (cf. Clementini & Felice 1996, Cohn & Gotts 1996a, Cohn & Gotts 1996b). However, neither these qualitative theories nor theories based on rough sets have been developed to cope with specific challenges of gradual transitions of vague regions. To formalize vague regions and gradual transitions between them, this article proposes a geometric characterization of spatial vagueness that is motivated by the theory of supervaluation.

In the theory of supervaluation (cf. Dummett 1975, Fine 1975, Lewis 1993) vagueness is considered as a semantic indecision: a vague predicate distinguishes entities to which it definitely applies, its *positive extension*, and entities to which it definitely does not apply, its *negative extension*. However, for some entities it is indefinite whether the predicate applies. They are called the *penumbra* of the predicate. According to the theory of supervaluation, this semantic indecision results from different interpretations. An interpretation assigning a meaning to a predicate like 'forest' is called *admissible* if it makes the predicate true in the positive extension, false in the negative extension, and either true or false in the penumbra. Since every admissible interpretation is precise, it is called a *precisification*. The theory of supervaluation is able to maintain crucial features of classical logic like the law of excluded middle and the law of non-contradiction.

The concept of degrees of truth seems to be tightly connected to many-valued logics, especially fuzzy logic. However, Kamp (1975) has shown that it is possible to introduce a notion of truth within the theory of supervaluation that admits different degrees or grades of truth. A predicate is true for an entity to a certain degree, if it applies to the entity for some but not all precisifications. The idea of Kamp is to measure the set of precisifications of a predicate that apply to the entity relative to the set of all possible precisifications of the predicate. In the general case, it is impossible to define a measure for (unrelated) interpretations of a vague predicate. Accordingly, the theory of supervaluation has not been applied in geography or computer science (except for the work of Bennett 1998, Bennett 2001a, Bennett 2001b). We propose a geometric theory that avoids a general measure. Instead, we use orders as well as pre-orders to compare two points with respect to a vague region in a relative manner (see Section 3.2 for details). A relative comparison does not require an assignment of numbers.

The theory of supervaluation subdivides the application range of a predicate denoting a spatial object into its positive extension, its negative extension, and its penumbra. If the assignment of spatial locations into one of these classes is unique then the predicate is vague of order one. Following Russell (1923) most vagueness theorists assume the opposite: there are locations that cannot be exactly assigned to one of the three classes, the borderline cases of these classes. The vagueness of these classes is called *second-order vagueness*. This idea can be generalized even further to higher orders of vagueness (cf. Williamson 1999). In general, many accounts in philosophy consider the characterization of higher-order vagueness as a crucial feature of every theory of vagueness. To quote Keefe & Smith (1996, p. 15): "Any putative theory of vagueness must accommodate the apparent lack of sharp boundaries to the borderline cases and address the issue of higher-order vagueness."

3 Geometric Theory of Vague Regions and Gradual Transitions

The introductory example of the forest and the snow region is the motivation for the approach developed in Section 3. The forest region can be characterized by several criteria: the height of the trees, the density of the trees, the diameter of the trees, or the overall size of the forest region (for an in-depth discussion of a forest cf. Bennett 2001b). If we take one of these criteria, e.g., the height of the trees, there are trees that are clearly taller than a predefined height. These trees constitute a region, the core of the forest. It is clear that the trees being slightly smaller than the predefined threshold value also belong to the forest to some degree. If we use finitely many additional threshold values, we obtain finitely many sharp regions determining the vague region of the forest. If we use any value between zero and the minimal value to be considered in the core of the forest, we get infinitely many sharp regions. All sharp regions are possible representations of the spatial extension of the forest. In contrast to sharp objects, it is not adequate to represent the forest as a vague object by a single sharp region. Thus, the presented account associates to every vague object a vague region, which is characterized as a family of sharp regions (see Section 3.1). The basic idea is to consider sharp regions, like the theory of supervaluation, to be different precisifications of a vague region. The sharp regions of the forest do not have to be defined by numbers. They could also be the result of assessments of different botanists during their field work. In this case, the sharp regions do not have to be included in each other. If the botanists agree on the criteria determining a forest, such that the regions can be assumed at least to overlap, we can introduce a vague region for the forest by a procedure discussed at the end of Section 3.1.

The forest and the snow region can be seen as vague regions with a gradual boundary. A vague object with a gradual boundary suggests that spatial locations belong to the object region in different degrees. The geometric description introduces an order relation in Section 3.2 for points. The order relation provides a relative characterization of vagueness that determines for two points of a vague region which of the two points belongs to the vague region to a higher degree. If we take the vegetation density or the height of the trees as criterion to determine the forest and the snow region, the transition of the forest and the snow region can be described by a gradual transition. Points that belong more to the forest region, belong less to the snow region. Gradual transitions are discussed in Section 3.3. If we need a numerical representation of the forest region, for example, for a graphical representation of the vague region using gray or color values, we cannot use a relative description of vagueness. In Section 3.4 we propose two techniques to obtain a numerical representation of vagueness from a relative one.

The basic geometric entities are points, sharp regions, and vague regions. Vague regions denote the spatial extensions of geographic objects and points represent locations or positions of point-like objects. The capitals P, P', Q, and R denote points; $\mathcal{R}$, $\mathcal{R}'$, $\mathcal{R}''$, $\mathcal{R}_1$, and $\mathcal{R}_2$ denote sharp regions; and $\mathcal{V}$, $\mathcal{V}'$, $\mathcal{V}_1$, and $\mathcal{V}_2$ denote vague regions. The entities are related by an incidence relation (ι). On the basis of the incidence relation we define an order relation ($\trianglerighteq$) for points and sharp regions with respect to vague regions. Therefore, the formal framework is based on ordering geometry. Some of the axioms and definitions are taken from Kulik (2001). We omit the formal description of sharp regions. In principle, any account of (topologically open) regular regions can be used. The regions do not need to be convex or (self-)connected. The characterization is based on the assumption that the regions do not include their topological boundary. However, only minor modifications are necessary if we assume that the regions are topologically closed. We further assume that a sharp region is uniquely determined by its points. In particular, the approach is compatible with mereotopological calculi like the work of Randell, Cui & Cohn (1992).

3.1 Axiomatic Characterization of Vague Regions

The incidence relation relates sharp and vague regions: In the same way as a point is incident with a straight line or a region, a sharp region is incident with a vague region. Axiom (VI1) requires that a vague region is uniquely determined by its sharp regions.

$$\forall \mathcal{V} \mathcal{V}' \, [\forall \mathcal{R} \, [\mathcal{R} \, \iota \, \mathcal{V} \Leftrightarrow \mathcal{R} \, \iota \, \mathcal{V}'] \Rightarrow \mathcal{V} = \mathcal{V}'] \tag{VI1}$$

To enable a comparison of the sharp regions of a vague region, we introduce an order relation $\trianglerighteq$. A similar relation, although with different properties, was introduced by Cohn and Gotts (1996b). If $\mathcal{R}$ and $\mathcal{R}'$ are two sharp regions of a vague region $\mathcal{V}$, and the region $\mathcal{R}$ is a part of the region $\mathcal{R}'$, then the region $\mathcal{R}$ is called *at least as restrictive as* the region $\mathcal{R}'$ with respect to the vague region $\mathcal{V}$ (symbolized as $\trianglerighteq(\mathcal{V}, \mathcal{R}, \mathcal{R}')$). A region $\mathcal{R}$ is a *part* of another region $\mathcal{R}'$ (symbolized as $\sqsubseteq$) if all points of the region $\mathcal{R}$ are also points of the region $\mathcal{R}'$.

$$\mathcal{R} \sqsubseteq \mathcal{R}' \quad \Leftrightarrow_{\text{def}} \quad \forall P \, [P \, \iota \, \mathcal{R} \Rightarrow P \, \iota \, \mathcal{R}']$$
$$\trianglerighteq(\mathcal{V}, \mathcal{R}, \mathcal{R}') \Leftrightarrow_{\text{def}} \quad \mathcal{R} \, \iota \, \mathcal{V} \wedge \mathcal{R}' \, \iota \, \mathcal{V} \wedge \mathcal{R} \sqsubseteq \mathcal{R}'$$

From the definition of the relation $\sqsubseteq$ immediately follows its transitivity. Accordingly, the relation $\trianglerighteq$ is also transitive for a fixed vague region (TV1). Moreover, the relation $\sqsubseteq$ is antisymmetric, and therefore for a given vague region the antisymmetry holds for the $\trianglerighteq$-relation (TV2).

$$\forall \mathcal{V} \mathcal{R} \mathcal{R}' \mathcal{R}'' \, [\trianglerighteq(\mathcal{V}, \mathcal{R}, \mathcal{R}') \wedge \trianglerighteq(\mathcal{V}, \mathcal{R}', \mathcal{R}'') \Rightarrow \trianglerighteq(\mathcal{V}, \mathcal{R}, \mathcal{R}'')] \tag{TV1}$$
$$\forall \mathcal{V} \mathcal{R} \mathcal{R}' \quad [\trianglerighteq(\mathcal{V}, \mathcal{R}, \mathcal{R}') \wedge \trianglerighteq(\mathcal{V}, \mathcal{R}', \mathcal{R}) \Rightarrow \mathcal{R} = \mathcal{R}'] \tag{TV2}$$

Corresponding to the positive and negative extension of a vague predicate, we define the core and the hull of a vague region. The minimal extension of a vague object is called the *core*, the maximal extension the *hull*. The core and the hull of a vague region $\mathcal{V}$ are symbolized as core($\mathcal{V}$) and hull($\mathcal{V}$), respectively. The core of a vague region of a geographic object is the region that definitely counts as part of the spatial extension of the geographic object. Thus, the core of a vague region is defined as the most restrictive region of all regions that are incident with the vague region. Therefore, the core is contained in all regions of the vague region. The hull of a vague region, on the other hand, contains every region of a vague region. Hence, the hull is defined as the least restrictive region of a vague region.

$$\mathcal{R} = \text{core}(\mathcal{V}) \Leftrightarrow_{\text{def}} \quad \mathcal{R}\,\iota\,\mathcal{V} \wedge \forall \mathcal{R}'\,[\mathcal{R}'\,\iota\,\mathcal{V} \Rightarrow \trianglerighteq(\mathcal{V},\mathcal{R},\mathcal{R}')]$$

$$\mathcal{R} = \text{hull}(\mathcal{V}) \Leftrightarrow_{\text{def}} \quad \mathcal{R}\,\iota\,\mathcal{V} \wedge \forall \mathcal{R}'\,[\mathcal{R}'\,\iota\,\mathcal{V} \Rightarrow \trianglerighteq(\mathcal{V},\mathcal{R}',\mathcal{R})]$$

The core of a vague region comprises all points that are contained in every sharp region of a vague region (TV3). The core of a geographic object corresponds in supervaluational terms to the positive extension of a predicate denoting this object. A point belongs to the hull of a vague region, if there is at least one sharp region of the vague region including the point (TV4). Thus, a point belongs to the negative extension of a predicate denoting an object, if it is not included in the hull of the object region.

$$\forall \mathcal{V}\,P\,[P\,\iota\,\text{core}(\mathcal{V}) \Leftrightarrow \forall \mathcal{R}\,[\mathcal{R}\,\iota\,\mathcal{V} \Rightarrow P\,\iota\,\mathcal{R}]] \tag{TV3}$$

$$\forall \mathcal{V}\,P\,[P\,\iota\,\text{core}(\mathcal{V}) \Leftrightarrow \exists \mathcal{R}\,[\mathcal{R}\,\iota\,\mathcal{V} \wedge P\,\iota\,\mathcal{R}]] \tag{TV4}$$

Axiom (VB1) guarantees that there are at least two sharp regions representing the vague region, the core and the hull of a vague region. If the core and the hull of a vague region are equal, all sharp regions of the vague region are equal to the core and hull. In this case, the extension of the vague region is described by a single sharp region. Thus, a sharp region can be seen as a special case of a vague region. Cohn and Gotts (1996b) require that a vague region has no core region, which means that there is not a single region for a geographic object that belongs undeniable to the object's spatial extension. Axiom (VB2) states that if two sharp regions are incident with the same vague region, one of the sharp regions is more restrictive than the other one. By assuming Axiom (VB2) the characterization departs from the theory of supervaluation. A supervaluational account does not integrate a linearity condition for its precisifications. However, the objective of the formalism is a characterization of vague regions with gradual boundaries; accordingly, the formalism has to guarantee that two points (or two regions) can be compared regarding their degree of membership to a vague region. To supply (non-numerical) degrees of membership of regions to a vague region, the Axiom (VB2) ensures that two regions can always be compared with respect to the relation $\trianglerighteq$.

$$\forall \mathcal{V}\,\exists \mathcal{R}\,\mathcal{R}'\,[\mathcal{R} = \text{core}(\mathcal{V}) \wedge \mathcal{R}' = \text{hull}(\mathcal{V})] \tag{VB1}$$

$$\forall \mathcal{V}\,\mathcal{R}\,\mathcal{R}'\,[\mathcal{R}\,\iota\,\mathcal{V} \wedge \mathcal{R}'\,\iota\,\mathcal{V} \Rightarrow \trianglerighteq(\mathcal{V},\mathcal{R},\mathcal{R}') \vee \trianglerighteq(\mathcal{V},\mathcal{R}',\mathcal{R})] \tag{VB2}$$

Axioms (VB1) and (VB2) combined with Theorems (TV1) and (TV2) describe a geometric ordering structure for the sharp regions of a vague region. The axioms contain no assumption whether the sharp regions of a vague region are a discrete or a dense structure. Thus, a vague region can be characterized by finitely or infinitely many regions. In the finite case, the sharp regions of a vague region could be represented as an ordered array. Axiom (VB1) guarantees that a vague region can be described by two distinct sharp regions. If there are no other regions than the core and the hull, we obtain the egg-yolk model of Cohn and Gotts (1996a). The egg-yolk model can be considered as a minimal model of vague spatial regions.

We give a second model to illustrate the geometric structure specified by Axioms (VI1), (VB1), and (VB2): the alpha-cuts of fuzzy set theory. An *alpha-cut* (α-cut) M_α of a set $M \subset M'$ is the set of elements of M' whose membership value (denoted by the characteristic function χ_M) is bigger than or equal to the threshold value $\alpha \in]0, 1]$:

$$M_\alpha := \{x \in M' \,|\, \chi_M(x) \geq \alpha\}, \ \alpha \in]0, 1], \ M_0 := \{x \in M' \,|\, \chi_M(x) > 0\}.$$

The sets M_α fulfill the following consistency condition: the smaller the threshold value, the larger the set M_α: $\alpha' \leq \alpha \Rightarrow M_\alpha \subseteq M_{\alpha'}$. Thus, Axiom (VB2) is fulfilled. The core is given M_1 by and the hull by M_0. Since for every set M_α holds $M_1 \subseteq M_\alpha \subseteq M_0$ Axiom (VB1) follows. The vague region $\mathcal{V}$ then is defined by the sets of all α-cuts: $\mathcal{V} := \{M_\alpha \,|\, \alpha \in [0, 1]\}$, which implies Axiom (VI1).

If an imprecise region is described by finitely many sharp regions and the sharp regions do not fulfill Axiom (VB2) (i.e., the imprecise region is not a vague region in the sense of the axiomatic structure), it is possible to introduce an ordering structure, if all the region share at least a common intersection. If the imprecise region is described by the regions $\mathcal{R}_i, i \in \{1, \ldots, n\}$, then we can construct regions $\mathcal{R}'_i, i \in \{1, \ldots, n\}$ that satisfy Axiom (VB2) in the following manner:

$$\mathcal{R}'_i := \bigcup_{\{j_1, \ldots, j_i\} \subseteq \{1, \ldots, n\}} \left(\bigcap_{k=1}^{i} \mathcal{R}_{j_k} \right)$$

In the case $n = 3$, for example, we would obtain the regions:

$$\mathcal{R}'_1 = \mathcal{R}_1 \cup \mathcal{R}_2 \cup \mathcal{R}_3, \quad \mathcal{R}'_2 = (\mathcal{R}_1 \cap \mathcal{R}_2) \cup (\mathcal{R}_1 \cap \mathcal{R}_3) \cup (\mathcal{R}_2 \cap \mathcal{R}_3),$$
$$\mathcal{R}'_3 = \mathcal{R}_1 \cap \mathcal{R}_2 \cap \mathcal{R}_3$$

Formally, we are associating to the imprecise region a vague region $\mathcal{V}$—described by the regions $\mathcal{R}'_i, i \in \{1, \ldots, n\}$—that fulfills Axioms (VI1), (VB1), and (VB2). According to the construction, we obtain $\text{core}(\mathcal{V}) = \mathcal{R}'_n$, $\text{hull}(\mathcal{V}) = \mathcal{R}'_1$, and $\mathcal{R}'_j \subseteq \mathcal{R}'_i \ \forall i, j \in \{1, \ldots, n\}, i < j$. Using the regions $\mathcal{R}'_i, i \in \{1, \ldots, n\}$, we are then able to compare two points in a relative manner with respect to the vague region $\mathcal{V}$. The details for a relative comparison of two points to a vague region are given in the next section.

3.2 Relative Degrees of Membership as Pre-Orders

The characterization of vague regions by sharp regions allows us to compare points in a relative manner regarding their degree of membership to a vague region. Relative characterizations enable more abstract representations of spatial vagueness. It is not necessary to decide for individual points, which absolute value has to be assigned. Moreover, relative characterizations are generalizable to partial orderings. A representation that avoids an assignment of numerical values is favorable, if no comparability of the degree of membership to two different vague regions like a forest and a mountain is intended. For example, assume that the degree of membership that a point belongs to the mountain region is 0.5 and that it belongs to the forest region is 0.6. It follows by the order of numbers that it is also the case that the point belongs more to the forest than to the mountain, even if this comparison is not wanted by an application.

The crucial feature of vague regions with gradual boundaries—which distinguish them from imprecise or general vague regions—is their ordering information. In the previous section we have used the "part of"-relation to introduce an ordering structure for the sharp regions of a vague region. The order of sharp regions of a vague region allows us to compare points regarding their degree of membership to the vague region in a relative manner. *A point P belongs to a vague region* $\mathcal{V}$ *at least to the same degree as a point Q* (symbolized as $\trianglerighteq(\mathcal{V}, P, Q)$) if P belongs to every region of the vague region to which Q belongs. Vice versa, if Q belongs to every sharp region of $\mathcal{V}$ that P belongs to then Q *belongs at most to the same degree to* $\mathcal{V}$ *as P* (symbolized as $\trianglelefteq(\mathcal{V}, P, Q)$). *P and Q belong to the same degree to a vague region* $\mathcal{V}$ (symbolized as $\approx(\mathcal{V}, P, Q)$), if the points cannot be distinguished with respect to the sharp regions.

$$\trianglerighteq(\mathcal{V}, P, Q) \Leftrightarrow_{\text{def}} \forall \mathcal{R} \left[\mathcal{R} \iota \mathcal{V} \Rightarrow (Q \iota \mathcal{R} \Rightarrow P \iota \mathcal{R}) \right]$$
$$\trianglelefteq(\mathcal{V}, P, Q) \Leftrightarrow_{\text{def}} \trianglerighteq(\mathcal{V}, Q, P)$$
$$\approx(\mathcal{V}, P, Q) \Leftrightarrow_{\text{def}} \trianglerighteq(\mathcal{V}, P, Q) \wedge \trianglelefteq(\mathcal{V}, P, Q)$$

The characterizations of $\trianglerighteq$, $\trianglelefteq$, and $\approx$ are not restricted to linear orders. They are also applicable, if we only assume that the relation $\trianglerighteq$ for the regions of a given vague region is a partial order. We consider relative point comparisons only for a fixed vague region and do not compare different vague regions. Thus, we can treat the relation $\trianglerighteq_{\mathcal{V}}(P, Q) := \trianglerighteq(\mathcal{V}, P, Q)$ as a binary relation for a fixed vague region $\mathcal{V}$. Correspondingly, the relations $\trianglelefteq_{\mathcal{V}}$ and $\approx_{\mathcal{V}}$ are binary relations for a fixed vague region $\mathcal{V}$. The relations $\trianglerighteq_{\mathcal{V}}$, $\trianglelefteq_{\mathcal{V}}$, and $\approx_{\mathcal{V}}$ are pre-orders since they are transitive and reflexive but not anti-symmetric. For any two points P and Q of a

Figure 2. The figure illustrates a vague region described by three sharp regions denoted by three different gray values. The light gray region includes the medium gray region, which includes the dark gray region. The points P and Q belong to the same degree to the vague region, whereas the point R has higher a degree of membership than the points P and Q.

vague region $\mathcal{V}$ it follows that one of them belongs at least to the same degree to $\mathcal{V}$ as the other one (TV5), i.e. the relation $\trianglerighteq_\mathcal{V}$ is a linear pre-order (cf. for a more detailed discussion on pre-orders Kulik, Eschenbach, Habel & Schmidtke 2002). Theorem (TV5) follows from Theorem (TV8).

$$\forall \mathcal{V}\, P\, Q\, [\trianglerighteq_\mathcal{V}(P, Q) \vee \trianglerighteq_\mathcal{V}(Q, P)] \tag{TV5}$$

We can simplify the determination of the relation $\trianglerighteq$ for two points under certain conditions. If two points belong to a region $\mathcal{R}$ of a vague region $\mathcal{V}$, then they also belong to every less restrictive region of $\mathcal{V}$. Thus, if we know that two points belong to a sharp region of a vague region, we only have to check their relation for more restrictive regions of the vague region (see also Axiom (VB2)). A point of the core of a vague region belongs at least to the same degree to the vague region as any other point (TV6). Conversely, if a point P is not in the hull of a vague region, every other point belongs at least to the same degree to vague region as P (TV7).

$$\forall \mathcal{V}\, P\, Q\, [P \iota\, \mathsf{core}(\mathcal{V}) \Rightarrow \trianglerighteq_\mathcal{V}(P, Q)] \tag{TV6}$$
$$\forall \mathcal{V}\, P\, Q\, [\neg(P \iota\, \mathsf{hull}(\mathcal{V})) \Rightarrow \trianglerighteq_\mathcal{V}(Q, P)] \tag{TV7}$$

We consider the strict variant of the relation $\trianglerighteq$: *A point P belongs more to a vague region than a point Q* (symbolized by $\triangleright_\mathcal{V}$) if P belongs to every region of the vague region to which Q belongs but Q does not belong to every region to which P belongs.

$$\triangleright_\mathcal{V}(P, Q) \Leftrightarrow_{\mathrm{def}} \trianglerighteq_\mathcal{V}(P, Q) \wedge \neg\trianglerighteq_\mathcal{V}(Q, P)$$

The definition of the relation $\triangleright$ ranges over all sharp regions of a vague region $\mathcal{V}$. The next theorem (TV8) states that the condition of the definition of $\triangleright$ can be

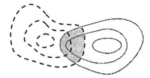 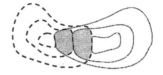

Figure 3. The figure shows two different ways for two vague regions to overlap resulting in two different gradual transitions of the vague regions. The left figure illustrates a weak gradual transition and the right figure a strong one.

rephrased using an existential quantifier: A point P belongs more to the vague region $\mathcal{V}$ than a point Q if and only if there is a region $\mathcal{R}$ that contains P but not Q. Theorem (TV8) follows from Axiom (VB2) and the definition of $\triangleright_{\mathcal{V}}$.

$$\forall \mathcal{V}\, P\, Q\, [\triangleright_{\mathcal{V}}(P, Q) \Leftrightarrow \exists \mathcal{R}\, [\mathcal{R} \iota \mathcal{V} \wedge P \iota \mathcal{R} \wedge \neg (Q \iota \mathcal{R})]] \qquad \text{(TV8)}$$

3.3 Axiomatic Characterization of Gradual Transitions of Vague Regions

This section characterizes gradual transitions of two vague regions. We can distinguish at least two types of gradual transitions, the *weak gradual transition* and the *strong gradual transition* (see Figure 3). These two types of gradual transitions can be seen as generalizations of the relations *overlapping* and *external contact* of sharp regions for vague regions. In the case of a weak gradual transition, two vague regions overlap in an arbitrary manner, whereas in the case of a strong gradual transition, one region completely blends into another region. Every location of a strong gradual transition belongs (depending on the interpretation) to one of the two regions. The more one location belongs to one region, the less it belongs to the remaining one.

There are two ways of introducing gradual transitions, as primitives like regions and vague regions, or via relations. We employ the second approach and consider transitions as spatial relations like disjointness or inclusion. Two vague regions have a weak gradual transition if their hulls overlap. The two hulls overlap if there is a common region that is included in both hulls. Therefore, a weak gradual transition (denoted by wgt) is modeled as a binary relation of two vague regions $\mathcal{V}$ and $\mathcal{V}'$. The overlapping region that consists of all the points that are incident with the hulls of $\mathcal{V}$ and $\mathcal{V}'$ is uniquely determined and is a function of $\mathcal{V}$ and $\mathcal{V}'$.

$$\text{wgt}(\mathcal{V}, \mathcal{V}') \Leftrightarrow_{\text{def}} \quad \exists \mathcal{R}\, \forall P\, [P \iota \mathcal{R} \Rightarrow P \iota \, \text{hull}(\mathcal{V}) \wedge P \iota \, \text{hull}(\mathcal{V}')]$$

In the case of a weak gradual transition, the two vague regions are unrelated. Thus, we cannot employ their ordering structure to draw inferences for points of the weak gradual transition from one vague region to the other one. For instance, if two points P and Q are in the hulls but not in the cores of the two vague regions $\mathcal{V}$ and $\mathcal{V}'$, and P belongs more to the vague region $\mathcal{V}$ than Q does, then it is still possible that P also belongs more to $\mathcal{V}'$ than Q does. The following notion of a strong gradual boundary ensures the compatibility of the ordering structure of vague regions.

Two vague regions have a strong gradual transition (denoted by sgt) if for every sharp region $\mathcal{R}$ of one of the vague regions there is a uniquely determined sharp region $\mathcal{R}'$ of the remaining vague region that is in external contact with $\mathcal{R}$. If the two vague regions are each described by a single sharp region (see the remarks to Axiom (VB1)), we obtain the external contact of two regions as a special case of a strong gradual transition. If two sharp regions $\mathcal{R}$ and $\mathcal{R}'$ are in external contact we write ect($\mathcal{R}, \mathcal{R}'$). Two regions are in external contact if the boundaries of both regions coincide and the regions do not share a point. Details on the contact of two regions and its implications can be found, for example, in Varzi (1997).

$$
\begin{aligned}
\text{sgt}(\mathcal{V}, \mathcal{V}') \Leftrightarrow_{\text{def}} \quad & \forall \mathcal{R} \, [\mathcal{R} \iota \, \mathcal{V} \Rightarrow \exists \mathcal{R}' \, [\mathcal{R}' \iota \, \mathcal{V}' \wedge \text{ect}(\mathcal{R}, \mathcal{R}')] \, \wedge \\
& \forall \mathcal{R}'' \, [\mathcal{R}'' \iota \, \mathcal{V}' \wedge \text{ect}(\mathcal{R}'', \mathcal{R}) \Rightarrow \mathcal{R}'' = \mathcal{R}']] \, \wedge \\
& \forall \mathcal{R}' \, [\mathcal{R}' \iota \, \mathcal{V}' \Rightarrow \exists \mathcal{R} \, [\mathcal{R} \iota \, \mathcal{V} \wedge \text{ect}(\mathcal{R}, \mathcal{R}')] \, \wedge \\
& \forall \mathcal{R}'' \, [\mathcal{R}'' \iota \, \mathcal{V} \wedge \text{ect}(\mathcal{R}'', \mathcal{R}') \Rightarrow \mathcal{R}'' = \mathcal{R}]]
\end{aligned}
$$

In the finite case this definition implies that two vague regions with a strong gradual transition have the same number of sharp regions. This is a consequence of the uniqueness condition for the sharp regions in the definition. If we drop this condition two vague regions that share a strong gradual transition could have a different number of sharp regions. However, such a modified definition would allow the case that all sharp regions of one vague region are in external contact with all sharp regions of the other vague region at a single point or a single line.

A consequence of the definition sgt is that for two vague regions with a strong gradual transition the core of one vague region is in external contact with the hull of the other vague region (TV9).

$$
\forall \mathcal{V} \, \mathcal{V}' \, [\text{sgt}(\mathcal{V}, \mathcal{V}') \Rightarrow \text{ect}(\text{core}(\mathcal{V}), \text{hull}(\mathcal{V}')) \wedge \text{ect}(\text{hull}(\mathcal{V}), \text{core}(\mathcal{V}'))] \quad \text{(TV9)}
$$

Proof. We outline the proof since we have not introduced a complete topological structure for regions. We show the statement for hull($\mathcal{V}'$). Because of sgt($\mathcal{V}, \mathcal{V}'$) there is a region $\mathcal{R} \iota \, \mathcal{V}$ such that ect($\mathcal{R}$, hull($\mathcal{V}'$)). First, core($\mathcal{V}$) cannot overlap hull($\mathcal{V}'$), because in this case all sharp regions of $\mathcal{V}$ would overlap hull($\mathcal{V}'$), which means that there is no region in external contact with hull($\mathcal{V}'$). If it is not the case that ect(core($\mathcal{V}$), hull($\mathcal{V}'$)), there would be no common boundary point of core($\mathcal{V}$) and hull($\mathcal{V}'$). Since every region of $\mathcal{V}'$ is included in hull($\mathcal{V}'$), there would not be a single region of $\mathcal{V}'$ being in external contact with core($\mathcal{V}$), in contradiction to sgt($\mathcal{V}, \mathcal{V}'$).

This characterization of a strong gradual transition of two vague regions ensures that it is a "blend-in constellation" in sense of Hadzilacos (1996): for two points in the gradual transition it holds that one point belongs more to one vague region than the other point and the second point belongs more to other vague region than the first point. This idea is stated precisely in the next theorem. If two vague regions V and V' have a strong gradual transition and there are two sharp regions R and R' of V and V', respectively, being in external contact, then all points in R belong more to V than the points in R' and vice versa (TV10). The proof follows from Theorem (TV8).

$$\forall V\, V'\, R\, R'\, P\, Q\, [\mathsf{sgt}(V, V') \wedge R \iota V \wedge R' \iota V' \wedge \mathsf{ect}(R, R') \wedge P \iota R \wedge Q \iota R'$$
$$\Rightarrow \triangleright_V(P, Q) \wedge \triangleleft_{V'}(Q, P)] \qquad \text{(TV10)}$$

If we determine the degree of membership of a point to a vague region by the number of sharp regions containing the point, we can summarize (TV10) in the following way: the more one point belongs to one vague region, the less it belongs to the other one. More details are given in the next section.

3.4 From a Relative to an Absolute Description of Vagueness

The characterization developed in the previous two sections provides a relative description of vagueness. An alternative characterization of vagueness—typically used in fuzzy theories—relies on an absolute description of vagueness. An absolute representation assigns a fixed value to every point of a vague region. Fuzzy theories generally employ numbers for absolute values, each number representing the degree of membership of a point to a vague region. For some tasks like the visualization of the (vague) area of a forest an absolute representation of vagueness is necessary. We present two alternatives to obtain an absolute representation of vagueness from a relative representation. For the first alternative we assume that the vague region is determined by finitely many sharp regions. In the case of a finite structure, the degree of membership of a point P incident with a vague region V (symbolized as $\mu(P \iota V)$) can be characterized by the number of sharp regions of the vague region that contain the point, relative to the number of all sharp regions of the vague region. Let $\|\Omega\|$ denote the cardinality of a set Ω.

$$\mu(P \iota V) := \|\{R \mid P \iota R \wedge R \iota V\}\| / \|\{R \mid R \iota V\}\|$$

For the second alternative, a vague region may be determined by finitely or infinitely many regions. We assume now a metric structure and presuppose that a sharp region is a set of points and a vague region a set of sharp regions. For the sharp regions of a vague region we cannot use the idea that the metric of two sets is the minimal distance of two arbitrary points of each set. This function is equal to zero, if two sets overlap, and for two sharp regions of a vague region it always holds that one is contained in the other. Thus, we use the Hausdorff metric of sets. This metric is zero, if and only if the two sets are identical. To characterize the Hausdorff metric we first introduce the ε-neighborhood. The ε-neighborhood of a set S, abbreviated as $N_\varepsilon(S)$, is the set of all points with a distance smaller than ε:

$$N_\varepsilon(S) := \{P \mid \exists Q \in S \, [\text{dist}(P, Q) < \varepsilon]\}$$

The Hausdorff metric D of two sets S_1 and S_2 is the infimum of all distances ε such that S_1 is contained in an ε-neighborhood of S_2 and S_2 is contained in an ε-neighborhood of S_1:

$$D(S_1, S_2) := \inf\{\varepsilon \mid S_1 \subset N_\varepsilon(S_2) \wedge S_2 \subset N_\varepsilon(S_1)\}$$

We can use the Hausdorff metric to characterize the degree of membership of a sharp region for a vague region. First, we normalize the degree of membership by requiring the following boundary conditions: the degree of membership of the core of a vague region is 1 and of its hull 0. Each of the remaining sharp regions $\mathcal{R}$ obtain a degree of membership between 0 and 1:

$$\mu(\mathcal{R}) := 1 - \frac{D(\mathcal{R}, \text{core}(\mathcal{V}))}{D(\text{hull}(\mathcal{V}), \text{core}(\mathcal{V}))}$$

The degree of membership of a point P incident with a vague region $\mathcal{V}$ is then given by the infimum of the membership degrees of the sharp regions of $\mathcal{V}$ containing P:

$$\mu(P \iota \mathcal{V}) := \inf\{\mu(\mathcal{R}) \mid \mathcal{R} \iota \mathcal{V}\}$$

4 Second-Order Vagueness

In the previous section we provided a formal characterization of first-order vagueness based on orders and pre-orders. Even if we consider first-order vagueness as sufficient, a vague region can be indeterminate in several respects. First, a geographic object is usually characterized by different criteria: the region of a forest, for instance, can be determined by the height of its trees, the density of its trees, the diameter of its trees, its overall size, and so forth. A description that offers an integrative perspective incorporating these criteria leads to different vague regions for the forest. We use this idea in Section 4.1 to characterize a second-order vague region by (first-order) vague regions. If we consider each vague region as a layer in a geographic information system, then a description using second-order vagueness can be seen as an overlay of these layers assuming a certain compatibility between the layers. Second, different experts might have different opinions as to which vague region in the case of a forest is the right one. We call the indeterminacy resulting from different interpretations of the localization of a vague region *higher-order indeterminacy*. The proposed approach deals with higher-order vagueness as well as with higher-order indeterminacy.

If we assume that the extension of a forest is characterized as a second-order vague region, which is determined, for instance by the the height and the diameter of the trees, and we assume that the two criteria are compatible such that the resulting two (first-order) vague regions are overlapping in a certain way, then we can infer order relations for points regarding the second-order vague region of the forest (see Section 4.1.2). An example: Suppose only trees that are definitely in the core of the second-order vague region should be felled since insects might require the (vague) boundary of the forest as a habitat. A tree is in this area if it has at least a certain height and diameter. For a biologist it might be easier to determine the diameter of the trees than the height of the trees. If the height and the diameter are compatible, i.e. the diameter of the trees implies an ordering for height information, then the vague habitat can be identified using observations of the diameter alone.

For a second-order vague region of the forest we can distinguish between points that belong to the same degree to one of the vague regions of the forest and points that belong to the same degree to all vague regions and thus cannot be distinguished regarding their membership degree for any criterion characterizing the forest. Therefore, an interpretation of a forest region based on second-order vagueness introduces a finer description for points with respect to the relative degree of membership (see Section 4.1.3).

Gradual transitions of second-order vague regions enable the representation of a vague transition. If two spatial regions are determined by more than one criteria, like the forest and the snow region in the introduction (see Figure 1), a second-order transition gives us an integrated view of their possible transitions. As elaborated in the introduction, a gradual transition of second-order vague regions enables the possibility of transitions within transitions. If we assume that the gradual transition of the forest and the snow area is defined by two criteria, the height of the trees and their density, then the meadow with trees can be seen as a vague transition, where both criteria vary; whereas in the case of the sparse forest only the density (but not the height) varies, and in the case of the stunted trees only the height (but not the density) varies. Section 4.2 presents the formal characterization of gradual transitions of second-order vague regions.

4.1 Axiomatic Characterization of Second-Order Vague Regions

We enrich the geometry of Section 3.1 by *vague regions of order two*. They are also called *second-order vague regions* and are denoted by $\mathcal{V}^2$, $\mathcal{V}_1^2$, and $\mathcal{V}_2^2$. The incidence (ι) relation and the precisification relation ($\unrhd$) are employed again to relate them to sharp and vague regions. In the same way as a vague region is uniquely determined by its sharp regions, a vague region of order two is uniquely determined by its vague regions (VI2). The sharp regions can be considered as *vague regions of order zero* and the vague regions as *vague regions of order one*. We also refer to vague regions as vague regions of order one to distinguish them from second-order vague regions.

$$\forall \mathcal{V}_1^2 \, \mathcal{V}_2^2 \, [\forall \mathcal{V} \, [\mathcal{V} \iota \, \mathcal{V}_1^2 \Leftrightarrow \mathcal{V} \iota \, \mathcal{V}_2^2] \Rightarrow \mathcal{V}_1^2 = \mathcal{V}_2^2] \qquad (\text{VI2})$$

Different criteria determining the spatial extension of an object usually lead to different possible regions. Axiom (VI2) does not impose any restrictions for the vague regions of a second-order vague region, hence the hulls of two vague regions do not even have to overlap. Moreover, there is no restriction for the extension of the vague regions of a second-order vague region, and the hulls of each vague region can grow or shrink without limit. Thus, we require Axiom (VB3) similar to Axiom (VB1) for vague regions: For every second-order vague region there is a sharp region included in each core of the characterizing vague regions and another sharp region including each hull the vague regions.

$$\forall \mathcal{V}^2 \, \exists \mathcal{R} \, \mathcal{R}' \, \forall \mathcal{V} \, [\mathcal{V} \iota \, \mathcal{V}^2 \Rightarrow \mathcal{R} \sqsubseteq \text{core}(\mathcal{V}) \wedge \text{hull}(\mathcal{V}) \sqsubseteq \mathcal{R}'] \qquad (\text{VB3})$$

4.1.1 Point Pre-Orders on Second-Order Vague Regions.

We provide a relative description of the degree of membership of two points to a second-order vague region. The following characterization also works without any assumptions about the vague regions of a second-order vague region. However, without Axiom (VB3) there might be no points at all that are comparable with respect to a second-order vague region. A point P *belongs at least to the same degree to a vague region $\mathcal{V}^2$ as a point Q*, if P belongs at least to the same degree to every vague region $\mathcal{V}$ of $\mathcal{V}^2$ as Q does:

$$\unrhd(\mathcal{V}^2, P, Q) \Leftrightarrow_{\text{def}} \quad \forall \mathcal{V} \, [\mathcal{V} \iota \, \mathcal{V}^2 \Rightarrow \unrhd(\mathcal{V}, P, Q)]$$

We can treat the relation $\unrhd_{\mathcal{V}^2}(P, Q) := \unrhd(\mathcal{V}^2, P, Q)$ as a binary relation for a fixed vague region $\mathcal{V}^2$. Analog to Section 3.2 we can define the second-order relations $\approx_{\mathcal{V}^2}$ and $\rhd_{\mathcal{V}^2}$ as well as the duals $\unlhd_{\mathcal{V}^2}$ and $\lhd_{\mathcal{V}^2}$. In general, second-order relations enable a finer distinction for points regarding the relative degree of vagueness. If two points are indistinguishable with respect to one of the vague regions of a second order vague region, they might still be distinguishable with respect to another vague region of $\mathcal{V}^2$. All second-order relations are pre-orders since they are transitive and reflexive but not anti-symmetric. Without any additional assumptions the relations are not linear.

4.1.2 Uniformly Vague Regions of Order Two.

We give an example that shows how we can employ the order on each vague regions of a second-order vague region to provide a pre-order for points. In the example we assume that every vague region of a second-order vague region is uniquely determined by the same finite number n of sharp regions. The sharp regions of every vague region $\mathcal{V}$ can be ordered such that $\mathcal{R}_i \sqsubseteq \mathcal{R}_{i+1}$, $\forall i \in \{1, \ldots, n-1\}$. In addition, we assume that every sharp region with index i of one vague region is contained in a sharp region with index $i+1$ of another vague region of the second-order vague region (see Figure 4). A second-order vague region $\mathcal{V}^2$ fulfilling this condition is called *uniformly vague*, symbolized as $\mathrm{uv}(\mathcal{V}^2)$.

$$\mathrm{uv}(\mathcal{V}^2) \Leftrightarrow_{\mathrm{def}} \quad \forall \mathcal{V} \, \mathcal{V}' \, i \, [\mathcal{V} \iota \mathcal{V}^2 \wedge \mathcal{V}' \iota \mathcal{V}^2 \wedge 1 \le i < n \wedge \mathcal{R}_i \iota \mathcal{V} \wedge \mathcal{R}'_{i+1} \iota \mathcal{V}'$$
$$\Rightarrow \mathcal{R}_i \sqsubseteq \mathcal{R}'_{i+1}]$$

We call a point P an *intersection point of degree i*, abbreviated as $\mathrm{ip}_i(\mathcal{V}^2, P)$, if P is included in all sharp regions with index i of the vague regions of a second-order vague region: $\forall \mathcal{V} \, [\mathcal{V} \iota \mathcal{V}^2 \wedge \mathcal{R}_i \iota \mathcal{V} \Rightarrow P \iota \mathcal{R}_i]$. For uniformly vague regions, we can prove two consequences. First, if P is an intersection point of a second-order vague region $\mathcal{V}^2$ of degree i and a point Q is not included in at least one sharp region $\mathcal{R}_i$ of a vague region of $\mathcal{V}^2$, then P belongs at least to the same degree to the second-order vague region as Q (TV11). More briefly: the order of two points with respect to a second-order vague region is known by the order of the points with respect to one of its vague regions. The proof of (TV11) is similar to the proof of (TV13).

$$\forall \mathcal{V}^2 \, \mathcal{V} \, i \, P \, Q \, [\mathrm{uv}(\mathcal{V}^2) \wedge \mathcal{V} \iota \mathcal{V}^2 \wedge 1 \le i \le n \wedge \mathcal{R}_i \iota \mathcal{V} \wedge \mathrm{ip}_i(\mathcal{V}^2, P) \wedge \neg(Q \iota \mathcal{R}_i)]$$
$$\Rightarrow \unrhd(\mathcal{V}^2, P, Q)] \tag{TV11}$$

Second, we obtain a generalized version of transitivity as an immediate consequence of (TV11). If an intersection point P of degree i belongs more to a vague region of a second-order vague region $\mathcal{V}^2$ than an intersection point Q of degree j, and Q belongs more to a vague region of $\mathcal{V}^2$ than a point R, and if there are regions $\mathcal{R}_i$ and $\mathcal{R}_j$ including P but not Q and Q but not R, respectively, then P belongs at least to the same degree to $\mathcal{V}^2$ as R (TV12) (see Figure 4).

$$\forall \mathcal{V}^2 \, \mathcal{V} \, \mathcal{V}' \, i \, j \, P \, Q \, R \, [\mathrm{uv}(\mathcal{V}^2) \wedge \mathcal{V} \iota \mathcal{V}^2 \wedge \mathcal{V}' \iota \mathcal{V}^2 \wedge 1 \le i, j \le n \wedge i < j \wedge$$
$$\mathcal{R}_i \iota \mathcal{V} \wedge \mathrm{ip}_i(\mathcal{V}^2, P) \wedge \neg(Q \iota \mathcal{R}_i) \wedge \mathcal{R}_j \iota \mathcal{V}' \wedge \mathrm{ip}_j(\mathcal{V}^2, Q) \wedge \neg(R \iota \mathcal{R}_j)]$$
$$\Rightarrow \unrhd(\mathcal{V}^2, P, R)] \tag{TV12}$$

4.1.3 A Linear Order for Second-Order Vague Regions.

The previous two sections showed how we can introduce a pre-order for points with respect to second-order vague regions. However, none of the assumptions

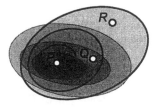 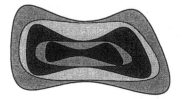

Figure 4. The left figure shows a second-order vague region that is uniformly vague. The point P has an intersection degree of 1, Q a degree of 2, and R no degree. The point P belongs more to the vague region with the fat bordered sharp regions than Q, Q belongs more to the vague region with the thin bordered regions than R. Thus, P belongs at least to the same degree to any of the vague regions as R. The right figure shows two vague regions of an order-preserving, second-order vague region.

guarantees that the relation $\trianglerighteq$ for second-order vague regions is linear. In Section 3.2 we have used the linear order of the sharp regions of a vague region to ensure the linearity of the pre-order for points with respect to a first-order vague region. It turns out that it is not necessary to order vague regions, since the pre-order of points can be imported by the order of the sharp regions of the vague regions of a second-order vague region. Therefore, we introduce the following compatibility condition for two vague regions: Two vague regions $\mathcal{V}$ and $\mathcal{V}'$ are called *compatible*, abbreviated as $c(\mathcal{V}, \mathcal{V}')$, if for each pair of sharp regions of the vague regions one of the sharp regions is included in the other. Thus, every fixed sharp region $\mathcal{R}$ of one vague region separates all sharp regions of the other vague region into two classes, the ones contained in $\mathcal{R}$ and the ones containing $\mathcal{R}$.

$$c(\mathcal{V}, \mathcal{V}') \Leftrightarrow_{\text{def}} \forall \mathcal{R}\, \mathcal{R}'\, [\mathcal{R}\, \iota\, \mathcal{V} \wedge \mathcal{R}'\, \iota\, \mathcal{V}' \Rightarrow \mathcal{R} \sqsubseteq \mathcal{R}' \vee \mathcal{R}' \sqsubseteq \mathcal{R}]$$

A second-order vague region $\mathcal{V}^2$ is called *order-preserving* if all of its vague regions are compatible, symbolized as $\text{op}(\mathcal{V}^2)$ (see Figure 4). The next theorem shows that an order for the vague regions of a second-order vague region is not necessary to be able to characterize a pre-order for points with respect to a second-order vague region. If a point P belongs more to a vague region of an order-preserving, second-order vague region $\mathcal{V}^2$ than a point Q does, then the point P belongs at least to the same degree to $\mathcal{V}^2$ as Q does (TV13). An immediate consequence is that the pre-order $\trianglerighteq$ is linear for order-preserving, second-order vague regions (TV14).

$$\forall \mathcal{V}^2\, \mathcal{V}\, P\, Q\, [\text{op}(\mathcal{V}^2) \wedge \mathcal{V}\, \iota\, \mathcal{V}^2 \wedge \triangleright_\mathcal{V}(P, Q) \Rightarrow \trianglerighteq_{\mathcal{V}^2}(P, Q)] \qquad \text{(TV13)}$$

$$\forall \mathcal{V}^2\, P\, Q\quad [\text{op}(\mathcal{V}^2) \Rightarrow \trianglerighteq_{\mathcal{V}^2}(P, Q) \vee \trianglerighteq_{\mathcal{V}^2}(Q, P)] \qquad \text{(TV14)}$$

Proof (TV13). Given the assumptions for $\mathcal{V}^2$, $\mathcal{V}$, P, and Q, we have to show that $\forall \mathcal{V}' \, \mathcal{R}' \, [\mathcal{V}' \iota \mathcal{V}^2 \wedge \mathcal{R}' \iota \mathcal{V}' \wedge Q \iota \mathcal{R}' \Rightarrow P \iota \mathcal{R}']$. Because of $\triangleright_{\mathcal{V}}(P, Q)$ Theorem (TV8) implies: $\exists \mathcal{R} \, [\mathcal{R} \iota \mathcal{V} \wedge P \iota \mathcal{R} \wedge \neg(Q \iota \mathcal{R})]$. If $\mathcal{R} \sqsubseteq \mathcal{R}'$ holds, it follows $P \iota \mathcal{R}'$. Otherwise, op($\mathcal{V}^2$) implies $\mathcal{R}' \sqsubseteq \mathcal{R}$ and thus $\neg(Q \iota \mathcal{R}')$, which concludes the proof.

Proof (TV14). If there is a vague region $\mathcal{V}$ of $\mathcal{V}^2$ with $\triangleright_{\mathcal{V}}(P, Q)$, then we obtain by (TV13) $\trianglerighteq_{\mathcal{V}^2}(P, Q)$. If there is no such region, i.e. it holds $\trianglerighteq_{\mathcal{V}}(Q, P) \, \forall \mathcal{V} \iota \mathcal{V}^2$, then it follows by definition $\trianglerighteq_{\mathcal{V}^2}(Q, P)$.

The vague regions of an order-preserving, second-order vague region do not need to contain the same number of sharp regions in the finite case. An example is the second-order vague region determined by two vague regions $\mathcal{V}$ and $\mathcal{V}'$, if $\mathcal{V}$ is determined by the sharp regions $\mathcal{R}_1$, $\mathcal{R}_2$, and $\mathcal{R}_3$, $\mathcal{V}'$ by $\mathcal{R}_1'$ and $\mathcal{R}_2'$, and if the sharp regions fulfill the condition: $\mathcal{R}_1 \sqsubseteq \mathcal{R}_1' \sqsubseteq \mathcal{R}_2 \sqsubseteq \mathcal{R}_2' \sqsubseteq \mathcal{R}_3$.

We introduce the core and the hull for second-order vague regions that are order-preserving. The core of a vague region is a sharp region; correspondingly, the core of a second-order vague region will be characterized as a vague region (of order one). This captures the fact that even the points that definitely belong to vague objects do not constitute a uniquely determined set with fixed boundaries. The same considerations also apply to the hull of a second-order vague region. The *core* and the *hull* of a second-order vague region are defined by the cores and hulls of the vague regions of the second-order vague region.

$$\mathcal{V} = \mathsf{core}(\mathcal{V}^2) \Leftrightarrow_{\mathsf{def}} \quad \mathsf{op}(\mathcal{V}^2) \wedge \forall \mathcal{R} \, [\mathcal{R} \iota \mathcal{V} \Leftrightarrow \exists \mathcal{V}' \, [\mathcal{R} = \mathsf{core}(\mathcal{V}') \wedge \mathcal{V}' \iota \mathcal{V}^2]]$$

$$\mathcal{V} = \mathsf{hull}(\mathcal{V}^2) \Leftrightarrow_{\mathsf{def}} \quad \mathsf{op}(\mathcal{V}^2) \wedge \forall \mathcal{R} \, [\mathcal{R} \iota \mathcal{V} \Leftrightarrow \exists \mathcal{V}' \, [\mathcal{R} = \mathsf{hull}(\mathcal{V}') \wedge \mathcal{V}' \iota \mathcal{V}^2]]$$

The core and the hull of an order-preserving, second-order vague region fulfill Axiom (VI1) by definition. Because the second-order vague region is order-preserving, the core and the hull also fulfill Axiom (VB2). To ensure that the core and hull are indeed vague regions, we have to require that each of them has a core and hull (VB4) & (VB5).

$$\forall \mathcal{V}^2 \, \exists \mathcal{R} \, \mathcal{R}' \, [\mathcal{R} = \mathsf{core}(\mathsf{core}(\mathcal{V}^2)) \wedge \mathcal{R}' = \mathsf{hull}(\mathsf{core}(\mathcal{V}^2))] \tag{VB4}$$

$$\forall \mathcal{V}^2 \, \exists \mathcal{R} \, \mathcal{R}' \, [\mathcal{R} = \mathsf{core}(\mathsf{hull}(\mathcal{V}^2)) \wedge \mathcal{R}' = \mathsf{hull}(\mathsf{hull}(\mathcal{V}^2))] \tag{VB5}$$

In the case of first-order vagueness, for every vague region $\mathcal{V}$ holds $\mathsf{core}(\mathcal{V}) \iota \mathcal{V}$ and $\mathsf{hull}(\mathcal{V}) \iota \mathcal{V}$. A similar relation does not translate into second-order vagueness. The reason is that the core and the hull can be seen as limits for the sharp regions of vague regions of order one. The core and the hull of a second-order vague region, however, refer to the vagueness of the cores and hulls of the characterizing vague regions. They are not limits for the second-order vague region, since the concept of a limit in the sense of minimal and maximal element would require an order for the vague regions of the second-order vague region. Moreover, the core and the hull generally do not belong to a second-order vague region.

Williamson (1999) has given an approach to higher-order vagueness based on a logic of vagueness, an idea already proposed by Fine (1975). The main idea of his approach is to introduce a 'definitely'-operator (abbreviated as Δ) in a similar way as the necessary-operator $\square$ in modal logic (cf., for instance, Hughes & Cresswell 1996). The idea of the Δ-operator is to single out all those instances of a vague predicate where a predicate definitely applies to (cf. Fine 1975). Using the Δ-operator the points of the core of the core of a second-order vague region are all the points for which it is definitely the case that they definitely belong to the second-order vague region. If $p(P, \mathcal{V}^2)$ denotes the fact that P belongs to a second-order vague region $\mathcal{V}^2$ the above statement can be written as $\Delta(\Delta p(P, \mathcal{V}^2))$. Correspondingly, the points not contained in the hull of the hull of a second-order vague region $\mathcal{V}^2$ are all the points for which it is definitely the case that they definitely do not belong to $\mathcal{V}^2$, i.e., $\Delta(\Delta\neg(p(P, \mathcal{V}^2)))$.

4.2 Characterization of Gradual Transitions of Second-Order Vague Regions

The characterization of a strong gradual transition between two second-order vague regions is based on the formalization of strong gradual transitions between first-order vague regions. The second-order vague regions are assumed to be order-preserving throughout this section. A gradual transition has to be characterized in a way that it makes room for gradual transitions within the gradual transition. *Two second-order vague regions $\mathcal{V}_1^2$ and $\mathcal{V}_2^2$ have a strong gradual transition* if for every vague region $\mathcal{V}_1$ of one of the second-order vague regions there is a region $\mathcal{V}_2$ of the remaining second-order vague region such that $\mathcal{V}_1$ and $\mathcal{V}_2$ have a strong gradual transition. We omit the modifier "strong" in the following.

$$\mathsf{sgt}(\mathcal{V}_1^2, \mathcal{V}_2^2) \Leftrightarrow_{\text{def}} \quad \forall \mathcal{V}_1 \, [\mathcal{V}_1 \, \iota \, \mathcal{V}_1^2 \Rightarrow \exists \mathcal{V}_2 \, [\mathcal{V}_2 \, \iota \, \mathcal{V}_2^2 \wedge \mathsf{sgt}(\mathcal{V}_1, \mathcal{V}_2)]] \wedge$$
$$\forall \mathcal{V}_2 \, [\mathcal{V}_2 \, \iota \, \mathcal{V}_2^2 \Rightarrow \exists \mathcal{V}_1 \, [\mathcal{V}_1 \, \iota \, \mathcal{V}_1^2 \wedge \mathsf{sgt}(\mathcal{V}_1, \mathcal{V}_2)]]$$

The next theorem is a generalization of Theorem (TV 10) to second-order vague regions. It shows that the notion of a "blend-in constellation" can be translated into second-order vagueness. If two (order-preserving) second-order vague regions $\mathcal{V}_1^2$ and $\mathcal{V}_2^2$ have a gradual transition and any two vague regions of them also have a gradual transition, then for all pair of points in two sharp regions that are in external contact and belong to the vague regions, one point belongs at least to the same degree to $\mathcal{V}_1^2$ as the other point and the second point belongs at least to the same degree to $\mathcal{V}_2^2$ as the first point (TV 15). The proof follows from Theorem (TV 10) and Theorem (TV 13).

$$\forall \mathcal{V}_1^2 \, \mathcal{V}_2^2 \, \mathcal{V}_1 \, \mathcal{V}_2 \, \mathcal{R}_1 \, \mathcal{R}_2 \, P \, Q \, [\mathsf{sgt}(\mathcal{V}_1^2, \mathcal{V}_2^2) \wedge \mathcal{V}_1 \, \iota \, \mathcal{V}_1^2 \wedge \mathcal{V}_2 \, \iota \, \mathcal{V}_2^2 \wedge \mathsf{sgt}(\mathcal{V}_1, \mathcal{V}_2) \wedge$$
$$\mathcal{R}_1 \, \iota \, \mathcal{V}_1 \wedge \mathcal{R}_2 \, \iota \, \mathcal{V}_2 \wedge \mathsf{ect}(\mathcal{R}_1, \mathcal{R}_2) \wedge P \, \iota \, \mathcal{R}_1 \wedge Q \, \iota \, \mathcal{R}_2$$
$$\Rightarrow \, \trianglerighteq_{\mathcal{V}_1^2}(P, Q) \wedge \trianglelefteq_{\mathcal{V}_2^2}(Q, P)] \qquad \text{(TV 15)}$$

We associate a spatial referent to a gradual transition of two second-order vague regions (denoted by rsgt) if there is a first-order vague region $\mathcal{V}$ determined by the cores of the second-order vague regions in the following way: for every sharp region $\mathcal{R}$ either of $\mathcal{V}$ or of one of the cores of the two second-order vague regions there are two sharp regions of the two remaining vague regions being in external contact with $\mathcal{R}$. Given three regions $\mathcal{R}$, $\mathcal{R}_1$, and $\mathcal{R}_2$, we use the abbreviation ect$(\mathcal{R}, \mathcal{R}_1, \mathcal{R}_2)$ for ect$(\mathcal{R}, \mathcal{R}_1) \wedge$ ect$(\mathcal{R}, \mathcal{R}_2)$. Note that not every gradual transition has a vague region as spatial referent.

$$\text{rsgt}(\mathcal{V}, \mathcal{V}_1^2, \mathcal{V}_2^2) \Leftrightarrow_{\text{def}}$$
$$\forall \mathcal{R}\,[\mathcal{R} \iota \mathcal{V} \Rightarrow \exists \mathcal{R}_1\,\mathcal{R}_2\,[\mathcal{R}_1 \iota \text{core}(\mathcal{V}_1^2) \wedge \mathcal{R}_2 \iota \text{core}(\mathcal{V}_2^2) \wedge \text{ect}(\mathcal{R}, \mathcal{R}_1, \mathcal{R}_2)]] \wedge$$
$$\forall \mathcal{R}_1\,[\mathcal{R}_1 \iota \text{core}(\mathcal{V}_1^2) \Rightarrow \exists \mathcal{R}\,\mathcal{R}_2\,[\mathcal{R} \iota \mathcal{V} \wedge \mathcal{R}_2 \iota \text{core}(\mathcal{V}_2^2) \wedge \text{ect}(\mathcal{R}, \mathcal{R}_1, \mathcal{R}_2)]] \wedge$$
$$\forall \mathcal{R}_2\,[\mathcal{R}_2 \iota \text{core}(\mathcal{V}_2^2) \Rightarrow \exists \mathcal{R}\,\mathcal{R}_1\,[\mathcal{R} \iota \mathcal{V} \wedge \mathcal{R}_1 \iota \text{core}(\mathcal{V}_1^2) \wedge \text{ect}(\mathcal{R}, \mathcal{R}_1, \mathcal{R}_2)]]]$$

If rsgt$(\mathcal{V}, \mathcal{V}_1^2, \mathcal{V}_2^2)$ holds, $\mathcal{V}$ is a vague region and we can consider its core, which is a sharp region. The core describes all the points that definitely belong to the vague gradual transition of $\mathcal{V}_1^2$ and $\mathcal{V}_2^2$. It is in external contact with the (sharp) regions hull$(\text{core}(\mathcal{V}_1^2))$ and hull$(\text{core}(\mathcal{V}_2^2))$.

The example of the introduction shows that a gradual transition can have a finer subdivision, which suggests considering gradual transitions within a gradual transition. If a vague region $\mathcal{V}$ is the spatial referent of the transition sgt$(\mathcal{V}_1^2, \mathcal{V}_2^2)$, then there are two gradual transitions within this transition: the strong gradual transition of $\mathcal{V}$ and core$(\mathcal{V}_1^2)$

$$\text{sgt}(\mathcal{V}, \text{core}(\mathcal{V}_1^2)) = \text{sgt}(\text{core}(\mathcal{V}_1^2), \text{hull}(\mathcal{V}_2^2)),$$

and the strong gradual transition of the vague regions $\mathcal{V}$ and core$(\mathcal{V}_2^2)$

$$\text{sgt}(\mathcal{V}, \text{core}(\mathcal{V}_2^2)) = \text{sgt}(\text{core}(\mathcal{V}_2^2), \text{hull}(\mathcal{V}_1^2)).$$

The equations follow from Theorem (TV9).

We relate the characterization to the vagueness logic of Williamson (1999) using the definitely-operator (see the end of Section 4.1). If we characterize the spatial location of the forest by a second-order vague region $\mathcal{V}_1^2$ and the location of the snow area by $\mathcal{V}_2^2$, then the points for which it is definitely the case that they definitely belong to the forest or the snow region are given by the regions core$(\text{core}(\mathcal{V}_1^2))$ and core$(\text{core}(\mathcal{V}_2^2))$, respectively. If $\mathcal{V}$ is the spatial extension of the gradual transition of the forest and snow region, i.e., rsgt$(\mathcal{V}, \mathcal{V}_1^2, \mathcal{V}_2^2)$ holds, then the sharp region core$(\mathcal{V})$ describes the points that definitely constitute the meadow region with trees. The gradual transition between the forest region and the meadow region with trees, the sparse forest, is given by sgt$(\mathcal{V}, \text{core}(\mathcal{V}_1^2))$, and the gradual transition between the meadow region with trees and the snow region, the stunted trees, is given by sgt$(\mathcal{V}, \text{core}(\mathcal{V}_2^2))$.

5 Conclusion

This article shows how to incorporate first- and second-order vagueness in the framework of ordering geometry. It provides a formal representation for geographic objects whose spatial extension is characterized by first- or second-order vague regions and for gradual transitions between vague geographic objects. This work has provided a relative characterization of spatial vagueness that determines for two given points, which one belongs more to a vague region. In contrast to an absolute representation as employed by fuzzy theories, it is not necessary to decide for an individual point, which numerical value has to be assigned to a point in order to describe its degree of membership to a vague region. We have offered two ways to obtain an absolute representation from a relative representation of vagueness, if an absolute representation is necessary, like in visualization tasks. The relative characterization of vagueness is based on a linear order but can be generalized to partial orders. However, even if the sharp regions of an indeterminate region only overlap and are not included in each other, we showed how to introduce a linear pre-order to relate points with respect to the indeterminate region.

Using a linear order in the case of first-order vagueness has the advantage that it implies a (linear) order for second-order vagueness under certain assumptions. In general, second-order vagueness can be used in at least three cases: (a) to model the lack of a sharp core or hull of a vague region, (b) to integrate different opinions of experts regarding the spatial localization of a vague geographic object, and (c) to incorporate different vague representations of the object resulting from different criteria determining the spatial localization of an object. The integration of spatial vagueness and context-dependency can be considered as higher-order indeterminacy. The analysis of second-order vagueness reveals that it is not necessary to assume a separate order to relate two points, since the ordering structure can be imported from the first-order vague regions. An order for second-order vagueness gives us a finer distinction for points of a second-order vague region: If for one criterion two points belong to the same degree to it, for a different criterion one point might belong more to it than the other point. To summarize, the ordering structure for second-order vagueness offers an integrated perspective that incorporates different views of vagueness.

Future research could include the analysis of partial orders and their implication for second-order vagueness. This article addresses second-order vagueness but does not consider higher-order vagueness in general. For second-order vagueness there are natural interpretations, like cases (b) and (c), that show why a representation of geographic objects should include second-order vagueness or indeterminacy, even if one denies the necessity of vague boundary cases like in (a). The question, whether it is necessary to integrate higher-order vagueness for degrees greater than two in the geographical or spatial domain, remains open. An integration of the interpretation of the cases (b) and (c) possibly suggests third-order vagueness or indeterminacy. However, even this interpretation would not require a theory much more general than the one presented in this paper, and would in particular not require incorporating arbitrary degrees of vagueness.

Acknowledgments

The research reported in this paper has been supported by the Deutsche Forschungs-gemeinschaft in the project 'Axiomatics of Spatial Concepts' (Ha 1237-7) and by the National Imagery and Mapping Agency under grant number NMA201-01-1-2003 (Principal Investigator: Max Egenhofer). I am in particular indebted to Thomas Barkowsky, Matt Duckham, Max Egenhofer, Carola Eschenbach, Jim Farrugia, Christopher Habel, Alexander Klippel, Inga Mau, Michael Worboys, and the anonymous reviewers for their valuable comments.

References

Ahlqvist, O., Keukelaar, J. & Oukbir, K. (2000). Rough classification and accuracy assessment, *International Journal of Geographical Information Science, 14*, 475–496.

Beaubouef, T. & Petry, F. E. (2001). Vagueness in spatial data: Rough set and egg-yolk approaches. In L. Monostori, J. Váncza & M. Ali (Eds.), *Engineering of Intelligent Systems, 14th International Conference on Industrial and Engineering Applications of Artificial Intelligence and Expert Systems, IEA/AIE 2001* (pp. 367–373). Berlin: Springer.

Bennett, B. (1998). Modal semantics for knowledge bases dealing with vague concepts. In A. G. Cohn, L. K. Schubert & S. C. Shapiro (Eds.), *Proceedings of the 6th International Conference on Principles of Knowledge Representation and Reasoning (KR'98)* (pp. 234–244). San Mateo, CA: Morgan Kaufmann.

Bennett, B. (2001a). Application of supervaluation semantics to vaguely defined spatial concepts. In D. R. Montello (Ed.), *Spatial information theory: Foundations of geographic information science*, COSIT'01, Vol. 2205 Lecture Notes in Computer Science (pp. 108–123). Berlin: Springer.

Bennett, B. (2001b). What is a forest? on the vagueness of certain geographic concepts, *Topoi, 20*, 189–201.

Brown, D. G. (1998). Classification and boundary vagueness in mapping presettlement forest types, *International Journal of Geographical Information Science, 12(2)*, 105–129.

Burrough, P. A. (1996). Natural objects with indeterminate boundaries. In P. A. Burrough & A. U. Frank (Eds.), *Geographic objects with indeterminate boundaries* (pp. 3–28). London: Taylor & Francis.

Burrough, P. A. & Frank, A. U. (1996). *Geographic objects with indeterminate boundaries*, Vol. 2 of *GISDATA*. London: Taylor & Francis.

Clementini, E. & Felice, P. d. (1996). An algebraic model for spatial objects with indeterminate boundaries. In P. A. Burrough & A. U. Frank (Eds.), *Geographic objects with indeterminate boundaries* (pp. 155–169). London: Taylor & Francis.

Cohn, A. G. (1997). Qualitative spatial representation and reasoning techniques. In G. Brewka, C. Habel & B. Nebel (Eds.), *KI-97: Advances in artificial intelligence, 21st Annual German Conference on Artificial Intelligence* (pp. 1–30). Berlin: Springer.

Cohn, A. G. & Gotts, N. M. (1996a). The egg-yolk representation of regions with indeterminate boundaries. In P. A. Burrough & A. U. Frank (Eds.), *Geographic objects with indeterminate boundaries* (pp. 171–187). London: Taylor & Francis.

Cohn, A. G. & Gotts, N. M. (1996b). Representing spatial vagueness: A mereological approach. In L. C. Aiello, J. Doyle & S. C. Shapiro (Eds.), *Proceedings of the 5th International Conference on Principles of Knowledge Representation and Reasoning (KR'96)* (pp. 230–241). San Mateo, CA: Morgan Kaufmann.

Couclelis, H. (1996). A typology of geographic entities with ill-defined boundaries. In P. A. Burrough & A. U. Frank (Eds.), *Geographic objects with indeterminate boundaries* (pp. 45–55). London: Taylor & Francis.

Dubois, D., Ostasiewicz, W. & Prade, H. (2000). Fuzzy sets: History and basic notions. In D. Dubois & H. Prade (Eds.), *Fundamentals of fuzzy sets*, Vol. 7 of *The handbooks of fuzzy sets* (pp. 21–124). Boston: Kluwer.

Duckham, M., Mason, K., Stell, J. & Worboys, M. F. (2001). A formal approach to imperfection in geographic information, *Computers, Environment and Urban Systems, 25*, 89–103.

Dummett, M. (1975). Wang's paradox, *Synthese, 30*, 301–324.

Egenhofer, M. J. & Franzosa, R. D. (1991). Point-set topological relations, *International Journal of Geographical Information Systems, 5*, 161–174.

Erwig, M. & Schneider, M. (1997). Vague regions. In M. Scholl & A. Voisard (Eds.), *Advances in Spatial Databases, 5th International Symposium, SSD'97* (pp. 298–320) Springer.

Fine, K. (1975). Vagueness, truth and logic, *Synthese, 30*, 265–300.

Fisher, P. (2000). Sorites paradox and vague geographies, *Fuzzy Sets and Systems, 113(1)*, 7–18.

Guesgen, H. W. & Albrecht, J. (2000). Imprecise reasoning in geographic information systems, *Fuzzy Sets and Systems, 113*, 121–131.

Hadzilacos, T. (1996). On layer-based systems for undetermined boundaries. In P. A. Burrough & A. U. Frank (Eds.), *Geographic objects with indeterminate boundaries* (pp. 237–255). London: Taylor & Francis.

Hughes, G. & Cresswell, M. J. (1996). *A new introduction to modal logic.* Routledge: New York.

Kamp, J. A. (1975). Two theories about adjectives. In E. L. Keenan (Ed.), *Formal semantics of natural language* (pp. 123–155). Cambridge: Cambridge University Press.

Keefe, R. & Smith, P. (1996). *Vagueness: A reader.* Cambridge, Mass.: MIT Press.

Kulik, L. (2001). A geometric theory of vague boundaries based on supervaluation, In D. R. Montello (Ed.), *Spatial Information Theory: Foundations of Geographic Information Science,* COSIT'01, Vol. 2205 Lecture Notes in Computer Science (pp. 44–59). Springer.

Kulik, L., Eschenbach, C., Habel, C. & Schmidtke, H. R. (2002). A graded approach to directions between extended objects. In M. J. Egenhofer & D. M. Mark (Eds.), *Geographic information science, Second International Conference, GIScience 2002* (pp. 119–131). Berlin: Springer.

Kulik, L. & Klippel, A. (1999). Reasoning about cardinal directions using grids as qualitative geographic coordinates. In C. Freksa & D. M. Mark (Eds.), *Spatial information theory: Cognitive and computational foundations of geographic information science,* COSIT'99, Vol. 1661 Lecture Notes in Computer Science (pp. 205–220) Berlin: Springer.

Lewis, D. K. (1993). Many, but almost one. In J. Bacon, K. Campbell & L. Reinhardt (Eds.), *Ontology, causality, and mind* (pp. 23–38). Cambridge: Cambridge University Press.

Morreau, M. (2002). What vague objects are like, *Journal of Philosophy, 99,* 333–361.

Pawlak, Z. (1982). Rough sets, *International Journal of Computer and Information Sciences, 11,* 341–356.

Pawlak, Z. (1991). *Rough sets: theoretical aspects of reasoning about data,* Dordrecht; Boston: Kluwer.

Randell, D. A., Cui, Z. & Cohn, A. G. (1992). A spatial logic based on regions and connection. In B. Nebel, C. Rich & W. R. Swartout (Eds.), *Proceedings 3rd International Conference on Knowledge Representation and Reasoning (KR'92)* (pp. 165–176). San Mateo, CA: Morgan Kaufmann.

Russell, B. (1923). Vagueness. *The Australian Journal of Philosophy and Psychology, 1,* 84–92.

Schneider, M. (1999). Uncertainty management for spatial data in databases: Fuzzy spatial data types.. In R. H. Güting, D. Papadias & F. H. Lochovsky (Eds.), *Advances in spatial databases, 6th International Symposium, SSD'99* (pp. 330–351). Berlin: Springer.

Schneider, M. (2003). Design and implementation of finite resolution crisp and fuzzy spatial objects, *Data & Knowledge Engineering, 44*, 81–108.

Tye, M. (1990). Vague objects, *Mind, 99*, 535–557.

Varzi, A. C. (1997). Boundaries, continuity, and contact, *Noûs, 31*, 26–58.

Varzi, A. C. (2001). Vagueness in geography, *Philosophy & Geography, 4*, 49–65.

Williamson, T. (1999). On the structure of higher-order vagueness, *Mind, 108*, 127–143.

Worboys, M. F. (1998a). Computation with imprecise geospatial data, *Computers, Environment and Urban Systems, 22*, 85–106.

Worboys, M. F. (1998b). Imprecision in finite resolution spatial data, *GeoInformatica, 2*, 257–280.

Zadeh, L. A. (1965). Fuzzy sets, *Information and Control, 8*, 338–353.

Zadeh, L. A. (1975). Fuzzy logic and approximate reasoning, *Synthese, 30*, 407–428.

SPATIAL COGNITION AND COMPUTATION, 3(2&3), 185–204

Where's Downtown?: Behavioral Methods for Determining Referents of Vague Spatial Queries

Daniel R. Montello, Michael F. Goodchild,
Jonathon Gottsegen, and Peter Fohl
University of California at Santa Barbara

Humans think and talk about regions and spatial relations imprecisely, in terms of vague concepts that are fuzzy or probabilistic (e.g., *downtown*, *near*). The functionality of geographic information systems will be increased if they can interpret vague queries. We discuss traditional and newer approaches to defining and modeling spatial queries. Most of the research on vague concepts in information systems has focussed on mathematical and computational implementation. To complement this, we discuss behavioral-science methods for determining the referents of vague spatial terms, particularly vague regions. We present a study of the empirical determination of *downtown Santa Barbara*. We conclude with a discussion of prospects and problems for integrating vague concepts into geographic information systems.

Keywords: Vagueness, Spatial Queries, Cognitive Regions, Geographic Information

People typically think and communicate about the world in terms of vague concepts. Unlike formal languages, natural languages used in everyday speaking and writing typically refer to categories that do not have precise referents and are not delimited by sharp semantic boundaries. Furthermore, unlike formal concepts such as those of geometry, exemplars of vague concepts vary in the degree to which they are members of a category or the chance that they are members of a category; that is, they are *fuzzy* or *probabilistic* (Lakoff, 1987; Smith & Medin, 1981; Zadeh, 1965). For example, Rosch and Mervis (1975) showed that lay people generally consider robins to be better examples of

Correspondence concerning this article should be addressed to Daniel R. Montello, Department of Geography and the NCGIA, The University of California, Santa Barbara, CA 93106, USA; email montello@geog.ucsb.edu

birds than are penguins, though both are birds to some degree, and both are birds according to the more rigorously-defined criteria of ornithology.

Natural language about space and place is no exception. Two classes of vague spatial terms are commonly used in geographic communication and thought: *spatial relations* and *regions*. Vague (qualitative) spatial relations include such terms as *near, around,* and *to the east* (Altman, 1994; Mark & Frank, 1989; Retz-Schmidt, 1988). Similarly, regions, which are essentially categories of land surface area, are typically vague (Mark & Csillag, 1989). *Administrative* regions such as a states or land parcels have sharp boundaries imposed on them (Smith & Varzi, 1997). But other region concepts used by lay people refer to probabilistically graded or fuzzy entities (as do the concepts of *thematic* and *functional* regions used in geo-science research contexts—see Montello, 2003). Examples of such *cognitive* or *perceptual* regions include *downtown, Riviera neighborhood* (in Santa Barbara, California), and *Midwest*. For our purposes, the two classes of spatial relations and regions share many similarities. Both refer to spatial extents without precise boundaries, and for which there are no exact criteria for membership—no finite set of necessary and sufficient characteristics. A formal test of the relationship "A is to the east of B," for example, might require that there exists at least one due east-west line that intersects both A and B. Informally, however, such a directional reference is likely to be used under a range of conditions that are difficult to identify precisely (Frank, 1996). Similarly there is no formally defined, universally accepted line that demarcates the Midwest, and any two individuals will agree only partially about which areas of the United States are part of the Midwest. Some areas (typically near the center of the region) are considered to be better or more typical examples of the Midwest than are other areas.

In this paper, we discuss the use of vague spatial concepts, particularly vague regions, in geospatial thought and communication. Given the ubiquitous use of vague spatial concepts, we agree with the premise (e.g., by Kuhn, 2001) that the functionality of geographic information systems (and other spatial information systems) will be enhanced if they can interpret queries containing vague terms. Our focus in this paper is on ways to determine the referents of queries about vague regions in geospatial information systems; what do people mean when they ask for a map of "Northern California" or the "area around the Eiffel Tower?" The importance of understanding vagueness has been widely recognized in geographic information science for at least a decade (e.g., contributions in Burrough and Frank, 1996) and even longer in other disciplines (e.g., Zadeh, 1965). There are many examples of work that discuss how to mathematically or computationally represent vagueness; solutions have included fuzzy logic, multivalued logic, probabilistic logic, and more (Altman, 1994; Cobb et al., 2000; Cohn & Gotts, 1996; De Bruin, 2000; Mark & Csillag, 1989; Papadias et al., 1999; Wahlster, 1989; Wang & Hall, 1996). Our focus in this paper is not on the formal structure of vague spatial concepts, though this work is obviously critically important to implementing vagueness in information systems. With few exceptions (discussed below), however, work on formally implementing vagueness does not discuss how to determine *what* should be implemented (this "behavioral omission" is discussed by Montello and Frank, 1996). This is especially problematic for vague regions, because nothing in the formal mechanics of representing the "Midwest" specifies what land area should be included—what the "content" of the region is. In the present paper, we address the problem of how behavioral methods can be used to determine what people mean when they use vague terms, particularly vague spatial terms[1]. To demonstrate these methods, we present a detailed example of the empirical determination of *downtown Santa Barbara*. The paper concludes with a return to the general question of the impacts of geographic information technologies on interactions among humans, technology, and the environment.

Precise and Vague Spatial Concepts in Practice

Traditionally, a complex set of arrangements has allowed formal and informal approaches to defining spatial concepts to coexist in relative harmony. These arrangements are being disrupted, however, by the rapid introduction of digital information-processing technologies into the geographic domain (Goodchild & Proctor, 1997). A digital system is inherently precise, and thus favors rigorously defined concepts. There has been much discussion over the extent to which such technologies bias, filter, or otherwise intrude on the interactions between humans and their environment (e.g., Pickles, 1995).

In-vehicle navigation systems provide an example of a GIS that would benefit from the capacity to handle vague spatial concepts. Systems that use natural-language interfaces now exist. Some research suggests that natural language provides a better medium for communicating spatial information in this context than does a strict reliance on maps (Streeter et al., 1985). Further research will attempt to determine the types of features and spatial relations that are most useful to include in computer-generated instructions, and how these features and relations should be verbalized (e.g., Allen, 1997).

Another example of a GIS that would benefit from the ability to handle vague spatial concepts is a digital map and imagery library (e.g., the Alexandria Digital Library at UCSB; Smith, Andresen, Carver, Dolin, Fischer, Frew, et al., 1996, and see http://www.alexandria.ucsb.edu). Users of conventional map and

---

[1] Many of the issues discussed in this paper also apply to a variety of other vague terms that are not explicitly spatial, including vague features, themes, and linguistic hedges, e.g., *pond, cold,* and *very* (e.g., Mark, 1993; Wallsten et al., 1986; Wang, 1994). An important distinction between explicitly spatial and nonspatial vague terms is that spatial terms involve delineation of portions of space as a literal entity, while nonspatial terms may be mapped onto space as a metaphorical entity (as in "semantic" space).

imagery libraries frequently pose queries based on vague regions, and a complex interaction between user and librarian is often needed before the query can be satisfied; furthermore, the result rarely meets the user's needs exactly. By contrast, the digital world is inherently precise, and approaches to queries are often essentially Boolean. For example, the Federal Geographic Data Committee's Content Standards for Digital Geospatial Metadata (http://www.fgdc.gov) include a number of fields, each corresponding to some defining characteristic of geographic data sets. The process of searching for data sets that fit defined needs is thus precise, since each data set either matches or does not match the specification of the search. It is difficult to incorporate the essential vagueness and trial-and-error of the conventional approach in a precise digital system.

In practice, geographic regions are more likely to be identified by their limits than by enumerating their contents. In response to a query, a digital library system must decide the extent of area to return to the user, and this is essentially the problem of identifying the limits, or boundaries, of the region in question. But there is a more conceptually interesting reason for a focus on boundaries. Because the geographic surface is continuous, a finite region will contain an infinite number of locations; thus, definition by enumeration is possible only if a region is defined as an aggregate of a finite number of smaller regions. Specification of a region is therefore often reduced to specification of its boundary. Even in the case of a well-defined region, however, specification of a boundary is ultimately insufficient to define a geographic region. Suppose, for example, that a boundary is defined as following a parallel of latitude. In principle, it would be possible to determine whether a point was inside or outside the region by measuring its latitude. Unfortunately, our ability to measure latitude is limited by the nature of our measuring procedures. Thus, the traditional response has been to replace a boundary defined by latitude with a series of physical monuments on the ground, together with the rule that the boundary between any adjacent pair of monuments follows a straight line. Additional uncertainty results when the monuments are lost, subject to tectonic movement, or represented digitally. In an important sense, then, all geographic regions can only be ultimately identified in a vague way, because the location of a point can never be measured accurately with unlimited precision.

These difficulties are even more profound for the vague spatial concepts we consider in this paper. They are vague in part because people are unsure about their precise referent— essentially a variant of measurement error, many spatial concepts reflect *epistemological* vagueness. But these concepts are vague in a fundamental *ontological* sense too, not just because of limitations due to measurement error, disagreements among experts, or inattention to temporal and scale issues (Burrough & Frank, 1996), though all of these are important reasons why GIS needs to deal better with vague information. They are cognitively vague, represented in people's conceptual understandings of the world as vague entities.

In many contexts, vague terms have either been replaced with precisely-defined ones, or ignored. Thus the adjectives *hot* and *cold* have been replaced by precise scales of temperature. Similarly, certain vague geographic regions have been replaced by precisely-defined regions by surveying their boundaries, by arbitrarily identifying precise boundaries, or by defining them as aggregates of well-defined component parts (e.g., biogeographic regions are discussed by Gray, 1997). But many regions lack official recognition, remain the subject of debate, or are tacitly accepted as being part of an informal geographic language. Gazetteers, used to describe the index of place-names found in atlases, have connotations of official recognition, typically including only the names of administrative entities that have some level of formal definition. The gazetteer of the Geographic Names Information System (GNIS) of the U.S. Geological Survey (http://mapping.usgs.gov/www/gnis/), a list of place-names derived from the USGS's topographic maps and arguably a digital equivalent of an atlas gazetteer, similarly reflects a preference for places with some form of official recognition, and omits less formal terms such as *Riviera* or *Midwest*, terms in common use and likely subjects of library searches.

Determining the Referents of Vague Spatial Queries

Behavioral-science methods are needed to determine the referents of vague queries. As we stated above, the various formal approaches to defining vague spatial concepts (fuzzy logic, etc.) may provide the computational mechanics for implementing vague concepts but do not provide a principled basis for determining the actual content of the implemented concept. This content is an empirical question, and requires empirical observation or interrogation of human conceptualizers.   In the study we report here, we demonstrate a method for empirically determining from human subjects the referent of a vague region, *downtown Santa Barbara.*

Aside from the traditional solutions of ignoring vague queries or making them artificially precise, there are two approaches one might take to empirically determining their referents (Burrough, 1996; Robinson, 2000). The first is the *a priori* approach, in which an understanding of particular vague terms is stored in the system. For example, a representation of a commonly used but informal term, such as *downtown Santa Barbara*, could be stored in the system's database along with formally-defined terms, using appropriate representations.   To implement this approach, one would need to conduct empirical tests or interviews with human informants and store the results. The second approach is *interactive*; no prior understanding of the vague term is stored in the system. Instead, the system interrogates users in some way to determine the referents of their vague queries. Conveniently, the methods useful for an a priori approach can be applied to an interactive approach. To do this, one or more of the data collection procedures we describe below would be implemented into the interface of the system as a series of system-generated queries. The system would process the responses to those queries in real time in order to make decisions about what areas of space to represent to users as the referents of their queries.

Robinson (1990, 2000) introduced such an interactive method for determining the referents of vague spatial relations like *near* and *far*; in doing so, he provides a rare example of an empirical attempt to determine the content of geospatial natural-language concepts (Mark, 1993, is another early example). Like our research, Robinson's work represents an attempt to help solve the problems of creating natural-language GIS. In his research, Robinson programmed a computer to ask a series of yes/no questions of a user, such as "is Alma near Douglas?" The program presents a series of such questions, based in part on the pattern of answers it gets. The research we present below may be seen in part as an attempt to replicate and extend Robinson's research, but focusing on vague regions rather than relations.

The empirical methods we propose to determine the referent of a user's vague spatial query are based on two assertions. The first is that a region like *downtown* is in fact vague rather than precise in respondents' conceptual structures. The second, shared with Robinson, is that respondents will be willing to make discrete judgments about area membership even though they believe that the areas do not have precise boundaries. In other words, we assume that users will typically be comfortable making "judgment calls" about the regional membership status of any small piece of the Earth. The responses we obtained in our study reported below support both of these assertions.

We conceive of a vague object as a field $z(X)$, giving a measure of the object's presence at any point in the plane (or on the surface of the Earth). A well-defined object is a binary field, $z = \{0,1\}$. But for vague objects, various interpretations of z are possible. Blakemore (1984) and others have suggested that z be three-valued, with an intermediate value denoting "X may be in A." In the egg-yolk model of Cohn and Gotts (1996), the "yolk" is "in A," the "white" is "may be in A," and the two sets together form the "egg." Since z has only three values in this model, its spatial variation can be treated as a simple variant of the standard Boolean two-valued case. In the more general case, however, the scale of z is continuous. It could be interpreted as a probability, $0 \leq z \leq 1$, either strictly frequentist as the probability that a randomly chosen person or observer would assign the point to A, or subjectively as a measure of an observer's confidence in assigning the point to A. Alternatively, it could be interpreted as a measure of the membership of X in the fuzzy set A (Zadeh, 1965).

In principle, determining the field $z(X)$ could require an infinite (or at least very large) amount of sampling, if the value of the field were independent at every location. In practice, however, vague spatial concepts tend to be strongly autocorrelated, so that effective determination may be possible with fairly sparse sampling. If we give $z(X)$ a frequentist interpretation, a surface can be constructed by interrogating a sufficiently large sample of users. Each user would be asked to identify locations that lie within the region [z(X)=1] and locations that lie outside [z(X)=0]. Again, sampling would continue until sufficiently dense. After a sufficient number of users have provided input, z(X) would be computed by some appropriate method of convolution over the inputs. For example, if every user provides input at the same set of sample locations, z(X) can be obtained by a simple average at every point. If point sample locations do not coincide between users, z(X) could be obtained by a convolution such as:

$$z(X) = \sum_i x_i W_i \Big/ \sum_i W_i$$

where j is a sample point, $x_j=\{0,1\}$ the value assigned at that point, and W_j is a decreasing function of the distance d_j between x and point j, such as $\exp(-bd_j)$. We term the result a *frequentist* z(X).

Interpreting z(X) as a subjective probability or fuzzy membership, we could ask users to assign values of z directly to locations. For example, users could be asked to indicate locations that they are "50% confident" lie within the region, or to draw the location of the "50% confidence" isoline. The process could be continued until the entire area is sampled sufficiently densely for a representation of z(X) to be built. An appropriate method of spatial interpolation would then be used to determine z(X) at any remaining locations. We term this a *subjectivist* z(X).

The specific methods we use in this study employ both of these approaches. The first method is distinctly frequentist in concept and probably the most efficient in placing minimal demands on the user. Presented with an inclusive base map, a user simply draws a line around the area believed to constitute the referent of the query (Figure 1a). Aitken and Prosser (1990) employed this method to determine residents' beliefs about the extents of their neighborhoods. Similarly, Brown (1991) had respondents identify downtown Tacoma, Washington, by verbally describing the boundaries or by marking the boundaries on a street map overlaid on an aerial photograph of the area. A frequentist z(X) can be obtained by averaging the binary surfaces obtained in this way from a number of users.

Other designs might be used to elicit similar binary information. For example, we could present the user with a series of sample points or raster cells, asking in each case for a binary response—the point or cell lies inside the region, or outside the region (Figure 1b). Points could be presented on a regular grid, with a spacing determined by the resolution needed and by the ergonomics of the task. But clearly it would be more efficient to concentrate sample points in the region of the boundary, where the variation of the frequentist z(X) is highest (Figure 1c). This is essentially the method Robinson (1990) used to elicit meanings of *near* and *far*. While complex algorithms might be devised to selectively sample the boundary region, this is effectively what happens when

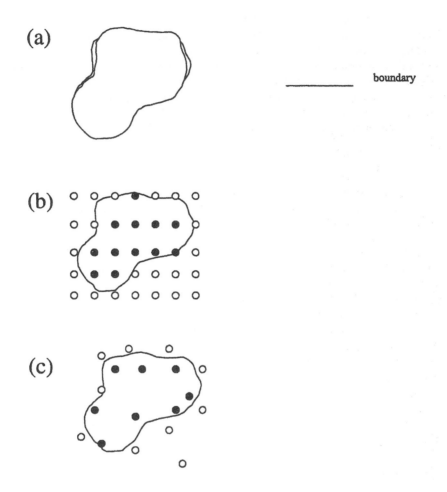

Figure 1. Strategies for eliciting individual representations of regions: a) by sketching a boundary; b) by responses over a grid; c) by selective trial-and-error sampling.

the user is asked to draw the actual boundary, and we conclude that the strategy of asking users to draw the boundary samples the plane very efficiently.

From a subjectivist perspective, the binary nature of the surface elicited from an individual respondent using the methods just described reflects a precise view of a region rather than a vague view. So as an alternative, various subjectivist methods might be devised that would interrogate the respondent for subjective probabilities or vague memberships at sample locations. We examine one of these below by asking respondents to draw the boundaries that they are 50% and 100% confident delimit downtown.

The base map. A technical problem arises in all of these methods because of the need to display a base map before eliciting representations of a region. To elicit an estimate of the region *downtown Santa Barbara*, for example, it is necessary to display and sample an area that includes the entire region. But until the region has been estimated, it is not possible to know whether the area displayed is sufficient. The interpretation of a region term will likely depend somewhat on the context of the user's specific problem; for instance, the location of downtown depends somewhat on whether one is thinking of shopping, dining, or attending the theater (though locations of these functions are clustered in space). Moreover, it is likely that a user's estimate will depend to a degree on the area shown; he or she will be more likely to underestimate a region that is large relative to the displayed area, and to overestimate a region that is small. We propose the following strategies to deal with these considerations:

1. Request that the user define the display area, by manipulating a comprehensive base map (panning, zooming, and clipping) until satisfied.

2. Request that the user delimit the boundary on the display. If the boundary approaches within a threshold distance of the edge at any time, interrupt and ask the user if the display should be redefined. If yes, return to 1. The threshold distance could be set to some proportion of the smaller of the linear dimensions of the screen, e.g., 0.15.

Empirical Study of Downtown Santa Barbara

To investigate the empirical determination of referents of vague regions, we conducted a study on people's beliefs about the extent of *downtown Santa Barbara*. We addressed several issues in this study: How well does a method for measuring vague regions work? What is the nature of the region that results? How do people understand and respond to instructions to draw boundaries of varying confidence? How feasible would it be to implement such regions in a GIS?

Method

Participants. Participants were pedestrians stopped at one of eleven locations on sidewalks near or within the area we anticipated that most people would consider downtown. These locations were chosen out of convenience as places with an intermediate amount of foot traffic. Potential participants were stopped at random at these locations. Our request informed them that we were "doing a research project on the way people identify neighborhoods," and that we wanted to ask "a few questions about the area that you consider to be downtown Santa Barbara." Thirty-nine people agreed to participate, 17 females and 22 males. One female and two males were excluded from data analysis because they did not complete the task. The remaining 36 participants ranged in age from 20 to

70 years, with a median age of 42. All except one lived and/or worked in the South Coast area of Santa Barbara County, which includes the city of Santa Barbara and the surrounding communities. Nearly half lived and/or worked in or near what they identified as the downtown area.

Materials. A base map showing the entire City of Santa Barbara and surrounding area on all sides was used for the mapping tasks. The base map was printed on American legal-size paper (8.5 x 14 in [21.6 x 35.6 cm]). The administrative boundary of the City was not visible on the map. A reduced version of the base map can be seen in Figures 2-5.

Procedures. Data collection involved three simple mapping tasks. The first task elicited participants' beliefs about the size and shape of downtown Santa Barbara. Participants were told to draw a line on the base map to "outline the area of the city that you consider to be downtown." Pilot tests had shown that some people would not delineate a closed area in response to this request, given that the city of Santa Barbara borders an ocean (we assume they meant us to consider their downtowns as ending at the waterfront). Closed areas were considered necessary for aggregating and displaying the vague regions, so for the regular data collection, we explicitly instructed participants to "enclose an area [around downtown] on the map." We refer to the regions generated from this first task as *default* regions, because they were elicited before we discussed the concept of vagueness with participants. They reflect a frequentist conception of vague regions, aggregated over participants.

The second task attempted to explicitly capture the subjectivist vagueness of an individual's conception of downtown. We introduced the second task to participants by explaining that downtown is not formally defined, that there is no official boundary for downtown. We explained that they might feel that some places are more representative, more clearly part, of downtown than others. We checked to make sure that participants understood what we meant by this; in fact, nearly all participants understood this readily and expressed agreement with it. The map with the default polygon drawn on it was removed and a new base map was given to participants. We instructed them to draw a line on the new base map to show the area that they were "100% confident was downtown," pointing out that this might or might not be different than their first line. We then asked participants to draw, on the same map, the area that they were "50% confident was downtown." Thus, the second task generated *100% regions* and *50% regions*. For convenience, either might be termed *confidence regions*.

The third and final task captured participants' conceptions of the most representative point in downtown. Participants put an x at the location that they considered to be the "core or focal point of downtown." We carefully avoided referring to the *center* of downtown because we did not necessarily want to elicit their conceptions of downtown's geometric centroid. Rather, we were interested in their assessment of the point that most represents downtown, that was most clearly *in* downtown. Finally, we collected basic information about how long participants had lived in the Santa Barbara area, and the neighborhoods in which they lived and worked.

Results and Discussion

The raw-data polygons for each participant's default region are displayed in Figure 2. These are a set of overlapping polygons, the smaller being mostly contained within the larger ones. Figure 2 makes evident that *downtown Santa Barbara* is a vague region, when that is understood in the frequentist sense (i.e., participants drew nonidentical regions). However, the large degree of overlap, particularly around a central core, suggests that the vague regions of different participants are similar enough so that an attempt to measure and display a single region is a meaningful exercise.

The polygons were digitized and entered into a GIS. Figure 3 is a representation of these data in the aggregate, mapped using dot-density shading (Lavin, 1986). In order to produce these, the continuous function describing goodness of fit is approximated using discrete raster representations of the vague regions. The resulting map of downtown apparently communicates vague boundaries effectively, though this method produces some noncontinuous gradations near the periphery that are artifacts of sparse data in the boundary areas of the largest raw data polygons.

After the default regions were drawn, participants were asked to show 100% and 50% regions on a new base map. The 100% and 50% raw-data polygons are shown in Figure 4. Aggregated dot-density maps for both confidence regions are shown in Figure 5.

It appears that the instruction to draw confidence regions of varying degrees of confidence (as expressed in percentages) was interpretable in sensible ways by most participants. Of the 36 participants, 33 drew 50% regions that are larger than their 100% regions, the other three drawing them as equal. Furthermore, all but 2 participants drew 50% regions that wholly contained their 100% regions.

It is interesting to compare the default regions to the two confidence regions because it suggests how participants interpreted the default instructions. Nearly all participants drew different polygons in response to the three tasks. Specifically, only 2 people drew the same regions for all three tasks. What were the sizes of the three regions? Given default instructions, where do people assign boundaries to a cognitive region they understand has no crisp boundary? We did not have any particular prior guess about this. In fact, 12 participants drew the 50% region as larger than the default, 12 drew it as smaller, and 12 drew them as the same size. That is, equal numbers of participants interpreted default instructions as weaker than 50% confidence, stronger than 50% confidence, or equal to 50% confidence. In contrast, no participant drew the 100% region as larger than the default; 32 drew it as smaller, and 4 drew it the same size. These results suggest that on average, people interpret a default

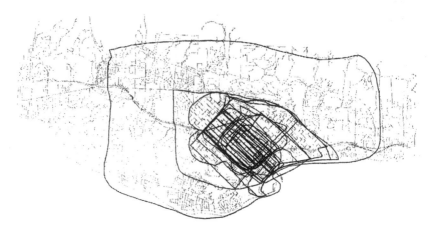

Figure 2. Raw-data polygons for each participant's default concept of downtown Santa Barbara.

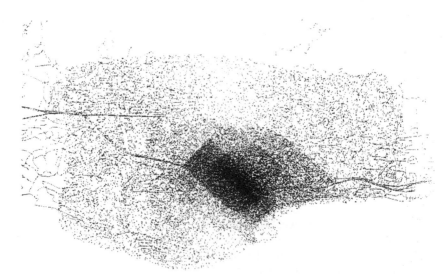

Figure 3. Default downtown region displayed with dot-density shading.

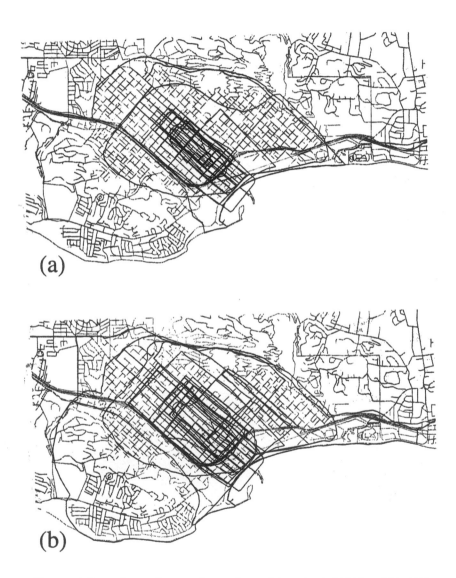

Figure 4. Raw-data polygons for each participant's a) 100% and b) 50% confidence downtowns.

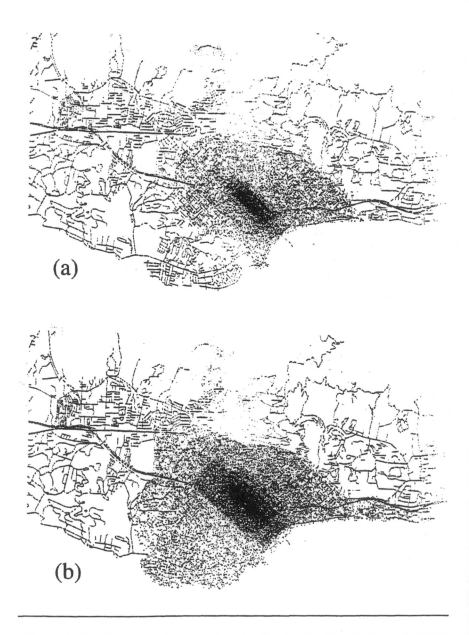

Figure 5. Confidence regions displayed with dot-density shading: a) 100% confidence.

request for *downtown* as calling for a boundary near the line of their 50% confidence. In general, smaller regions were wholly contained within larger regions, and no participant drew completely noncontiguous regions. But 9 participants did draw smaller or equal-sized regions that were only partially contained within the other region (typically 50% and/or 100% regions that only partially overlapped the default region).

In addition to the sizes and locations of the downtown regions, we examined their shapes. Twenty-three participants drew only convex polygons, with either rounded or rectangular corners. The remaining 13 participants drew at least one of their regions as concave, 8 drawing all of their regions as concave. Comments made by participants provided some insight into their bases for determining their regions, including their shapes. The presence of commercial enterprises was a common reason, consistent with a dictionary definition of downtown as central business district. But several people mentioned that downtown was the area in which people (presumably tourists) would walk. And one participant stated that the presence of City Hall and the courthouse defined downtown.

Participants readily understood our request for a core location in downtown. And the core was located in the most stringently defined downtown, the 100% confidence region, for all but 2 participants (2 others did not answer this question). As stated above, we tried to avoid suggesting to participants that the core had to be the spatial centroid of their regions. In fact, participants did not necessarily interpret the instructions to be a request for a spatial centroid. The core was located an average of nearly 300 meters from the centroid of the 100% region (to understand the scale of this, the average 100% region was only 600-800 m in width). It appears that participants' concepts of downtown were graded (whether fuzzy or probabilistic) but not symmetric around the core of downtown.

Summary and Conclusions

Many commentators have claimed that spatial information systems will benefit from applying knowledge of human conceptualizations of space and place to system design. There is little doubt that these conceptualizations are replete with categories, both spatial and nonspatial, that are vague, having imprecise and graded boundaries. Attempts to understand these conceptualizations must involve both theoretical and empirical work on the structures and processes of vague entities such as cognitive regions. In this paper, we have discussed some of the difficulties of representing vague regions in traditionally precise ways in digital systems. In addition to modeling and representing the structure of vague regions, it is important to develop methods for determining their content: To what do these terms refer? In this paper, we discussed empirical methods for answering this question in a specific context. Both a priori and interactive approaches were described. We reported a study in which participants drew lines around areas they believed constituted *downtown Santa Barbara*. Vagueness in the boundaries was elicited in two ways, by comparing variation in boundary locations across participants and by having participants draw different boundaries to indicate their varying confidence in region membership for different parts of the area. The results provide evidence that our method is a viable approach to externalizing people's representations of vague cognitive regions.

Interactive and a priori approaches to determining the referents of vague spatial queries are based on similar empirical methods. There are important differences between them. Interactive approaches are much more labor intensive for the user querying a database, but they allow determination of idiosyncratic meanings for any particular user. A priori approaches require prior data collection but do not place extra demand on the user at the time the query is placed. However, they require that there is sufficient agreement among different users that the stored vague concept applies generally, not just to a single user. In his study of vague spatial relations, Robinson (2000) concluded that there was little consistency among users, that it was "apparent from these results that one can expect little agreement among individual users on the exact definition of simple spatial relations" (p. 140). Our results suggest instead that people's conceptual understandings do reflect a fair amount of agreement, though clearly two people are unlikely to agree exactly on the meaning of a vague region like *downtown* (indeed, that is the frequentist notion of vagueness). Still, a consideration of the ultimate idiographic nature of conceptual structure may support the viability of an interactive approach over an a priori approach.

All approaches depend on the willingness of people to make discrete and precise judgments about region membership, even though they do not conceptualize boundaries as discrete and precise. Our study found that people were in fact quite willing and able to draw discrete boundaries around downtown, even though we also found that most people readily accepted the notion that downtown does not actually have a single precise boundary but a "band" of area of diminishing membership strength around a high confidence core (or possibly multiple discrete boundaries varying in degree of membership strength). Comments we recorded from participants indicated that they clearly believed downtown has a "core" location of greatest prototypicality, though not necessarily at the spatial centroid.

Of course, a person's concept of downtown is not a single context-free representation. The concept of "downtown" as expressed in thought and behavior (including language and mapping) is not due just to a static representation (or set of representations) stored in long-term memory. When a person uses knowledge about regions (or other conceptual entities), long-term memory representations are activated into working memory. The representations are thus subject to various processes of memory integration, transformation, etc., that take account of the particular context of the situation (including the purpose of querying about downtown, the form by which downtown is expressed, whether one is speaking to a local resident or a tourist, and so on). The precise referent of "downtown" may thus vary somewhat depending on contextual factors. The degree and nature of this variation is an empirical possibility; it should not be assumed necessarily to be great in magnitude. Questions about the effects of contextual factors make up critical research agenda for cognitive- and information-science communities.

An important example of such a contextual factor in the present case concerns the determination and presentation of appropriate base maps that include the entire area that might, even slightly, be considered to be part of a particular vague region. It is possible that using a base map could introduce some type of a map bias. For example, the area covered by the base map might influence the size of estimated regions (e.g., a smaller downtown might be elicited if the base map depicted less area). One could avoid such a bias by using a method not dependent on a base map. For example, one could stop participants at many different places around town and ask them to say whether they were downtown or not at that moment. From a research perspective, this would be an interesting technique to explore, though very labor intensive. However, its applicability to the situation of a user sitting at a terminal requesting spatial information is limited.

Natural language is inherently vague and imprecise; human communication often proceeds by a series of iterations when greater precision is needed. There is no single reason for the vagueness of conceptual structure—both epistemological and ontological vagueness are characteristic of human thought (though precision and certainty do occur as well). The user entering a map library without a precise definition of need enters into a dialog with an assistant in which both iterate towards an agreement. The assistant helps the user to refine the need and to identify the best solution in the form of an information object. So far, systems like digital libraries work fundamentally differently than this in their assumption that the user is able to approach the system with a precise need and that all of the objects available can be characterized precisely.

The tension between precise and vague specification extends far beyond the context of digital libraries to many other aspects of the interaction of society with information and the environment. Standard digital systems are inherently precise, requiring everything to be reduced to a binary alphabet. Traditional maps are also precise, forcing gradual transitions between regions to appear as sharp boundaries. Precision is relatively easy to achieve in a centralized authoritarian system where uniformity can be imposed. Thus an obvious solution to the *downtown Santa Barbara* problem posed in this paper would be to establish a standard that applies to all users of digital information systems, or even to society as a whole. But the precise agreement reached between the individual user and the map library assistant is a standard for two people only, and very different in its implications for the broader community. Thus the challenge for designers of digital libraries and other information systems is to achieve precision in a user's interaction with the system, without at the same time forcing that version of precision on all users.

Acknowledgments

The National Center for Geographic Information and Analysis (NCGIA), and the Alexandria Digital Library, are supported by the National Science Foundation. The National Imagery and Mapping Agency University Research Initiative also provided support for this work. Thanks to David Mark, the editors of this special issue, and anonymous reviewers of an earlier version for helpful comments.

References

Aitken, S. C., & Prosser, R. (1990). Residents' spatial knowledge of neighborhood continuity and form. *Geographical Analysis, 22,* 301–325.

Allen, G. L. (1997). From knowledge to words to wayfinding: Issues in the production and comprehension of route directions. In S. C. Hirtle & A. U. Frank (Eds.), *Spatial information theory: A theoretical basis for GIS,* COSIT'97, Vol. 1329 Lecture Notes in Computer Science (pp. 363–372). Berlin: Springer-Verlag.

Altman, D. (1994). Fuzzy set theoretic approaches for handling imprecision in spatial analysis. *International Journal of Geographical Information Systems, 8,* 271–289.

Blakemore, M. J. (1984). Generalization and error in spatial databases. *Cartographica, 21,* 131–139.

Brown, R. F. (1991). *Delimiting the perceived downtown: A perceptual approach.* Unpublished doctoral dissertation, The University of Pennsylvania, Philadelphia.

Burrough, P. A. (1996). Natural objects with indeterminate boundaries. In P. A. Burrough & A. U. Frank (Eds.), *Geographic objects with indeterminate boundaries* (pp. 3–28). London: Taylor & Francis.

Burrough, P. A., & Frank, A. U. (Eds.) (1996). *Geographic objects with indeterminate boundaries.* London: Taylor & Francis.

Cobb, M., Petry, F., & Robinson, V. E. (2000). Special issue on "Uncertainty in geographic information systems and spatial data." *Fuzzy Sets and Systems, 113.*

Cohn, A. G., & Gotts, N. M. (1996). The 'egg-yolk' representation of regions with indeterminate boundaries. In P. A. Burrough & A. U. Frank (Eds.), *Geographic objects with indeterminate boundaries* (pp. 171–188). London: Taylor & Francis.

De Bruin, S. (2000). Querying probabilistic land cover data using fuzzy set theory. *International Journal of Geographical Information Science, 14,* 359–372.

Frank, A. U. (1996). Qualitative spatial reasoning: Cardinal directions as an example. *International Journal of Geographical Information Systems, 10,* 269–290.

Goodchild, M. F., & Proctor, J. (1997). Scale in a digital geographic world. *Geographical & Environmental Modelling, 1,* 5–23.

Gray, M. V. (1997). Classification as an impediment to the reliable and valid use of spatial information: A disaggregate approach. In S. C. Hirtle & A. U. Frank (Eds.), *Spatial information theory: A theoretical basis for GIS,,* Vol. 1329 Lecture Notes in Computer Science (pp. 137–149). Berlin: Springer-Verlag.

Kuhn, W. (2001). Ontologies in support of activities in geographical space. *International Journal of Geographical Information Science, 15,* 613–631.

Lakoff, G. (1987). *Women, fire, and dangerous things.* Chicago, IL: University of Chicago Press.

Lavin, S. (1986). Mapping continuous geographical distributions using dot-density shading. *The American Cartographer, 13,* 140–150.

Mark, D. M. (1993). Toward a theoretical framework for geographic entity types. In A. U. Frank & I. Campari (Eds.), *Spatial information theory: A theoretical basis for GIS,* Vol. 716 Lecture Notes in Computer Science (pp. 270–283). Berlin: Springer-Verlag.

Mark, D. M., & Csillag, F. (1989). The nature of boundaries on "area-class" maps. *Cartographica, 26,* 65–78.

Mark, D. M., & Frank, A. U. (1989). Concepts of space and spatial language. *Proceedings, Ninth International Symposium on Computer-Assisted Cartography* (pp. 538–556). Baltimore, MD.

Montello, D. R. (2003). Regions in geography: Process and content. In M. Duckham, M. F. Goodchild, & M. F. Worboys (Eds.), *Foundations of geographic information science* (pp. 173–189). London: Taylor & Francis.

Montello, D. R., & Frank, A. U. (1996). Modeling directional knowledge and reasoning in environmental spaces: Testing qualitative metrics. In J. Portugali (Ed.), *The Construction of Cognitive Maps* (pp. 321–344). Dordrecht: Kluwer Academic.

Papadias, D., Karacapilidis, N., & Arkoumanis, D. (1999). Processing fuzzy spatial queries: A configuration similarity approach. *International Journal of Geographical Information Science, 13,* 93–118.

Pickles, J. (Ed.) (1995). *Ground truth: The social implications of geographic information systems.* New York, NY: Guilford.

Retz-Schmidt, G. (1988). Various views on spatial prepositions. *AI Magazine, Summer,* 95–105.

Robinson, V. B. (1990). Interactive machine acquisition of a fuzzy spatial relation. *Computers and Geosciences, 16,* 857–872.

Robinson, V. B. (2000). Individual and multipersonal fuzzy spatial relations acquired using human-machine interaction. *Fuzzy Sets and Systems, 113,* 133–145.

Rosch, E. H., & Mervis, C. B. (1975). Family resemblances: Studies in the internal structure of categories. *Cognitive Psychology, 7,* 573–605.

Smith, B., & Varzi, A. C. (1997). Fiat and bona fide boundaries: Towards an ontology of spatially extended objects. In S. C. Hirtle, & A. U. Frank (Eds.), *Spatial information theory: A theoretical basis for GIS,* Vol. 1329 Lecture Notes in Computer Science (pp. 103–119). Berlin: Springer-Verlag.

Smith, E. E., & Medin, D. L. (1981). *Categories and concepts.* Cambridge, MA: Harvard University Press.

Smith, T. R., Andresen, D., Carver, L., Dolin, R., Fischer, C., Frew, J., et al. (1996). A digital library for geographically referenced materials. *Computer, 29,* 14.

Streeter, L. A., Vitello, D., & Wonsiewicz, S. A. (1985). How to tell people where to go: Comparing navigational aids. *International Journal of Man/Machine Studies, 22,* 549–562.

Wahlster, W. (1989). One word says more than 1000 pictures—On the automatic verbalization of the results of image sequence analysis systems. *Computers and Artificial Intelligence, 8,* 479–492.

Wallsten, T. S., Budescu, D. V., Rapoport, A., Zwick, R., & Forsyth, B. (1986). Measuring the vague meanings of probability terms. *Journal of Experimental Psychology: General, 115,* 348–365.

Wang, F. (1994). Towards a natural language user interface: An approach of fuzzy query. *International Journal of Geographical Information Systems, 8,* 143–162.

Wang, F., & Hall, G. B. (1996). Fuzzy representation of geographical boundaries in GIS. *International Journal of Geographical Information Systems, 10,* 573–590.

Zadeh, L. A.(1965). Fuzzy sets. *Information and Control, 8,* 338–353.

SPATIAL COGNITION AND COMPUTATION, 3(2&3), 205–220

Buffering Fuzzy Maps in GIS

Hans W. Guesgen
University of Auckland

Joachim Hertzberg
*Fraunhofer Institute for
Autonomous Intelligent Systems, Germany*

Richard Lobb
University of Auckland

Andrea Mantler
University of North Carolina

In this paper, we show how standard GIS operations like the complement, union, intersection, and buffering of maps can be made more flexible by using fuzzy set theory. In particular, we present a variety of algorithms for operations on fuzzy raster maps, focusing on buffer operations for such maps. Furthermore, we show how widely-available special-purpose hardware (in particular, z-buffering in graphics hardware) can be used for supporting buffer operations in fuzzy geographic information systems (GIS).

Keywords: Geographic information systems, raster maps, buffering, fuzzy logic

1 Introduction

Geographic information systems (GIS) have been in use for quite a while now (Coppock and Rhind, 1991), but their functionality has changed only little over

---

Correspondence concerning this article should be addressed to Hans W. Guesgen, Department of Computer Science, University of Auckland, PMB 92019, Auckland, New Zealand; email hans@cs.auckland.ac.nz

the years. In spite of being called *geographic*, GIS have so far been mostly geometric in nature, ignoring the temporal, thematic, and qualitative dimensions of geographic features (Molenaar, 1996; Sinton, 1978; Usery, 1996). There are, however, several attempts to overcome these limitations and to incorporate qualitative (Egenhofer and Golledge, 1997; Frank, 1994; Frank, 1996; Peuquet, 1994) or fuzzy aspects (Altmann, 1994; Brimicombe, 1997; Molenaar, 1996; Plewe, 1997) in GIS. This paper focuses on the latter aspect, extending work that has been published previously (Guesgen and Hertzberg, 2000a; Guesgen and Hertzberg, 2000b; Guesgen and Hertzberg, 2001; Guesgen et al., 2001).

An essential operation in GIS is map overlay, where new maps are computed from existing ones by applying either:[1]

- Buffer operations, which increase the size of an object by extending its boundary, or

- Set operations, such as complement, union, and intersection.

In traditional GIS, these operations are exact quantitative operations. Humans, however, often prefer a qualitative operation over an exact quantitative one, which can be achieved by extending the standard map overlay operations to fuzzy maps and using fuzzy logic rather than crisp logic.

Consider, for example the simple raster maps in Figure 1. The first row shows raster maps for the location of roads (a-i), the location of water (a-ii), locations of residences (a-iii), and the location of native forest (a-iv) in a fictional region. The second row is an illustration of crisp buffering operations. It contains raster maps illustrating roads buffered by 200m (b-i), rivers buffered by 400m (b-ii), residences buffered by 200m (b-iii), and unbuffered native forest areas (b-iv). The third row shows the result of fuzzy buffering operations: areas close to roads, obtained with a cone buffer function (Guesgen et al., 2001) of radius 400m (c-i), areas close to rivers, obtained with a cone buffer function of radius 800m (c-ii), areas close to residences, obtained with an inverse-distance buffer function (c-iii), and a probability density distribution (Scott, 1992) based on the recorded location of native forest, obtained with a 50m-radius gaussian distribution (c-iv). Dark areas are areas of high membership, while light areas are those of low membership.

The last row illustrates how the fuzzy maps can be combined to find areas close to roads, not close to rivers or residences, and not on native forest. Such areas might be required for an industrial development, for example. The boolean classification of the crisp map (d-i) would generally be much less useful for decision making than the fuzzy map (d-ii), in which darkness (i.e., the membership grade) increases with suitability. The 3D membership surface illustration (d-iii) provides an alternative view of the fuzzy map (d-ii). Here, the membership grade

---

[1] A more detailed introduction to these operations can be found elsewhere (Guesgen and Histed, 1996).

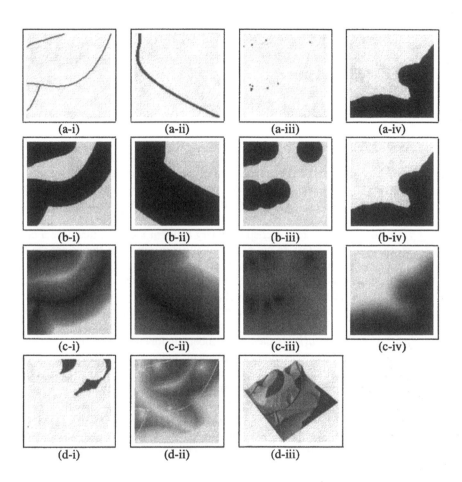

Figure 1. An illustration of buffering in a fuzzy GIS (Duff and Guesgen, 2002).

is represented by terrain height rather than greyscale (which is irrelevant in this illustration).

The rest of this paper is organized as follows. We start with a brief review of fuzzy maps and the definition of set operations for fuzzy maps; a more detailed introduction can be found elsewhere (Guesgen and Albrecht, 1998). We then continue with the introduction of various algorithms for buffering fuzzy maps, which is an extension of previously published work (Guesgen and Hertzberg, 2000a). Finally, we show how graphics hardware can be used to implement buffering algorithms more efficiently.

2 Fuzzifying Maps

In the following, we restrict ourselves to raster-based maps. Such a map consists of a grid of cells whose values specify certain attributes of the locations represented by the map. In the simplest case, the cell values are restricted to 0 and 1, where 0 signals the absence and 1 the presence of a certain attribute, like the attribute of a location being part of a road, waterway, residential area, commercial area, rural area, etc.

In some cases there is a crisp boundary between locations that have a certain attribute and those that do not have that attribute, but often this is not the case. For example, it is not always clear where a rural area stops and a residential area starts, or where a forest is not a forest any more. To cater for this fact, we extend the range of cell values from the set $\{0, 1\}$ to the interval $[0, 1]$, and thereby convert a regular raster map into a fuzzy raster map. Given a cell l in the fuzzy raster map, $\mu(l) \in [0, 1]$ indicates the degree to which l has the attribute represented by the map. The function $\mu(l)$ is called the membership function of the fuzzy raster map.

Performing a set operation (complement, union, and intersection) on fuzzy raster maps is straightforward. There are several ways of defining the complement, union, and intersection of membership functions (Driankov et al., 1996), but they all have in common that they are defined cell-wise for all cells L in the fuzzy raster map. In the case of the original max/min scheme (Zadeh, 1965), the membership functions for the complement, union, and intersection are defined as follows, where μ_1 and μ_2 denote the membership functions of the underlying maps and μ_3 the one of the resulting map:

$$
\begin{aligned}
&\text{Complement:} &&\forall l \in L : \mu_3(l) = 1 - \mu_1(l) \\
&\text{Union:} &&\forall l \in L : \mu_3(l) = \max\{\mu_1(l), \mu_2(l)\} \\
&\text{Intersection:} &&\forall l \in L : \mu_3(l) = \min\{\mu_1(l), \mu_2(l)\}
\end{aligned}
$$

Since the membership functions for the complement, union, and intersection are defined cell-wise, an algorithm for performing a set operation on fuzzy raster maps can just iterate through the set of cells and compute a new value for each cell based on the given value(s) for that cell, which means the algorithm is linear in the number of cells, i.e, its complexity is $O(|L|)$.

3   Iterative Buffering of Fuzzy Maps

Unlike the set operations, buffer operations cannot be defined cell-wise. To determine the new value of a cell l in a crisp raster map, the values of all cells in the neighborhood of l are considered. If at least one of these values is 1, then the value of l is changed to 1; otherwise it remains unchanged. In other words, the new value of l is the maximum of the original value of l and the values of all cells in the neighborhood of l. A fuzzy raster map can be buffered crisply in a similar way: the value of l is changed to the maximum fuzzy value in the neighborhood of l, which might be any value from the interval $[0, 1]$ (rather than the set $\{0, 1\}$).

Although buffering a fuzzy raster map as indicated above might be of use for many applications, we do not want to restrict ourselves to crisp buffer operations for fuzzy raster maps. Rather, we want the buffer operation to depend on the proximity of the cells under consideration. For example, if there is an area on the map with very high membership grades, then the buffer operation should assign high membership grades to cells that are very close to that area, medium high membership grades to cells close to the areas, and low membership grades to cells further away.

One way to achieve this behavior is to determine the direct neighbors of a cell and to apply a buffer function to determine the new membership grade of these neighbors. There are two types of direct neighbors:

- Edge-adjacent (4-adjacent) neighbors, or edge neighbors for short. Two cells of the grid are edge neighbors if and only if they have an edge in common.

- Vertex-adjacent (8-adjacent) neighbors, or vertex neighbors for short. Two cells of the grid are vertex neighbors, if and only if they have a vertex in common.

A buffer function is a monotonically increasing function $\beta : [0, 1] \rightarrow [0, 1]$ whose value never exceeds its input:

$$\forall m \in [0, 1] : \beta(m) \leq m$$

An example of a simple buffer function is $\beta(m) = \max\{0, m - 0.1\}$.

If l_0 is a neighbor of l_1, then the new membership grade of l_1 is determined by the maximum of the old membership grade of l_1 and the value of the buffer function applied to the membership grade of l_0:

$$\mu(l_1) \leftarrow \max\{\mu(l_1), \beta(\mu(l_0))\}$$

Brute-Force β-Buffering

Let μ be the membership function of the map.

Let β be a buffer function.

Let L be the set of all cells in the map to be buffered.

Repeat until μ is stable:

    For each $l_0 \in L$ do:

        For all neighbors l_i of l_0 do:

           $\mu(l_i) \leftarrow \max\{\mu(l_i), \beta(\mu(l_0))\}$

Figure 2. A brute-force algorithm for β-buffering raster fuzzy maps.

Since updating the membership grade of l_1 can have an impact on the membership grades of the neighbors of l_1, the update process has to be repeated for all cells of the map over and over again until a stable situation is obtained. In the following, we refer to the process of buffering a fuzzy raster map, using a buffer function β as defined above, as *iterative buffering*, or β-*buffering*.

A brute-force algorithm for β-buffering is shown in Figure 2. The algorithm visits each cell of the map and updates its membership grade based on the membership grades of the neighboring cells.[2] If any of the membership grades is changed, the algorithm repeats the updating process until all membership grades become stable. More precisely, the algorithm applies the buffer function β to the membership grade $\mu(l_0)$ of a cell l_0 and uses the result to update the membership grades of the four edge neighbors, or the eight vertex neighbors, of l_0, respectively. Since the maximum operator is commutative and associative, the order in which the cells are updated does not have an impact on the final result of the updating process.

Since the algorithm revisits each cell when repeating the updating process, even the ones whose neighbors have not been changed in the previous iteration, it performs many unnecessary checks. An improved approach is to keep track of the changed cells and to revisit a cell only if at least one of its neighbors has been changed. The algorithm in Figure 3 achieves this by applying the principle of local propagation: the membership grade of a cell is propagated to the neighbors of the cell, which are then put on to the list of cells to be visited in the future.

The local propagation algorithm is guaranteed to terminate: since the value of the buffer function never exceeds its input, we cannot get a cyclic set of updates.

---

[2]The membership grades of the neighboring cells are lower bounds for the new membership grade.

β-Buffering by Local Propagation

Let μ, β, and L be defined as before (Figure 2).

While $L \neq \emptyset$ do:

  Select $l_0 \in L$.
  $L \leftarrow L - \{l_0\}$
  For all neighbors l_i of l_0 do:
    $\mu(l_i) \leftarrow \max\{\mu(l_i), \beta(\mu(l_0))\}$
    If $\mu(l_i)$ has changed, then $L \leftarrow L \cup \{l_i\}$

Figure 3. A local propagation algorithm for β-buffering fuzzy raster maps.

At worst, a single cell can receive $|L| - 1$ updates, which correspond to paths of updates originating at each of the other cells in the map. (Also note that a path of updates cannot be longer than $|L| - 1$ cells.)

Although the propagation algorithm is guaranteed to terminate, it can be rather inefficient: many cells may be revisited repeatedly as their membership grades are overwritten by successively larger values. To prevent this from happening, we can select a cell l_0 from L with a maximum membership grade. The grade for l_0 cannot be increased by any buffer operation $\beta(m)$, since $\beta(m) \leq m$ for all $m \in [0,1]$, which means that the current grade of l_0 is the final membership grade for that cell. Since the membership grade of l_0 is both final and maximal, buffering the neighbors of l_0 results in assigning a final membership grade to the neighbors of l_0 as well. This means that none of the neighbors have to be revisited. The improved algorithm is shown in Figure 4.

4   From Iterative Buffering to Global Buffering

So far, our discussion of algorithms revolved about a buffer function β. Although propagating the result of β locally through a fuzzy raster map is a reasonable way to buffer such a map, it is not ideal for global effects, since the membership grade of a cell is determined by its original membership grade and the grade of its immediate neighbors, but not by the membership grade of cells further away from the cell under consideration. To achieve a more global effect, we replace β with a global buffer (or proximity) function ψ that is applied not only to the membership grades of the neighbors of a given cell l_0 but potentially to any cell l in the map. The function ψ has two arguments, one of which is $\mu(l_0)$, the membership grade

---

β-Buffering with Ordered Cells

Let μ, β, and L be defined as before (Figure 2).

While $L \neq \emptyset$ do:

Select $l_0 \in L$ such that $\mu(l_0)$ is maximal in L.
$L \leftarrow L - \{l_0\}$
For all neighbors l_i of l_0 do:
$\mu(l_i) \leftarrow \max\{\mu(l_i), \beta(\mu(l_0))\}$

Figure 4. An algorithm for β-buffering fuzzy maps using ordered cells.

of l_0, and the other is $\delta(l, l_0)$, the distance between l and l_0, which can be defined as follows:

1. $\delta(l_0, l_0) = 0$

2. $\forall l \neq l_0$:
   $\delta(l, l_0) = \min\{\delta(l', l_0) \mid l' \text{ neighbor of } l\} + 1$

We require ψ to be monotonically increasing in the first argument, i.e., the larger the membership grade of l_0, the larger the value of ψ, and monotonically decreasing in the second argument, i.e., the further away l is from l_0, the smaller the value of ψ. We further require that the value of ψ never exceeds the value of the first argument:

$$\forall m \in [0, 1] \text{ and } \forall d \in [0, \infty) : \psi(m, d) \leq m \tag{1}$$

The update of a membership grade is computed in a similar way as before:

$$\mu(l) \leftarrow \max\{\mu(l), \psi(\mu(l_0), \delta(l, l_0))\}$$

In addition, we have to ensure that the resulting membership grades are intuitively plausible. In particular, we want to avoid having a local effect override a more global one if they originate in the same cell. For example, if a cell l_0 has a distance of 1 to a cell l_1 and a distance of 2 to a cell l_2, then $\psi(\psi(\mu(l_2), 1), 1)$ should not exceed $\psi(\mu(l_2), 2)$, i.e., the new membership grade of l_0 is influenced by the membership grade of l_2 directly rather than the propagation of that membership from l_2 through l_1 to l_0. We can enforce this property by requiring:

$$\forall m \in [0, 1] \text{ and } \forall d_0, d_1, d_2 \in [0, \infty) : \tag{2}$$
$$d_2 = d_1 + d_0 \implies \psi(m, d_2) \geq \psi(\psi(m, d_1), d_0)$$

Figure 5. A raster map with its original fuzzy membership grades and its buffered version. Greyscale shades indicate membership grades. A white circle in the buffered map denotes a cell that received its membership grade directly or indirectly from the circled cell in the original map. Where two membership grades overlap, a larger value has precedence over a smaller one.

The buffer function $\psi(m, d) = \frac{m}{1+d}$, for example, satisfies this criterion, whereas $\psi(m, d) = \frac{m}{1+d^2}$ does not.

If we require equality instead of inequality in Formula (2), we achieve the same effect as with the function β as introduced in Section 3. If $\psi(m, d_2) = \psi(\psi(m, d_1), d_0)$, then the new membership grade of a cell l with distance d from cell l_0 can be computed by applying ψ successively to the membership grade of l_0, i.e., by defining $\beta(m) \equiv \psi(m, 1)$:

$$\mu(l) \leftarrow \max\{\mu(l), \underbrace{\psi(\psi(\ldots \psi(\mu(l_0), 1)\ldots), 1)}_{d}\}$$

Figure 5 shows a fuzzy map being buffered, using $\psi(m, d) = \frac{m}{1+d}$ as the proximity function and using a distance measure based on vertex adjacency. The original map has only membership grades of 0 (unfilled white cells), except for: (A) the filled black cells on the right of the map, which have a membership grade of 1 and (B) the single dark grey cell with a circle, which has a membership grade of $\frac{1}{2}$. An interesting effect occurs at the cell with the grid in Figure 5. This cell is closer to the single cell of Object B than to any cell in Object A. However, the effect of buffering Object A overtakes the effect of buffering Object B due to the larger membership grade of Object A:

$$\psi(\tfrac{1}{2}, 3) = \tfrac{1}{8} \quad < \quad \psi(1, 6) = \tfrac{1}{7}$$

A brute-force algorithm for global buffering (also referred to as ψ-*buffering*) a fuzzy map using a global buffer function ψ can be obtained by extending the update operations in the algorithm of Figure 2 to all cells in the map. The resulting algorithm is shown in Figure 6. The algorithm repeatedly iterates through the set of cells, using the membership grades of a cell to update the membership grades of

---

Brute-Force ψ-Buffering

Let μ be the membership function of the map.

Let ψ be a global buffer function.

Let L be the set of all cells in the map to be buffered.

Repeat until μ is stable:

    For each $l_0 \in L$ do:

        For all $l \in L - \{l_0\}$ do:

            $\mu(l) \leftarrow \max\{\mu(l), \psi(\mu(l_0), \delta(l, l_0))\}$

Figure 6. A brute-force algorithm for ψ-buffering fuzzy raster maps.

the other cells. This is done regardless of whether the membership grade of a cell can possibly have an effect on other cells or not. An improvement can be achieved by using only those cells that have the potential to influence other cells. This is the case if the current membership grade of the cell is not minimal and was not derived from the membership grade of another cell through buffering. Cells with minimal membership grade cannot increase the membership grade of another cell during buffering, because the buffer operation always returns a value smaller than or equal to the membership grade of the cell that is used as argument of the buffer operation (cf. Formula (1)). A cell whose membership grade was derived from the membership grade of another cell through buffering cannot make any contribution because the other cell has spread its influence to all cells of the map already, and since global effects dominate local ones (cf. Formula (2)), the current membership grade of the cell under consideration does not have any additional effect.

Figure 7 shows an improved algorithm, which restricts the outer loop to the set of cells that might have an influence on other cells. Initially, this set contains all cells of the map. However, when a cell is detected whose membership grade is updated through a buffer operation, the cell that was updated is removed from the set of influential cells, because it won't have any effect on the membership grades of other cells in a future iteration. In addition to that, the cells to be buffered are selected according to their membership grades. Cells with large membership grades are more likely to cause a cutoff than those with smaller grades. It therefore makes sense to consider cells with large membership grades first.

ψ-Buffering with Ordered Cells and Cutoffs

Let μ, ψ, and L be defined as before (Figure 6).

$L' \leftarrow L - \{l \mid \mu(l)$ is minimal in $L\}$

While $L' \neq \emptyset$ do:

    Select $l_0 \in L'$ such that $\mu(l_0)$ is maximal in L'.

    $L' \leftarrow L' - \{l_0\}$

    For all $l \in L - \{l_0\}$ do:

        $\mu(l) \leftarrow \max\{\mu(l), \psi(\mu(l_0), \delta(l, l_0))\}$

        If $\mu(l)$ has changed, then $L' \leftarrow L' - \{l\}$

Figure 7. An algorithm for ψ-buffering fuzzy raster maps using ordered cells and cutoffs.

5   Using Graphics Hardware for Buffering

So far, we have focussed on improving buffering by applying various software techniques and heuristics. In the rest of this paper, we adopt a different course: we describe an implementation of the brute-force algorithm that is efficient because we use special-purpose hardware. Since a fuzzy map can be viewed as a two-dimensional pixel image in which the colors represent the different membership grades of the fuzzy map, it is not surprising that techniques from the area of computer graphics can be used to buffer fuzzy maps more efficiently. (Hoff et al., 1999) suggest using graphics hardware to compute generalized Voronoi diagrams. (Mustafa et al., 2001) use hardware generated Voronoi diagrams as the basis for map simplification. We also adapt the idea of (Hoff et al., 1999) and will show how such hardware (in particular, the z-buffer of the hardware) can be used to buffer fuzzy maps.

The z-buffer (or depth buffer) is similar to the frame buffer in that it stores information for each pixel of the image. The value stored in the z-buffer is the depth of the closest object found so far that covers that pixel. Before a pixel is given the color of a new object, the depth of the object at that particular pixel is computed and compared with the depth stored in the z-buffer. If the new object is closer, its color will be stored in the frame buffer and its depth value in the z-buffer. Figure 8 shows this approach in algorithmic form.

In the context of buffering fuzzy maps, we use the z-buffer to mimic the current fuzzy map, i.e., we take the depth $\zeta(l_0)$ of a given pixel l_0 to uniquely represent

---

Z-Buffer Algorithm

Let L be the set of pixels of the image.

Let $\zeta(l)$ be the value of the z-buffer for the pixel $l \in L$.

Let $\pi(l)$ be the value of the frame buffer for the pixel $l \in L$.

Let O be the set of objects to be rendered.

For all $o \in O$ do:

    For each $l \in L$ covered by o do:

        Let z be the depth of o at l.

        Let p be the color of o at l.

        If $z < \zeta(l)$, then do:

            $\zeta(l) \leftarrow z$

            $\pi(l) \leftarrow p$

Figure 8. An algorithm showing the use of the z-buffer in graphics hardware.

the membership grade $\mu(l_0)$. A close depth indicates a high membership grade, whereas a far depth stands for a low membership grade.

To buffer the membership grade represented by the depth of the pixel, we render an object that approximates the buffer function ψ applied to $\mu(l)$. If we restrict ourselves to buffer functions of the type $\psi(m, d) = \max\{0, m - kd\}$, where k determines how fast the original membership m diminishes with the distance d, the object to be rendered is a right circular cone. Cones expand away from the camera, and thus the depth of the cone is determined by $\zeta(l) = (1 - \psi(\mu(l_0), \delta(l, l_0)))$. A membership grade of 1 is mapped to a depth of zero, and a membership grade of 0 is mapped to a depth of 1. Note that it is possible to use different values of k within the same map to obtain different buffering effects for the objects represented in the map. Beyond that, cones of a different shape (not necessarily with constant slopes) can be used to model other buffer functions.

To speed up the rendering process (i.e., to make the buffering process more efficient), we approximate each buffering cone as a triangle fan, as shown in Figure 9. To further speed up the process, we suppress the rendering process for certain pixels, if there are regions with equivalued pixels. In this case, we only need cones from the boundary pixels.

As mentioned in Section 3, distance is sometimes defined in a grid structure through neighborhood relationship. In the case of vertex neighbors, this means that our buffer function ψ can be represented by a cone with four triangles (i.e., a

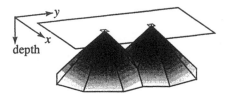

Figure 9. $\zeta(l_i)$ approximated by triangle fans.

pyramid) that is aligned parallel to the grid structure. In the case of edge neighbors, this is also possible, but the pyramid is rotated by 45 degrees.

In general, we cannot guarantee the soundness of hardware buffering, as the rendered objects are only approximations of the buffer function ψ.[3] On the other hand, there are experiments showing that fuzzy membership grades are quite robust, which means that it is not necessary to have exact membership grades (Bloch, 2000). The explanation given for this observation is twofold: first, fuzzy membership grades are used to describe imprecise information and therefore do not have to be exact, and second, each individual fuzzy membership grade plays only a minor role in the whole reasoning process, as it is usually combined with several other membership grades.

6 Evaluation of the Algorithms

The brute-force algorithm of Figure 6 iterates through the set of cells L, using the membership grades of a cell to update the membership grades of the other cells. Since this is done regardless of whether the membership grade of a cell can have an effect on other cells or not, the algorithm has an average complexity of $O(|L|^2)$.

The improved algorithm of Figure 7 still has the worst-case time complexity of $O(|L|^2)$, since it can happen that the algorithm does not change any membership grade and therefore has to iterate through all cells of the map. The time complexity is bound from below by the time complexity of selecting cells in the order of their membership grades. If the membership grades are discrete, bucket sorting can be used to sort the list beforehand, which makes sorting and selecting the cells linear; otherwise, sorting and selecting is $O(|L| \cdot \log |L|)$. In practice, the sorting time is negligible and the quadratic properties of the algorithm dominate on most data.

The worst-case time complexity for buffering a fuzzy map using graphics hardware is $O(|L|^2)$ in general and $O(|L|)$ for certain special cases (Duff and Guesgen,

---

[3]There are special cases where the result is identical with the one obtained through the software buffering algorithms (like the buffer function $\psi(m, d) = \max\{0, m - kd\}$, which corresponds to a right circular cone).

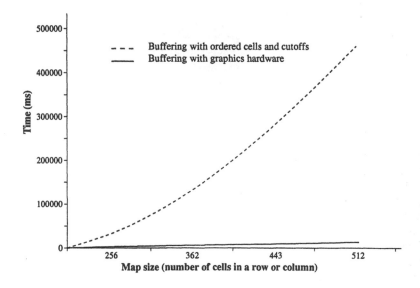

Figure 10. Processing time of buffering with ordered cells and cutoffs plotted against processing time of buffering using graphics hardware.

2002). In these cases, the graphics hardware method performs significantly better than any of the software algorithms. Figure 10 shows a plot of processing time for buffering with ordered cells and cutoffs and for buffering with graphics hardware, applied to a typical fuzzy map. The horizontal axis shows the number of cells in each row or column of the map, rather than the total number of cells of the map, and therefore a linear curve indicates quadratic processing time.

7 Conclusion

The idea of using fuzzy set theory to handle imprecision in spatial reasoning is not new (Altmann, 1994), and compared to other approaches our way of defining buffer operations in GIS might look like a step backwards. However, our more rigid way of looking at buffering of fuzzy maps has two advantages. Firstly, it allows us to apply algorithms that are practically more efficient than brute-force buffering, owing to restricting re-calculations of cell membership grades to candidates for potential value changes. And secondly, it enables us to implement a particular brute-force variant of buffering on widely-available special hardware.

Acknowledgement

Many thanks to Damien Duff, who performed the evaluation of the algorithms and provided some of the illustrations used in this paper.

References

Altmann, D. (1994). Fuzzy set-theoretic approaches for handling imprecision in spatial analysis. *International Journal of Geographical Information Systems, 8*,271–289.

Bloch, I. (2000). Spatial representation of spatial relationship knowledge. In *Proceedings of KR-00* (pp. 247–258). Colorado: Breckenridge.

Brimicombe, A. (1997). A universal translator of linguistic hedges for the handling of uncertainty and fitness-of-use in GIS. In Kemp, Z. (Ed.), *Innovations in GIS 4*. (pp 115–126). London, England: Taylor and Francis.

Coppock, J. and Rhind, D. (1991). The history of GIS. In Maguire, D., Goodchild, M., and Rhind, D., (Eds.), *Geographical information systems: Principles and applications* (pp. 21–43). Essex, England: Longman Scientific & Technical.

Driankov, D., Hellendoorn, H., and Reinfrank, M. (1996). *An Introduction to Fuzzy Control 2nd edition*. Berlin, Germany: Springer.

Duff, D. and Guesgen, H. (2002). An evaluation of buffering algorithms in fuzzy GISs. In *Proceedings of The International Conference on Geographic Information Science (GIScience-02)*. (pp 80–92). Boulder, Colarado: Springer.

Egenhofer, M. and Golledge, R. (1997). *Spatial and temporal reasoning in geographic information systems*. New York: Oxford University Press.

Frank, A. (1994). Qualitative temporal reasoning in GIS-ordered time scales. In *Proceedings of SDH-94* (pp. 410–431). Edinburgh, Scotland.

Frank, A. (1996). Qualitative spatial reasoning: Cardinal directions as an example. *International Journal of Geographical Information Systems, 10*,269–290.

Guesgen, H. and Albrecht, J. (1998). Qualitative spatial reasoning with a fuzzy distance operator. In *Proceedings of SDH-98*. Vancouver, Canada.

Guesgen, H. and Hertzberg, J. (2000a). Buffering in fuzzy geographic information systems. In *Proceedings of International Conference on Geographic Information Science (GIScience-00)* (pp. 189–192). Savannah, Georgia.

Guesgen, H. and Hertzberg, J. (2000b). Buffering in fuzzy geographic information systems. GMD Report 105, GMD. St. Augustin, Germany.

Guesgen, H. and Hertzberg, J. (2001). Algorithms for buffering fuzzy raster maps. In *Proceedings of FLAIRS-01* (pp. 542–546). Key West, Florida.

Guesgen, H., Hertzberg, J., Lobb, R., and Mantler, A. (2001). First steps towards buffering fuzzy maps with graphics hardware. In *Proceedings of FOIS-01 Workshop on Spatial Vagueness, Uncertainty and Granularity (SVUG-01)*. Ogunquit, Maine.

Guesgen, H. and Histed, J. (1996). Towards qualitative spatial reasoning in geographic information systems. In *Proceedings of AAAI-96 Workshop on Spatial and Temporal Reasoning* (pp. 39–46). Portland, Oregon.

Hoff, K., Culver, T., Keyser, J., Lin, M., and Manocha, D. (1999). Fast computation of generalized Voronoi diagrams using graphics hardware. In *Proceedings of SIGGRAPH-99* (pp. 277–286). Los Angeles, California.

Molenaar, M. (1996). The extensional uncertainty of spatial objects. In *Proceedings of SDH-96* (pp. 9B.1–13). Delft, The Netherlands.

Mustafa, N., Koutsofios, E., Krishnan, S., and Venkatasubramanian, S. (2001). Hardware-assisted view-dependent map simplification. In *Proceedings of The 17th ACM Symposium on Computational Geometry*. (pp 50–59). Medford, Massachusetts.

Peuquet, D. (1994). It's about time: A conceptual framework for the representation of temporal dynamics in geographic information systems. *Annals of the Association of American Geographers, 84*,441–461.

Plewe, B. (1997). A representation-oriented taxonomy of gradation. In Hirtle, S. and Frank, A. (Eds.), *Spatial information theory: A theoretical basis for GIS*, COSIT'97, Vol. 1329 Lecture Notes in Computer Science (pp. 121–136). Berlin, Germany: Springer.

Scott, D. (1992). *Multivariate density estimation: Theory, practice, and visualization*. Chichester, England: John Wiley & Sons.

Sinton, E. (1978). The inherent structure of information as a constraint to analysis: Mapped thematic data as a case study. In Dutton, G. (Ed.), *Harvard papers on geographic information systems* Vol. 6. Reading, Massachusetts: Addison-Wesley.

Usery, L. (1996). A conceptual framework and fuzzy set implementation for geographic features. In Burrough, P. and Frank, A. (Eds.), *Geographical objects with indeterminate boundaries*, GISDATA Series No. 2 (pp. 71–85). London, England: Taylor and Francis.

Zadeh, L. (1965). Fuzzy sets. *Information and Control, 8*,338–353.

SPATIAL COGNITION AND COMPUTATION, *3*(2&3), 221–237

Implications of a Data Reduction Framework to Assignment of Fuzzy Membership Values in Continuous Class Maps

Barry J. Kronenfeld
University at Buffalo (SUNY)

This paper develops a data reduction framework for assigning fuzzy membership values to continuous geographic data. The goal of classification is defined quantitatively using explicit criteria of error and confusion introduced by the classification process. A new method of assigning fuzzy membership values is designed to reduce overall error, and compared with standard, similarity-based methods. As a case study, a continuous forest-type map is created for an area of the northeastern United States using data from the U.S. Forest Service. Given certain reasonable assumptions regarding the interpretation of continuous classes, the new method is shown to provide small but consistent reductions in error and confusion. More generally, the data reduction framework provides explicit meaning to the use of continuous classes in ecological mapping, allowing for quantitative measurement of the error introduced by the classification process.

Keywords: continuous classification, fuzzy set theory, data reduction, fuzzy membership values, classification error, confusion index

A key question regarding the application of fuzzy set theory to geographic data has been how to assign class membership values to a given location that has a set of known underlying attribute values. Although various quantitative algorithms have been proposed, there is no general framework for evaluating the appropriateness of competing algorithms. Since the purpose of classification is to convey information, such evaluation should begin with an assessment of the information conveyed by each method. This leads to a fundamental question regarding fuzzy set theory: How should people extract information from a classification system in which each location is assigned simultaneously to more than one category? Answering this question explicitly provides a means of evaluating quantitative methods of continuous classification.

The use of class membership values to describe multivariate data has led several authors to observe that fuzzy set theory is implicitly a method of multivariate data reduction (Bezdek *et al.* 1983,Burrough & McDonnell 1998). If *m* relevant attributes are observed across the landscape, membership in a smaller set of *n* (*n<m*) classes is used to describe the landscape in a reduced form. The data reduction approach suggests a simple but useful criterion for evaluating a classification method: to minimize the difference between the original data and the classified representation.

In this paper I develop a quantitative framework for continuous classification based on an explicit procedure for interpreting class membership values. In order to capture the spatial complexity of ecological units as they occur in real-world mapping situations, data from the U.S. Forest Service is used to produce continuous forest region maps of the tri-state area of New York, Pennsylvania and New Jersey in the northeastern United States. The following two sections provide background to the concepts of continuous classification and the data used in the case study.

In the fourth section, the key ideas of a data reduction framework are presented. Three specific criteria are defined to evaluate procedures for quantitative classification: 1) overall classification error, 2) locational bias, and 3) tradeoff between accuracy and confusion. As an implementation of the data reduction framework, a new procedure for assigning class membership values, the *pairwise combination* method, is developed with the purpose of reducing overall classification error. The *pairwise combination* method is compared with the most common existing methods for assigning fuzzy membership values according to the criteria given. The results of the case study are presented and discussed in the final two sections.

Background

Fuzzy Set Theory

The common-sense notion of categories probably includes crisp partitions, non-spatial versions of the discrete lines that partition area-class maps. We "draw lines" between categories, and objects must neatly fall into one category or another. Rosch (1978) argued, however, that although categories must be clearly differentiated from one another for the purposes of cognitive economy, the formal delineation of boundary criteria is only one method for achieving this separation. A more common and less cumbersome method is to define prototypes representing the most typical attributes of a category. Prototype-based definitions are not new; in fact they are ubiquitous in multivariate data settings in the physical sciences. Most vegetation classification manuals, for example, describe in detail the species and structural features that one would expect to find in each vegetation type, but only general hints are given as to where to draw the line between one type and another (cf. UNESCO 1973). The key feature of prototype-based definitions is that they describe typical members of classes but do not provide explicit criteria for assigning observed entities into one class or another.

Fuzzy set theory is based on the observation that entities often do not fall neatly into a particular class, and is compatible with the graded prototypicality structure found in studies of cognitive categories (Rosch 1978). Classification using fuzzy sets can be broken into two steps: 1) class definition, and 2) assignment of class membership values. Classes are generally defined by specifying a precise vector of attribute values representing each class prototype. Membership of each location within a class is represented numerically by a class membership value ranging between 0 and 1 inclusive.

Methods for both classification steps are reviewed in Burrough & McDonnell (1998), who identify two general approaches. The *semantic import* approach is based on expert definition, and does not require quantitative data on underlying attributes. The data reduction framework applies to *natural* classification methods, in which attribute data is taken as input to compute optimal class prototypes and fuzzy membership values.

The most widely used natural classification procedure is the *fuzzy K-means* clustering algorithm (Bezdek et al 1983). Fuzzy K-means is a fuzzy version of discrete clustering algorithms, the objective of which is to determine data clusters that minimize total within-cluster variance and/or maximize between-cluster variance. The difference between fuzzy and ordinary K-means clustering is that in fuzzy K-means, variance within each cluster is computed as a weighted (as opposed to simple) average of the squared differences between each observation and the cluster mean. The weights used for each observation are the class membership values, which are computed as an inverse power function of distance to cluster centers.

An important parameter in fuzzy K-means clustering is the fuzzy exponent, q (Burrough & McDonnell 1998; denoted m in Bezdek et al 1983). The fuzzy exponent ranges from 1 to ∞, and affects both class definition and the assignment of membership values within each class. Class prototypes will be either more centered or more spread out in attribute space, and the steepness of the membership gradient between classes either can either be steep (approaching discrete classification) or gradual (with nearly equal membership in multiple classes over large areas) depending on the value of the fuzzy exponent (McBratney & de Gruijter 1992, McBratney & Moore 1985).

In using fuzzy sets to model geographic data, virtually all authors to date have constrained membership values to sum to one (cf. Bezdek *et al.* 1983, Burrough *et al.* 1992, Burrough 1996, but see Zhu 1997). This probably reflects a mental opposition of classes against one another within a classification scheme, emphasizing a negative or mutually exclusive relationship between classes (Freksa & Barkowski 1996). Summation constraints remove important information, however, on the degree to which the classification scheme as a whole is able to accurately describe a given unit of observation. A solution to this problem was given by McBratney & de Gruijter (1992), who introduced the concept of an *extragrade* class to capture the degree to which a data point is not well represented by the classification scheme; in their system, the sum of membership values in all classes *plus* the extragrade class must equal one.

Continuous Classification Fields

Although fuzzy set theory has frequently been applied to geographic data, the relation between spatial data structures and classification has received little attention. The purpose of spatial data structures is to generalize from an infinite number of geographic locations to a finite number of data elements. Two classes of generalization are widely recognized in geographic information systems: the *object* and *field* models.

Goodchild (1992) defined fields as data structures that assign a value to every possible location within a specified spatial domain, whereas objects are entities that populate the domain independently of one another. Although the individual spatial units (regions) that make up most ecological maps are often conceptualized as objects, in assigning of a nominal data value (a class) to every location within the spatial domain ecological maps correspond better to the field model (Mark 1999). Maps of ecological regions are not ordinarily thought of as fields, perhaps because the prototypical field representation consists of the distribution of a simple, numerical attribute, such as rainfall or elevation. Nevertheless, use of a nominal data value in maps of ecological regions is consistent with the field model.

Let us refer to the combination of a field-based spatial data structure with classification as a *classification field*. In this combination, the spatial data structure serves to generalize the geographic domain, while classification provides a method to generalize the attribute domain. When applied to geographic data, fuzzy sets can be said to produce a *continuous classification field*. Several authors have already chosen to use the term *continuous classification* as a better description of this process than *fuzzy sets* (McBratney & de Gruijter 1992, Burrough et al. 1992), emphasizing the descriptive utility of class membership values over the functional utility of fuzzy logic. A continuous classification field can be defined as any data structure that couples every location within a spatial domain to a set of membership values in a predefined set of classes.

Vagueness, Spatial Heterogeneity & Continuous Classification

Many solutions have been proposed to the general problem of fuzziness in geographic information, including supervaluation theory (Bennett 2001), evidence sets (Rocha 1999), and the egg-yolk representation of regions with indeterminate boundaries (Cohn & Gotts 1996). Two differences between these solutions and continuous classification will be noted:

1. Where other methods are formally precise, continuous classification is numerically precise.

2.   Most solutions deal with objects, whereas continuous classification creates a spatial field.

The precision of fuzzy sets has been a major source of criticism due to the fact that fuzzy set theory is often purported to address the problem of vagueness (or the related problems of imprecision & uncertainty; see Bennett 2001 for a good explanation of these concepts). In this paper, however, continuous classification is used as a tool for describing reality, and thus addresses the problems of gradation and spatial heterogeneity. Vagueness, uncertainty and imprecision here refer to characteristics of *descriptions* of reality, while gradation and spatial heterogeneity are seen as attributes of reality itself.

The problem of describing spatial heterogeneity is inherently grounded in a field-based conceptual model, and is thus different from the problem of modeling "objects with indeterminate boundaries." Any description, of course, may be more or less precise, vague or certain, and modeling these aspects of description is an important research challenge. These are meta-descriptive issues that are beyond the scope of the present paper.

It may be noted in this regard that a fairly weak form of fuzzy set theory is used in this paper. Haack (1996) distinguished between this weaker version, in which fuzzy membership values are used to describe entities, and a stronger version in which truth itself is measured in degrees. The use of logical operators such as fuzzy *union* and *intersection*, a key component of the application of fuzzy set theory to geographic analysis, depends on the logical formalism of the strong version. Recognizing this limitation, the term *continuous classification* (McBratney & de Gruijter 1992, Burrough & McDonnell 1998) is used in this paper to refer to the weaker form of fuzzy set theory. Nevertheless, any assessment of the truth of an assertion presupposes an understanding of *what* is being asserted. It is for this reason that a framework detailing the descriptive component of fuzzy set theory is important.

Case Study Preparation

Data

Data from the U.S. Forest Service Forest Inventory and Analysis (FIA) program was used to produce continuous forest-type maps for the area of New York, Pennsylvania and New Jersey in the northeastern United States. FIA data is compiled from periodic inventories conducted for every state in the United States, as mandated by Congress in the Forest and Rangeland Renewable Resources Planning Act of 1974 (Hansen *et al.* 1992). Data is currently available for free download on the world wide web at:

http://www.srsfia.usfs.msstate.edu/ewdata/

FIA data includes records of stand age and origin, and the species and diameter at breast height (dBh) of individual trees within each sample plot. Data from sample plots located in the tri-state area of New York, Pennsylvania and New Jersey was filtered to remove: a) saplings or small trees (<4 in. dBh), b) plots in immature forests (<30 yrs. old), and c) undersampled plots (w/ <15 trees/plot). After filtering, 4209 plots remained (Figure 1), with an average of 37 trees per plot. A total of 107 species were present in at least one sample plot.

Species were divided into 12 commonly known species groups for simplification purposes, with a 13th group, "other", reserved for species not included in any of the 12 main groups. At each plot, relative Importance Values (IV's) of each of the 13 species groups were computed. IV is a standard forestry measure of the percent composition of each species within an area, and was calculated as the average of 1) relative density (species count/total tree count), and 2) relative dominance (species basal area/total basal area).

Species group IV's were interpolated to a 350 x 333 cell raster grid (1 cell = 2 x 2 km) using inverse-distance squared interpolation. Although there is much uncertainty in these maps, this uncertainty was not considered in the present paper.

Class Definition

For all classification methods, seven classes were defined subjectively based on preliminary data exploration, but prior to classification. Each class was defined by a set of prototypical IVs for each of the 13 species groups.

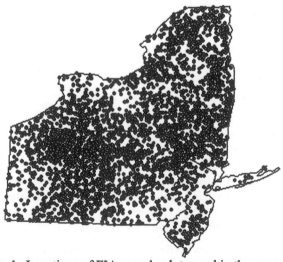

Figure 1. Locations of FIA sample plots used in the case study.

Classification Framework

Objectives

Let us suppose that a user is given a raster data set of class membership values assigned to each pixel in a number of well-defined classes. Suppose further that the user does not have access to the original attribute data – species group distributions in our case study - on which the classification was based. A reasonable goal of the classification system would be to allow the user to reconstruct the original data as accurately as possible. Any difference between the actual attribute values and an end user's reconstruction of those values at any location represents an error introduced by the classification process.

Given this primary criterion, a secondary goal of classification might be to provide a representation that is easy to interpret by the end user. It is reasonable to assume that discrete classification takes less effort to visualize and interpret than continuous classification. Thus, if continuous classification produces a more accurate representation, the "best" method will depend on the specific context of classification. We may provide a guideline for the map producer, however, by quantifying the tradeoff between accuracy on the one hand, and ease of interpretation on the other.

Criteria Definition

Let us first define *classification error* (E) as a measure of the inaccuracy of a classification. To define classification error computationally, it is necessary to specify how the end user is to reconstruct attribute values from class membership values. A simple but plausible method of interpreting class membership values was given by McBratney & Moore (1985) and Zhu (1997). Both authors suggested that attributes at any location could be reconstructed as a weighted average of class prototypes, using fuzzy membership as weights:

$$\hat{a}_i = \sum_{j=1}^{k} m_j c_{ij} \qquad (1)$$

where:

$\hat{a}_i$	=	reconstructed value of attribute i
k	=	total number of categories
m_j	=	membership value in class j
c_{ij}	=	value of attribute i in class j prototype

Let us define classification error *(E)* using a simple Euclidean measure of the difference between the actual and reconstructed attribute values at each location:

$$E = \sqrt{\sum (a - \hat{a})^2} \qquad (2)$$

Note that other measures of difference, such as Mahanolobis or Manhattan distance, could be substitued easily.

Next, let us define a *confusion index* (*CI*) to measure the difficulty in interpreting a classified location. Confusion indices are often used in fuzzy set theory to measure the degree to which a continuous classification differs from a discrete classification (membership of 1 in a single class, 0 in the remaining classes). Confusion indices are usually computed as a function of the two highest membership values (Burrough & McDonnell 1998), but this ignores information on membership in other classes. Here, a confusion index was devised to take into consideration all membership values at once:

$$CI = \left(1 - \sum_{j=1}^{k} m_j^2\right)\bigg/\left(1 - \frac{1}{k}\right) \tag{3}$$

CI ranges from 0 (discrete classification) to 1 (equal membership in all classes). One desirable property of this confusion index is that, given any vector of class membership values M, replacement of two membership values (m_a & m_b) with (m_a' & m_b') such that $|m_a' - m_b'| < |m_a - m_b|$ will always increase the value of the confusion index.

Assigning Fuzzy Membership Values

As noted above, continuous classification consists of the two steps of 1) class definition and 2) assignment of class membership values. Quantitative methods for each step may be developed to achieve the explicit objectives of a data reduction framework. For the purposes of this paper, three methods for assigning class membership values were compared within the context of a pre-determined category system. By focusing only on the assignment of class membership values, it is assumed that the performance of any specific algorithm should be independent of the initial set of classes used. Exploratory use of different sets of initial classes showed results similar to what follows, justifying this assumption.

Discrete model. The discrete model was used as a baseline for analysis, since it is the model most often used in forest type maps. A discrete model was represented with class membership values simply by assigning each pixel a membership value of 1 in the most similar category, and a membership value of 0 in each of the other categories.

Similarity Model. The similarity model is the basis of current quantitative methods to determined class membership values, including the fuzzy K-means clustering algorithm (Bezdek et al 1984), and is described more fully by Zhu (1997). First, a similarity index was calculated based on inverse distance to class prototypes:

$$s_k = \frac{1}{\sqrt{\sum_{i=1}^{n}(a_i - c_{ik})}} \qquad (4)$$

where: n =   total number of attributes (species)
a_i =   value (IV) of attribute (species) I
c_{ik} =   prototypical value (IV) of attribute (species) i
in class (forest type) k

The similarity index has a lower bound of zero, and no upper bound. Fuzzy membership values were calculated by normalizing these similarity indices with a fuzzy exponent:

$$m_k = s_k^q \Big/ \sum s^q \qquad (5)$$

The fuzzy exponent used here is simpler in form than that used in the fuzzy K-means clustering algorithm, owing to the fact that the problem of identifying optimal cluster centers (class prototypes) is not addressed here. In terms of the effect on class membership values, q here is equivalent to m in Bezdek et al (1984) except that the range is reversed. That is, the lowest value ($q=1$) will produce the most fuzzy classification, whereas higher values ($q\rightarrow\infty$) will produce more discrete classifications.

Pairwise Combination Method. Although the similarity model provides meaningful, quantitative information regarding the relationship between individual categories and the attributes at a given location, it ignores the utility of treating a set of categories as a cohesive system. The pairwise combination method was devised to take advantage of the fact that more than one category may be used in combination to describe the attributes of a location (Figure 2). First, each pair of categories was given a weight based on the inverse of the perpendicular distance between the pixel attribute values and the line intersecting the pair of category prototypes:

$$w_{ab} = \frac{1/d_{ab}}{\sum_{i=1}^{k}\sum_{j=1}^{k}1/d_{ij}} \qquad (6)$$

where: w_{ab} =   weight for category pair (A,B)
d_{ij} =   perpendicular distance (in attribute space)
from X to the line connecting categories i and j
(for example, d_{AB} in Figure 2)

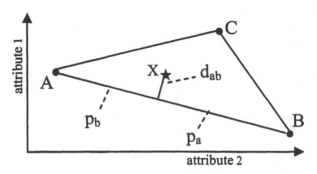

Figure 2. An entity (X) and three categories (A,B,C) in attribute space. Attribute values of X are poorly described by a simple similarity measure. Although the actual attribute values of X are most similar to category C, they can be better described as a mix of categories A and B.

Given these pair weights, membership values in each category were computed as:

$$m_a = \sum_{b=1}^{k} w_{ab} \times p_{a|b} / (p_{a|b} + p_{b|a}) \qquad (7)$$

where: $p_{a|b}$ =   the distance from category j to the nearest point to X on the line connecting categories i & j (for example, p_A, p_B in Figure 2)

Membership values were then normalized to sum to one:

$$m_j = (m_j)^q / \sum (m)^q \qquad (8)$$

The fuzzy exponent q was used to adjust the degree of fuzziness, as in the similarity method.

    Comparison. Indices of classification error and confusion (as defined above) were computed at each pixel for the discrete model and for both the similarity and pairwise combination methods of continuous classification for values of q ranging from 1 to 10. Note that the similarity method where (q = ∞) is mathematically equivalent to the discrete method of classification. Two types of error comparisons were made: 1) overall classification error was computed as the average of the classification error at each pixel, and 2) errors were mapped in order to detect locational bias.

Visualization. A simple but effective technique for visualizing fuzzy membership data was adopted from Goodchild et al (1994). Each category was assigned a single (legend) color, defined by RGB values; the color of each pixel was then computed as the weighted average of legend colors using class membership values as weights. Ideally, colors should be defined in a perceptual color space rather than RGB. Adequate results were achieved by a much simpler technique of differentially emphasizing the red, green and blue components when mixing colors. The resulting visualizations were important for conceptualizing the tradeoff between accuracy and confusion, providing a link between the abstract numerical value of the confusion index and the real difficulty encountered in interpreting continuously classified maps.

Results

The discrete map (Figure 3) produced relatively contiguous regions, and represents a reasonable facsimile of the product of current discrete mapping methods. The legend, shown in Figure 4, applies to both the discrete and fuzzy maps.

The similarity and pairwise combination methods of classification resulted in significantly different overall maps (Figure 5). The pairwise combination method produced lower values of *CI* and crisper maps than the similarity method at equal values of q. This was especially true for areas that did not fit well into the classification scheme, such as southern New Jersey (containing a number of southern species at their northern limit) and the area of high species variability to the northwest of the Adirondack region.

The average rate of error for the discrete map was 12.9%. Both continuous classification methods achieved lower rates of average classification error at optimal levels of the fuzzy exponent (Figure 6). As the fuzzy exponent decreased from $\propto$ to 1, error decrease to a minimal value, then rose again. Error

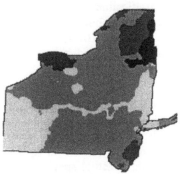

Figure 3. Discrete map of forest types in tri-state area.

▓	**Adirondack**	*(maple 28%, beech 22%, spruce 17%, birch 11%, aspen 4%, hemlock 4%, other 3%, ash 3%, cherry 3%, pine 3%, oak 2%, elm 1%, hickory 0%)*
▓	**Champlain**	*(maple 26%, hemlock 17%, pine 17%, birch 10%, beech 8%, other 6%, spruce 4%, ash 4%, aspen 2%, cherry 2%, elm 1%, oak 1%, hickory 0%)*
▓	**Dry Oak**	*(oak 40%, maple 17%, other 15%, birch 12%, ash 4%, hemlock 3%, pine 3%, hickory 2%, beech 2%, aspen 1%, cherry 1%, spruce 0%, elm 0%)*
▓	**Northern Hardwood**	*(maple 46%, beech 12%, hemlock 7%, birch 7%, oak 7%, other 6%, ash 5%, cherry 5%, aspen 2%, pine 2%, hickory 1%, spruce 0%, elm 0%)*
▓	**Lake Plain**	*(ash 25%, maple 23%, other 17%, hickory 7%, cherry 6%, beech 5%, oak 5%, hemlock 4%, elm 3%, aspen 3%, birch 2%, spruce 0%, pine 0%)*
▓	**Pine Barren**	*(pine 49%, oak 22%, other 16%, maple 10%, ash 1%, birch 1%, spruce 0%, hickory 0%, elm 0%, aspen 0%, beech 0%, hemlock 0%, cherry 0%)*
▓	**Allegheny**	*(maple 27%, oak 21%, cherry 13%, other 11%, hemlock 6%, elm 5%, hickory 4%, birch 4%, beech 3%, ash 3%, aspen 2%, pine 1%, spruce 0%)*

Figure 4. Forest type legend for Figures 3 & 5. Each forest type is defined by its prototypical species composition as shown.

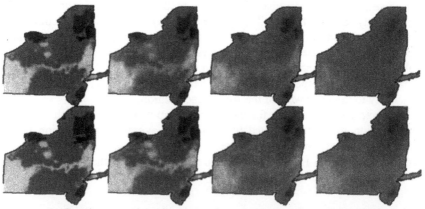

Figure 5. Continuous classification of study area using similarity (top) and pairwise combination (bottom) methods of assigning class membership values. Values of q from left to right are: 10, 4, 2, 1. Interpretation requires visual estimation of color combinations, and becomes more difficult as fuzziness increases.

under the similarity method at ($q=1$) was actually greater than the error of the discrete map. The pairwise combination method produced the most accurate classification overall, with a minimum overall error of 7.7% at ($q=1.9$). The accuracy of the similarity method peaked at ($q=3.0$) with an overall error of 8.3%. Figure 7 compares three actual species distributions chosen at random with reconstructions based on each classification method.

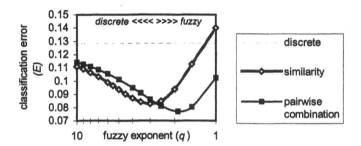

Figure 6. Effect of fuzzy exponent on classification error.   Error was minimized at *q*=3.0 for the *similarity* method, *q*=1.9 for the *pairwise combination* method.

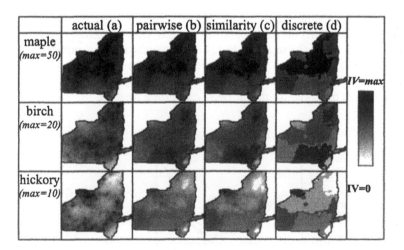

Figure 7. Evaluation of classification methods under a data reduction framework. Differences between actual and reconstructed distributions show the degree of error introduced by each method. Figure shows 3 groups selected at random from the 12 main species groups; fuzzy exponents of *q=1.9* and *q=3.0* were used for (b) and (c) respectively.

Locational bias was obvious in the map of the error distribution for the discrete classification (Figure 8a). Error was lowest towards the center of forest type regions and highest along the boundaries between forest types. For the continuous classification methods, high values of the fuzzy exponent produced significantly *lower* than average error along the boundaries between forest types as well as towards region centers. As the q was further decreased, the error distribution became increasingly random. This trend was observed for both the *similarity* and *pairwise estimation* methods.

Figure 9 plots overall error against the confusion index for each classification method. Error was minimized at $CI \approx 0.6$ for both methods, although this corresponded to different values of q. For every value of CI, the pairwise combination method slightly outperformed the similarity method.

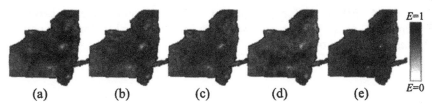

Figure 8. Locational bias. Maps of error distribution shown for discrete classification (left) and the *similarity method* with increasing fuzziness (q = 10, 5, 2, 1 from (b) to (e)). In (a), the greatest error occurred at regional boundaries. Error was least at regional boundaries in (b), with the error distribution becoming increasingly random in (c) through (e). A similar pattern was observed for the *pairwise estimation* method.

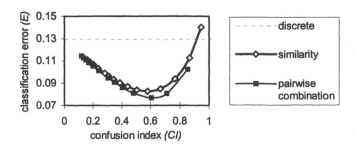

Figure 9. Tradeoff between accuracy and confusion. A map producer is able to choose any combination of error & confusion along the line between the upper left (crisp map) and the error minimum, which is achieved at $CI \approx 0.6$ for both the similarity and pairwise combination methods.

Discussion

If continuous classification is used to explicitly convey information about underlying attributes, then information loss can occur at one of three points in the communication process: 1) a map user may not be able to assess the fuzzy membership values at any given location, 2) a map user may not know how to interpret a given set of fuzzy membership values, or 3) the fuzzy membership values, even when interpreted correctly, may not accurately portray the attribute values at a location. These three sources of information loss correspond roughly to the terms *confusion, interpretation,* and *classification error.*

In terms of human users, confusion results from visual and cognitive processes, a thorough analysis of which is beyond the scope of this paper. However, two statements can be made from the maps in Figure 5. First, the general trend of greater difficulty in interpretation with higher values of the *confusion index* is apparent. Second, the difficulty in interpretation does not increase so quickly as to render the visualization method entirely ineffective. Thus, if visualization can be used as a surrogate for cognitive function, then it is reasonable to conclude that continuous maps can be more effective at conveying attribute information than discrete maps.

The question of how human users intuitively interpret a set of fuzzy membership values is an open one. The weighted-average method used here seems intuitive, and was the only proposed method that was encountered in the literature. However, other methods may be equally plausible; more research is needed in this area.

The third source of information loss is entirely dependent upon the method used for assigning class membership values, and thus can be termed *classification error.* Previous methods of assigning fuzzy membership values have not considered error in this context. Under the assumption of weighted-average interpretation, the *pairwise combination* method succeeded in producing less error than the widely used *similarity* method; the improvement was small but consistent. It should be noted that the *pairwise combination* method did not provide an optimal solution to the problem of minimizing classification error, but merely used a logical strategy to improve upon the *similarity method.*

Given an explicit method of interpretation, there will always be a tradeoff between the goals of minimizing confusion and classification error. Figure 9 demonstrates how this tradeoff can be quantified to provide a reference for a map producer to choose an appropriate fuzzy exponent. In the fuzzy K-means clustering algorithm, q has traditionally been chosen subjectively on the basis of trial and error, and has no theoretically optimum value (Bezdek *et al.* 1983). An external measure of classification error provides a means for defining such a theoretical optimum. The map producer can then choose from a continuum of possibilities ranging between a discrete map (high error, low confusion) to this optimal value (low error, high confusion).

The concept of data reduction can provide a useful framework for minimizing error in unsupervised computational procedures for continuous classification. Although this paper presented one specific implementation (the *pairwise combination* method) as an example, the framework is intended to be a general one. Variation in the interpretation procedure and the measure of *classification error* will produce different contexts for optimization. Furthermore, various strategies may be employed to minimize error, both in terms of defining class prototypes and assigning class membership values. It is hoped that the overall framework will lead to more explicit models of the continuous classification process.

Acknowledgement

This project is supported by IGERT award DGE-9870668 from the National Science Foundation and by the University at Buffalo. Support from NSF is gratefully acknowledged.

References

Bennett, B. (2001). What is a forest? On the vagueness of certain geographic concepts. *Topoi, 20*, 189–201.

Bezdek, J. C., Ehrlich, R. & Full, W. E. (1983). FCM: The fuzzy c-means clustering algorithm. *Computers & Geosciences, 10*, 191–203.

Burrough, P. A. (1996). Natural objects with indeterminate boundaries. In P. A. Burrough & A. W. Frank (Eds.), *Geographic objects with indeterminate boundaries*. London: Taylor & Francis.

Burrough, P. A. & McDonnell, R. A. (1998). *Principles of geographical information systems*. New York: Oxford University Press.

Cohn, A. G. & Gotts, N. M. (1996). The egg-yolk representation of regions with indeterminate boundaries. In P. A. Burrough & A. W. Frank (Eds.), *Geographic objects with indeterminate boundaries* (pp. 171–187). London: Taylor & Francis.

Freksa, C. & Barkowsky, T. (1996). On the relations between spatial concepts and geographic objects. In P. A. Burrough & A. W. Frank (Eds.), *geographic objects with indeterminate boundaries* (pp. 109-121). London: Taylor & Francis.

Goodchild, M. F. (1992). Geographical Data Modeling. *Computers & Geosciences, 18*, 401–408.

Goodchild, M. F., Chih-chang, L. & Leung, Y. (1994). Visualizing fuzzy maps. In H. Hearnshaw & D. Unwin (Eds.), *Visualization in geographical information systems*. New York: Wiley.

Haack, S. (1996). *Deviant logic, fuzzy logic*. Chicago: University of Chicago Press.

Hansen, M. H., Frieswyk, T., Glover, J. F. & Kelly, J. F. (1992). The Eastwide Forest Inventory Data Base: Users Manual. General Technical Report NC-151 (pp. 1–48). St. Paul, MN, U.S. Department of Agriculture, Forest Service, North Central Forest Experiment Station.

Mark, D. M. (1999). Spatial representation: a cognitive view. In D. Maguire, M. F. Goodchild, D. Rhind & P. Longley (Eds.), *Geographical information systems: Principles and applications* (pp. 81–89). Chichester: Wiley.

McBratney, A. B. & de Gruijter, J. J. (1992). A continuum approach to soil classification by modified fuzzy k-means with extragrades. *Journal of Soil Science, 43*, 159–175.

McBratney, A. B. & Moore, A. W. (1985). Application of fuzzy sets to climatic classification. *Agricultural and Forest Meteorology, 35*, 165–185.

Rocha, L. M. (1999). Evidence sets: modeling subjective categories. *International Journal of General Systems, 27*, 457–494.

Rosch, E. (1978). Principles of Categorization. In E. Rosch & B. B. Lloyd (Eds.), *Cognition and categorization*. Hillsdale, NJ: Lawrence Erlbaum Associates.

UNESCO (1973). *International classification and mapping of vegetation.* UNESCO, Switzerland.

Zadeh, L. A. (1965). Fuzzy sets. *Information and Control, 8*, 338–353.

Zhu, A.-X. (1997). A similarity model for representing soil spatial information. *Geoderma, 77*, 217–242.

SPATIAL COGNITION AND COMPUTATION, *3*(2&3), 239–255

Cognitive Evidence of Vagueness Associated with some Linguistic Terms in Descriptions of Spatial Relations

F. Benjamin Zhan
Southwest Texas State University

When describing spatial relations, humans often use qualitative linguistic terms. For example, it is fairly common for people to say "Region Q covers Region R a little bit." Unfortunately, current Geographic Information Systems (GIS) do not have the intelligence to directly represent and process linguistic descriptions containing qualitative linguistic terms such as 'a little bit,' 'somewhat,' 'nearly completely,' and 'completely.' An important step in developing more natural GIS that can process natural language-based queries is to quantify these qualitative linguistic terms. The purpose of this study is to find out how much of Region Q is covering Region R if "Region Q covers Region R a little bit, somewhat, or nearly completely" through experiments with people. Based on the experiments, it is concluded that (1) if the ratio between the area of region R covered by region Q and the area of region R is 0.50 or less, then one usually says "Region Q covers Region R a little bit," (2) if the ratio is greater than or equal to 0.15 but less than 0.70, then it is somewhat, and (3) if the ratio is greater than or equal to 0.55 but less than 1.00, then it is nearly completely.

Keywords: spatial relations, GIScience, fuzzy set, linguistic terms

---

Correspondence concerning this article should be addressed to Benjamin Zhan, Texas Center for Geographic Information Science, Department of Geography, Southwest Texas State University, San Marcos, TX 78666; e-mail: zhan@swt.edu

1   Introduction

A better understanding of how humans describe spatial relations is a key issue in the development of adequate models for representing and processing spatial relations in a computing environment such as Geographic Information Systems (GIS). While describing spatial relations, humans often tend to use qualitative terms. For example, in the case of topological relations between two regions, the degree of "region Q covering region R" can be described using *qualitative terms* in the four statements given below.

(1) Region Q covers region R *a little bit*;
(2) Region Q covers region R *somewhat*;
(3) Region Q *nearly completely* covers region R;
(4) Region Q *completely* covers region R.

In the rest of this paper, these four statements, in the order of appearance as shown above, will be called the first, second, third, and fourth statement. In addition, the qualitative terms in the four statements above will be called "qualitative linguistic terms." Using qualitative linguistic terms such as *a little bit, somewhat, nearly completely*, and *completely* in descriptions of spatial relations is very natural to humans, and people have little difficulty, if any, understanding each other as to "how much" is "a little bit" in these descriptions. This seemingly very intuitive and simple task can be hard to handle by a computer because current GIS are not *intelligent* enough to present and process topological relations described by statements containing qualitative linguistic terms. For example, it is still a fairly difficult task for current GIS to directly process the query given below.

"In the given area, find all polygons classified as soil type *S* that are *nearly completely* covered by vegetation *V*."

The main obstacle is that existing GIS do not have the "intelligence" to "understand" how much "nearly completely" is. The only way to accommodate this type of query in GIS is to build the necessary intelligence in GIS so that it can 'understand' qualitative linguistic terms in some systematic way. Long-term research issues in this area include what capabilities are expected from such an intelligent GIS, and what appropriate computational procedures would need to be built in a GIS in order to support these capabilities. The first step toward developing more natural GIS that are capable of handling this type of query is to try to understand better how the human mind processes linguistic descriptions containing qualitative terms. Only then can one develop adequate mathematical and computational models of qualitative spatial relations that can be used to represent and process those qualitative terms typically used by humans in GIS.

The focus of this study is to find out how much of Region Q is covering Region R if "Region Q covers Region R *"a little bit," "somewhat," "nearly completely,"* or *"completely"* in the four statements mentioned above. Intuitively, people use these qualitative linguistic terms to describe the relative size of the area of Region R covered by Region Q. This relative size can often be measured by dividing the area of Region R covered by Region Q by the entire area of Region R. In the spatial relation of region Q covering region R, three areas can be distinguished: the area of Region Q (denoted as A_Q), the area of Region R (denoted as A_R), and the area covered by the overlapping portion of Regions Q and R (denoted as A_O). The area-based ratio (R_A) is defined as the ratio between A_O and A_R. The support of the intuition that people use the linguistic terms based on the area-based ratio defined above is yet to be confirmed through experiments. Nevertheless, the author used this intuition and attempted to quantify the four qualitative linguistic terms through experiments with people. As a first step along this line of research, this study mainly focuses on regions without holes in relation to the four qualitative linguistic terms mentioned above

Although it is highly desirable to develop a GIS with the capabilities of understanding how much of Region Q is covering Region R if "Region Q covers Region R 'a little bit,' 'somewhat,' 'nearly completely,' or 'completely,'" it is possible that users of a GIS may prefer to have the GIS ask a user to specify what percentage of coverage the user is interested in. In that case, the user bears the burden of interpreting any natural language descriptions indicating the degrees of 'Region Q covering Region R' and translates the descriptions to different percentages of coverage. It should be emphasized that the focus of this discussion is on the concepts of 'covering a little bit,' 'covering somewhat,' and 'covering nearly completely.' It is not the intention of this study to address the vagueness related to the terms of 'a little bit,' 'somewhat,' and 'nearly completely' in other contexts. Therefore, results related to the area-based ratios corresponding to the qualitative linguistic terms obtained in this study will only hold in the context of 'one region covering another region.'

The work reported in this study falls within the general research area of spatial relations, an area that has received the attention of many scholars in the past 28 years (see, e.g., Freeman 1975; Peuquet and Zhan 1988; Egenhofer and Franzosa 1991; Mark and Egenhofer 1994). The study reported in this article is closely related to the understanding of the vague nature in the ways in which humans describe spatial relations and the development of models that can be used to represent and process vague descriptions of spatial relations in GIS. Past work along this line of research has been mainly related to the applications of fuzzy sets in modeling vague spatial objects and vague spatial relations (e.g., Freeman 1975; Rosenfeld 1979; Dubois and Jaulent 1987; Robinson 1990; Burrough and Frank 1991; Krishnapuram *et al.* 1993; Zhan 1998; Schneider 2000). The significance of linguistic descriptions of spatial relations and the roles of linguistic descriptions in helping us understand how humans process spatial relations have long been recognized (see, e.g., Talmy 1983; Mark 1989; Mark and Frank 1991; Shariff *et al.* 1998; Landau and Jackondoff 1993). However, there has been very limited published work on the cognitive aspect of qualitative linguistic terms in descriptions of spatial relations and the quantification of qualitative linguistic terms. This study addresses this issue.

In the remainder of this discussion, I will first discuss the experimental design and the methodologies used to analyze the responses obtained in the experiments in Section 2. Sections 3, 4, and 5 present the results. Conclusions and discussions are provided in Section 6.

2   Research Design and Method of Analysis

Three experiments were designed for this study. Experiment One aimed at finding the range of area-based ratios for each of the qualitative linguistic terms. For this experiment, subjects were given 10 diagrams showing different degrees of region Q covering region R. In the stimuli, Region Q was represented by a circle and Region R was depicted by an ellipse. These two shapes make the two regions easily distinguishable. The degrees of 'Region Q covering Region R' in the stimuli were set arbitrarily but with a clear progression in the degrees of coverage from Diagram 1 to Diagram 10. The four statements introduced above were put next to each of the 10 diagrams. These four statements are labeled A, B, C, D in the stimuli given to the participants of the experiment, i.e., (A) Region Q covers Region R a little bit; (B) Region Q covers Region R somewhat; (C) Region Q nearly completely covers Region R; (D) Region Q completely covers Region R. The 10 diagrams and the four statements are shown in Figure 1. The written instructions presented to the subjects who participated in Experiment One are given below.

> **Instructions to participants of Experiment One:**
> "On the next two pages, there are 10 diagrams showing different degrees of 'Region Q covers Region R.' For each diagram, there are four statements next to it. Please choose one and only one statement from the four statements that best describes the degree of 'Region Q covers Region R' in each diagram."

While arranging the 10 diagrams in the experiment, the author made sure that the progression of the degree of Region Q covering Region R in the diagrams was not the same as the sequence in which the diagrams appeared in the experiment. The 10 figures are put in a randomized sequence. That same sequence was presented to every participant.

It was clear from the results of Experiment One that there is no vagueness involved when the term 'completely' is used. This result was expected. Thus, the term 'completely' was not further tested in Experiments Two and Three. Experiment two was designed to obtain the average area-based ratio corresponding to each of the linguistic terms. For this experiment, subjects were given an example of Region Q (a circle) and an example of Region R (an ellipse) as well as the first three of the four statements. The subjects were then

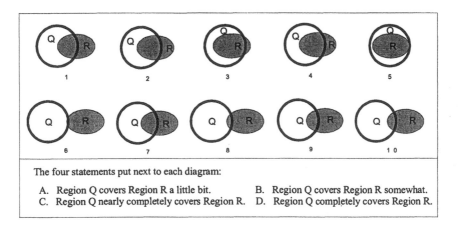

The four statements put next to each diagram:

A. Region Q covers Region R a little bit.   B. Region Q covers Region R somewhat.
C. Region Q nearly completely covers Region R. D. Region Q completely covers Region R.

Figure 1. Stimuli used in Experiment One (Note: The number below each stimulus indicates the order in which the stimuli were presented to the participants; the four statements were placed next to each stimulus).

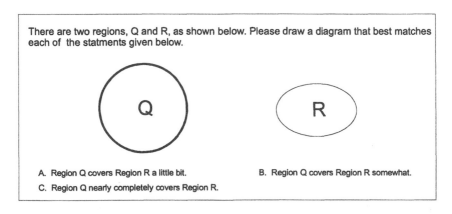

Figure 2. Instructions and Stimuli used in Experiment Two (Note: In the experiment, more space was left after each statement for a participant to make their drawings. No space is left in this figure in order to make better use of journal space.).

asked to draw one diagram that best matches each of the three statements. Figure 2 shows the instructions and stimuli used in Experiment Two.

The objective of Experiment Three was to test whether polygons with different shapes would have an effect on area-based ratios corresponding to the three linguistic terms. Experiment Three was conducted in three steps. In each

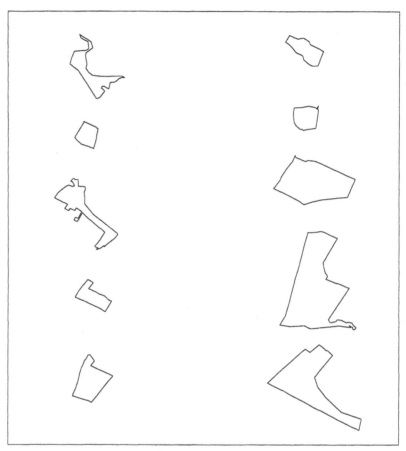

Figure 3. Stimuli used in Experiment Three

step, a set of 10 irregularly shaped polygons, extracted from U. S. census tracts in Travis County, Texas, were presented to the participants. These 10 polygons were arranged into two columns as shown in Figure 3 and presented in the same way to each participant in all three steps. The instructions used in the first step of Experiment Three are given below. For the second and third step, the instructions were the same except that the keyword 'a little bit' was changed to either 'somewhat' or 'nearly completely' accordingly.

Instructions to participants of Experiment Three: "On the computer screen, you will see a graphic containing ten irregularly shaped polygons arranged in two columns of five objects each. Using the computer mouse to point, click, and drag, move the five polygons from the left column, one at a

time, so that one of the polygons from the left column
covers one (and only one) of the polygons in the right
column *a little bit*. Any polygon from the left column may
be moved to cover any polygon in the right column."

All participants in the three experiments are graduate and undergraduate students at Southwest Texas State University. The participants were not paid. Stimuli used in Experiment One, all drawings in Experiment Two, and responses from Experiment Three were scanned and saved as TIFF image files. These image files were then imported to the ArcView GIS package in order to measure the A_R and A_O for each case and relate them to each corresponding stimulus in Experiment One, every drawing of two polygons in Experiment Two, and each pair of polygons in Experiment Three. Responses from all three experiments were analyzed based on the area-based ratio defined in the introduction section of this article. The area-based ratio associated with each of the 10 diagrams in Experiment One was calculated from the scanned images. For Experiment Two, the area-based ratio corresponding to each of the drawings produced by the participants was obtained from the scanned images. The area-based ratio corresponding to each pair of overlapping polygons produced by the participants in Experiment Three was also obtained from the scanned images.

3   Results from Experiment One

A total of 41 useful responses for Experiment One were obtained. Results from the responses are summarized in Table 1. For each of the four statements associated with the 10 diagrams, the number and percentage of subjects who chose that particular statement are given in Table 1. The area-based ratios corresponding to the 10 diagrams are also provided in the rightmost column of Table 1. As can be seen in Table 1, nearly all subjects chose the first statement of "Region Q covers Region R a little bit" for diagrams 1 and 2. The area-based ratios for diagrams 1 and 2 are 0.01 and 0.08. Some subjects also picked up diagrams 3 to 6 for this statement (Table 1). Among these participants, 31 out of the 41 participants selected diagram 4 for the first statement. Diagram 4 has an area-based ratio of 0.27. One subject chose diagram 10 for the first statement, which presumably was an error.

The distribution of the number of participants who selected a particular diagram for the statement of "Region Q covers Region R somewhat" is more complex compared to that of the statement of "Region Q covers Region R a little bit". The diagram picked up by most subjects (39 out of 41) for this statement was diagram 6 with an area-based ratio of 0.50. In addition, diagrams 3 and 5 were also picked up by 83% of the subjects. The two diagrams that were not chosen by any subject are diagrams 2 and 10 (Table 1).

For the statement of "Region Q nearly completely covers Region R," it was clear that most subjects (40 out of 41) selected diagram 9, which had an area-

Table 1

Results of Experiment One: Participants' choices of the four statements related to each of the ten diagrams

Stimuli		No. of subjects that chose the description				Percentage of subjects that chose the description				Area based ratio of `Q covers R` in the stimuli
ID	Diagram	A	B	C	D	A	B	C	D	
1	Q R	40	1			98%	2%			0.01
2	Q R	41				100%				0.08
3	Q R	7	34			17%	83%			0.15
4	Q R	31	10			76%	24%			0.27
5	Q R	6	34	1		15%	83%	2%		0.39
6	Q R	2	39			5%	95%			0.50
7	Q R		27	14			66%	34%		0.65
8	Q R		18	22	1		44%	54%	2%	0.70
9	Q R		1	40			2%	98%		0.90
10	Q R	1		1	39	2%		2%	95%	0.99

A. Region Q covers Region R a little bit.   B. Region Q covers Region R somewhat.
C. Region Q nearly completely covers Region R.   D. Region Q completely covers Region R.

based ratio of 0.90 (Table 1). In addition, some subjects also selected diagrams 5, 7, 8, and 10 for this statement. Almost all participants felt that diagram 10 is the diagram corresponding to the statement "Region Q completely covers Region R" with the exception of one subject who chose diagram 8 for this statement.

Table 2
Results from Experiment One

Qualitative linguistic term	Range of area-based ratio (RA)	Most agreed area-based ratio (RA)
A little bit	RA < 0.50	0.08
Somewhat	0.15 <= RA <= 0.70	0.50
Nearly completely	0.65 <= RA <= 0.90	0.90
Completely	RA = 1.00	1.00

Results from Experiment One give us some evidence to suggest that (1) the area-based ratio corresponding to the statement "Region Q covers Region R a little bit" may be as high as 0.50, but for the vast majority of people, the ratio should be less than 0.10; (2) the area-based ratio corresponding to the statement "Region Q covers Region R somewhat" may range from 0.15 to 0.70 with 0.50 as the most agreed ratio for the statement; (3) the range of area-based ratio corresponding to the statement of "Region Q nearly completely covers Region R" is between 0.50 and 1.00, and the vast majority of people believe that it is fine to say "Region Q nearly completely covers Region R" when the ratio reaches 0.90; and (4)) if the area-based ratio is 1.00, then it is definite that almost all people think "Region Q covers Region R completely." These results are summarized in Table 2.

4 Results from Experiment Two

A total of 32 useful responses were obtained from Experiment Two. One set of example drawings from a subject related to Experiment Two is shown in Figure 4. Area-based ratios related to those responses were calculated and are summarized in Table 3. As can be seen in Table 3, the mean area-based ratio related to the first statement, "Region Q covers Region R a little bit," is 0.10 with a standard deviation of 0.07; the average ratio related to the second statement, "Region Q covers Region R somewhat," is 0.36 with a standard deviation of 0.10; the average ratio related to the third statement, "Region Q nearly completely covers Region R," is 0.74 with a standard deviation of 0.18. The minimum area-based ratio for the first, second, and third statement are 0.02, 0.13, and 0.25, respectively. The maximum area-based ratio for the first, second, and third statement are 0.29, 0.55, and 1.00.

These results are fairly consistent with the results obtained in Experiment One. Based on the mean, the standard deviation, and the maximum values in the

1. Region Q covers Region R a little bit.

2. Region Q covers Region R somewhat.

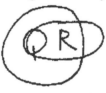

3. Region Q covers Region R nearly completely.

Figure 4. Example drawings by a participant in Experiment Two.

area-based ratios, the results from Experiment Two suggest that (1) if the area-based ratio is roughly 0.74, then one typically say "Region Q nearly completely covers Region R." Based on the resulting area-based ratios from the two experiments (Tables 2 and 3), the intervals of the area-based ratios and the average area-based ratios for each of the three qualitative linguistic terms are summarized in Table 4.

5   Results of Experiment Three: The Effect of Polygon Shape

The remaining question is to determine whether polygons with different shapes would significantly affect the results obtained from Experiments One and Two. A total of 32 useful responses were obtained from Experiment Three. In this case, a response is defined as any pair of polygons that was put together by a subject. A set of example responses is given in Figure 5.

Table 3

Results of Experiment Two

Subject ID	A_{R1}	A_{O1}	R_{A1}	A_{R2}	A_{O2}	R_{A2}	A_{R3}	A_{O3}	R_{A3}
1	15510.5	1790.2	0.12	22687.8	10927.5	0.48	14698.3	12114.2	0.82
2	27373.1	2289.4	0.08	29005.7	12615.5	0.43	22867.8	17450.1	0.76
3	10162.4	585.3	0.06	10554.9	1414.2	0.13	7943.0	6383.4	0.80
4	7500.4	1245.3	0.17	9782.7	3435.9	0.35	7906.3	6354.6	0.80
5	32243.2	2724.9	0.08	22243.2	4990.2	0.22	13443.8	10975.6	0.82
6	25755.0	1258.4	0.05	22295.5	6293.1	0.28	27421.9	24525.5	0.89
7	3121.3	78.1	0.03	3986.8	1433.2	0.36	7697.3	3238.9	0.42
8	3594.9	279.5	0.08	4015.3	1574.5	0.39	2281.4	2284.4	1.00
9	1279.7	63.3	0.05	1047.9	259.9	0.25	638.4	561.9	0.88
10	1464.0	419.6	0.29	849.7	420.5	0.49	1901.8	1477.7	0.78
11	1681.1	356.5	0.21	1950.0	1021.2	0.52	2012.5	1663.9	0.83
12	1390.2	358.1	0.26	1527.1	582.7	0.38	1202.4	970.2	0.81
13	1839.3	108.7	0.06	3003.1	707.7	0.24	2380.0	1625.4	0.68
14	2651.3	181.3	0.07	1054.1	423.0	0.40	879.5	220.4	0.25
15	2115.1	152.1	0.07	2243.0	549.4	0.24	3058.6	2074.2	0.68
16	2490.7	179.3	0.07	1404.7	449.3	0.32	1971.6	1697.1	0.86
17	777.0	110.3	0.14	1174.7	271.8	0.23	1208.7	1078.6	0.89
18	3114.1	252.6	0.08	3406.7	943.1	0.28	2007.1	858.3	0.43
19	3240.6	251.1	0.08	2364.9	1192.7	0.50	2142.4	1673.3	0.78
20	1090.4	74.1	0.07	1841.7	497.6	0.27	1123.5	683.2	0.61
21	3446.9	138.8	0.04	3615.8	1978.2	0.55	3278.6	3009.9	0.92
22	2353.7	485.0	0.21	1909.5	977.9	0.51	1909.5	977.9	0.51
23	584.8	47.0	0.08	584.7	248.4	0.42	522.0	326.4	0.63
24	2561.7	169.6	0.07	1876.8	604.4	0.32	1689.8	1478.0	0.87
25	2936.5	627.2	0.21	3302.8	1195.7	0.36	3652.8	2303.2	0.63
26	3718.2	200.0	0.05	3498.2	1707.9	0.49	4037.2	3638.8	0.90
27	1196.5	167.7	0.14	1050.9	346.0	0.33	909.8	837.9	0.92
28	2871.1	197.4	0.07	2158.6	705.6	0.33	2283.2	1869.9	0.82
29	3077.7	71.9	0.02	2820.3	844.1	0.30	2827.9	2008.7	0.71
30	3716.7	287.6	0.08	2275.7	1116.2	0.49	2896.4	2466.4	0.85
31	3035.9	223.0	0.07	2218.8	628.8	0.28	1630.5	1039.0	0.64
32	425.7	31.4	0.07	526.4	138.5	0.26	889.3	498.3	0.56
Average			0.10			0.36			0.74
StdDev			0.07			0.10			0.18
Min			0.02			0.13			0.25
Max			0.29			0.55			1.00

Note. Area-based ratios corresponding to the drawings from the subjects (A_{Ri}, - the area covered by Region R in the drawings corresponding to the ith statement; A_{Oi} - the area covered by the overlapping portion of Regions Q and R in the drawings corresponding to the ith statement; R_{Ai} – area-based ratio in the drawings corresponding to the ith statement).

Table 4
Overall Results of Experiments One and Two

Qualitative linguistic term	Interval of area-based ratio	Average area-based ratio
A little bit	$0 < RA1 < 0.50$	$RA1 = 0.10$
Somewhat	$0.15 <= RA2 <= 0.70$	$RA2 = 0.36$
Nearly completely	$0.55 <= RA3 < 1.00$	$RA3 = 0.74$

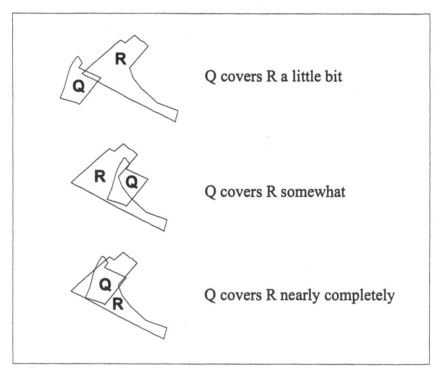

Figure 5. Examples of responses in Experiment Three (Note: Texts were added by the author for illustration purposes).

The area-based ratios for these responses were calculated. The resulting area-based ratios are summarized in Table 5. It can be seen from Table 5 that the mean area-based ratio is 0.08 for 'a little bit,' 0.24 for 'somewhat,' and 0.53 for 'nearly completely.' A *t* test was performed to test whether the corresponding means of the area-based ratios from Experiments Two and Three are

Table 5

Area-based Ratios of the Responses in Experiment Three

Response ID	A_{R1}	A_{O1}	R_{A1}	A_{R2}	A_{O2}	R_{A2}	A_{R3}	A_{O3}	R_{A3}
1	7570.9	1251.3	0.17	7570.9	4643.2	0.61	7570.9	5021.6	0.66
2	5338.2	1985.6	0.37	5338.2	3435.2	0.64	5338.2	5051.5	0.95
3	32197.4	1760.1	0.05	32197.4	5087.1	0.16	32197.4	9487.9	0.29
4	50212.2	2580.3	0.05	50212.2	7856.2	0.16	50212.2	9778.6	0.19
5	33192.8	963.0	0.03	33192.8	6321.0	0.19	33192.8	11833.6	0.36
6	7570.9	896.1	0.12	7570.9	2208.1	0.29	5338.2	5060.7	0.95
7	32197.4	561.6	0.02	32197.4	4096.1	0.13	33192.8	12290.7	0.37
8	50212.2	3302.5	0.07	50212.2	6810.0	0.14	7570.9	5217.7	0.69
9	33192.8	996.4	0.03	33192.8	3964.2	0.12	5338.2	4214.8	0.79
10	32197.4	6941.5	0.22	33192.8	8884.2	0.27	33192.8	11809.8	0.36
11	7570.9	1176.6	0.16	32197.4	12172.7	0.38	33192.8	11711.7	0.35
12	5338.2	938.0	0.18	50212.2	10676.3	0.21	7570.9	5420.2	0.72
13	32197.4	834.0	0.03	33192.8	12241.6	0.37	5338.2	4854.2	0.91
14	7570.9	676.9	0.09	32197.4	8391.7	0.26	33192.8	8427.5	0.25
15	5338.2	821.0	0.15	50212.2	1636.7	0.03	7570.9	5436.8	0.72
16	32197.4	278.7	0.01	33192.8	4757.7	0.14	5338.2	4937.6	0.92
17	50212.2	886.1	0.02	7570.9	2151.2	0.28	32197.4	12297.3	0.38
18	33192.8	560.4	0.02	32197.4	7296.1	0.23	50212.2	10620.0	0.21
19	5338.2	371.9	0.07	33192.8	3945.5	0.12	33192.8	12437.5	0.37
20	50212.2	656.9	0.01	7570.9	1948.2	0.26	7570.9	5202.9	0.69
21	33192.8	1634.8	0.05	5338.2	2761.5	0.52	5338.2	5005.6	0.94
22	5338.2	768.1	0.14	50212.2	4065.4	0.08	50212.2	12285.6	0.24
23	32197.4	1796.9	0.06	33192.8	5723.5	0.17	33192.8	9240.3	0.28
24	50212.2	1287.0	0.03	7570.9	1152.2	0.15	7570.9	5511.9	0.73
25	33192.8	1997.2	0.06	5338.2	1846.5	0.35	5338.2	4912.1	0.92
26	7570.9	212.8	0.03	32197.4	1729.2	0.05	32197.4	12263.5	0.38
27	5338.2	508.2	0.10	50212.2	5869.3	0.12	50212.2	6651.6	0.13
28	32197.4	1689.8	0.05	33192.8	7587.3	0.23	33192.8	8915.5	0.27
29	50212.2	512.5	0.01	7570.9	2525.5	0.33	7570.9	4481.8	0.59
30	33192.8	1694.8	0.05	5338.2	2579.9	0.48	5338.2	4450.7	0.83
31	5338.2	808.2	0.15	50212.2	5322.0	0.11	50212.2	12656.0	0.25
32	32197.4	636.7	0.02	33192.8	7646.9	0.23	33192.8	12435.8	0.37
Average			0.08			0.24			0.53
StdDev			0.08			0.15			0.27
Min			0.01			0.03			0.13
Max			0.37			0.64			0.95

Note. A_{Ri} - the area covered by a polygon in the right column of Figure 3; A_{Oi} - the area covered by the overlapping portion of a pair of polygons put together by a subject; R_{Ai} – area-based ratios.   The numbers in the subscripts indicate different approximate linguistic terms: a little bit (i=1), somewhat (i=2), and nearly completely (i=3).

Table 6

Comparison of the Means Corresponding to Each of the Three Linguistic Terms in Experiments One and Two Using a t-test (n_1=32, n_2=32; df=62)

	A little bit	Somewhat	Nearly completely
Results from Experiment Two			
Mean	0.10	0.36	0.74
Standard deviation	0.07	0.10	0.18
Results from Experiment Three			
Mean	0.08	0.24	0.53
Standard deviation	0.08	0.15	0.27
Results of t-test			
t value	1.05	3.72	3.62

significantly different. The results of the *t* test are given in Table 6. Based on the *t*-values, the means of area-based ratios corresponding to the statement 'Region Q covers Region R a little bit' from the two experiments are not significantly different (*t*=1.05, α=0.05). However, the means of area-based ratios corresponding to the statement 'Region Q covers Region R somewhat' are significantly different (*t* =3.72, α=0.01), and so are the means of area-based ratios corresponding to the statement ' Region Q covers Region R nearly completely' (*t* =3.62, α=0.01). These results suggest that polygon shape does not have an effect when the linguistic term 'a little bit' is used to describe the degree of 'Region Q covering R,' but polygon shape does have an effect when linguistic terms such as 'somewhat' and 'nearly completely' are used to describe the degree of 'Region Q covering R.'

One may notice from the examples shown in Figure 5 that the graphics appear more like 'R covering Q' rather than 'Q covering R' after the participant moved Polygon Q to cover Polygon R based on the instructions of the experiment. It is possible that the relative size of the polygons to cover and to be covered may also have an effect on the area-based ratio corresponding to different linguistic terms. However, it should be pointed out that the instructions given to the participants clearly stated that only polygons are to be moved to cover polygons in the right column (Figure 3). Therefore, whether or not the polygon size has an effect on the results is an issue subject to further investigation.

6 Conclusion and Discussion

The goal of this study was to quantify several qualitative linguistic terms such as 'a little bit,' 'somewhat,' and 'nearly completely' in descriptions involving varying degrees of 'Region Q covering Region R.' The results from the experiments presented in the previous sections can be summarized in Figure 6.

In the graphic shown in Figure 6, it is assumed that the area-based ratio corresponding to each of the three linguistic terms decreases linearly from the mean of area-based ratios to both ends of the range of that area-based ratio. The results suggest that one can definitely say 'Region Q covers Region R a little bit' if the area-based ratio is less than 0.10, but it is possible that some people would still consider that 'Region Q covers Region R a little bit' even if the area-based ratio is as high as 0.50. On average, people would consider 'Region Q covering Region R somewhat' if Region Q covers 36% of the area of Region R, but that percentage could range from 15% to 70%. If the percentage of coverage is more than 74%, then on average people would consider that 'Region Q covers Region R nearly completely' although in some cases that percentage may be as low as 55%.

It was evident from the experiment that polygon shape does not have a significant effect when the statement 'Region Q covers Region R a little bit' is used to describe the degree of 'Region Q covering Region R.' However polygon shape does have an effect when the statements 'Region Q covers Region R somewhat' and 'Region Q covers Region R nearly completely' are used. The findings are important because they suggest that polygons with different shapes have to be treated differently in a GIS when developing computational procedures to process queries related to descriptions involving different qualitative linguistic terms. How to treat polygons with different shapes differently in a GIS is an important area for further research.

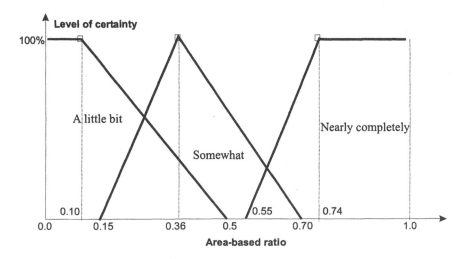

Figure 6. The ranges of values corresponding to three linguistic terms: `a little bit,' `somewhat,' and `nearly completely.'

It is important to recognize that the results are only valid in the context of one region covering another region. The results provide some cognitive evidence toward the development of computational procedures in a GIS that can be used to process queries related to linguistic descriptions corresponding to Region Q covering Region R a little bit, somewhat, or nearly completely. For the example given at the beginning of this discussion, all polygons classified as soil type S with 74% or more of their areas covered by vegetation V are considered "nearly completely" covered by vegetation V.

The results also clearly demonstrate that there are no precise and definite values associated with each of the three qualitative linguistic terms: 'a little bit,' 'somewhat,' and 'nearly completely' when they are used to describe different degrees of Region Q covering Region R. In fact, there are overlapping areas in the ranges of the area-based ratios corresponding to the three terms (Figure 6). While the purpose of this discussion is to find the range and the mean value associated with each of the three qualitative linguistic terms, the vagueness associated with the qualitative linguistic terms gives rise to some compelling research issues. These issues include what capabilities should be expected from a GIS when dealing with queries associated with descriptions involving qualitative linguistic terms, and what are the appropriate methods in a GIS that can be used to address the vagueness associated with descriptions of spatial relations involving qualitative terms. These are important issues that warrant further research.

In addition, there are several other important research issues that remain to be addressed in future research. The first extension is to determine how more complex regions with holes would affect the results. Secondly, additional qualitative linguistic terms (e.g., Region Q *almost* covers Region R) will need to be tested. Third, it is possible that the results may be different when humans describe regions of different phenomena (e.g., regions covered by vegetation versus regions flooded by water). Therefore, additional tests need to be conducted to validate the values in other situations. Fourth, it is not clear from this study as to how the relative size of the two regions involved would affect area-based ratios corresponding to different linguistic terms. Finally, computational procedures must be developed so that the values obtained in the experiments can be used in GIS to answer queries from a GIS user. These issues are currently under study and will be reported elsewhere.

Acknowledgments

Part of this study was presented at the *Joint COSIT-FOIS Workshop on Spatial Vagueness, Uncertainty and Granularity*. The author wishes to thank several referees whose suggestions on earlier versions of this article helped shape the article to its current form. Assistance from Ellen Lewis and Melissa Gray in helping conduct the experiments and preparing this article is greatly appreciated. The author is grateful to everyone who participated in the experiments.

References

Burrough, P., and Frank, A. U., (Eds.) (1996). *Geographic objects with indeterminate boundaries*. London: Taylor and Francis.

Dubois, D., Jaulent, M.-C. (1987). A general approach to parameter evaluation in fuzzy digital pictures. *Pattern Recognition Letters, 6*, 251–259.

Egenhofer, M. J., Franzosa, R. (1991). Point-set topological spatial relations. *International Journal of Geographical Information Systems, 5*, 161–174.

Freeman, J. (1975). The modeling of spatial relations. *Computer Graphics and Image Processing, 4*, 156–171.

Krishnapuram, R., Keller, J. M., Ma, Y. (1993). Quantitative analysis of properties and spatial relations of fuzzy image regions. *IEEE Transactions on Fuzzy Systems, 1*, 222–233.

Mark, D. M. (1989). Languages of Spatial Relations: Researchable Questions and NCGIA Research Agenda. Report 89-2A (Santa Barbara, California: National Center for Geographic Information and Analysis).

Mark, D. M., and Frank, A. U. (1991). *Cognitive and linguistic aspects of geographic space*. Dordrecht: Kluwer.

Peuquet, D J, and Zhan C-X. (1987). An algorithm to determine the directional relationship between arbitrarily-shaped polygons in the plane. *Pattern Recognition, 20*, 65–74.

Robinson, V. B. (1990). Interactive machine acquisition of a fuzzy spatial relation. *Computers and Geosciences, 16*, 857–872.

Rosenfeld, A. (1979). Fuzzy digital topology. *Information and Control, 40*, 76–87.

Schneider, M. (2000). Metric operations on fuzzy spatial objects in databases. In Li, K-J., Makki, K., Pissinou, N., Ravada, S. (eds.): *Proceedings of 8th ACM Symposium on Geographic Information Systems (ACM GIS)* (pp. 21–26).

Shariff, A. R., Egenhofer, M. J., and Mark, D. M. (1998). Natural-language spatial relations between linear and areal objects: the topology and metric of English-language terms. *International Journal of Geographical Information Science, 11*, 215–246.

Talmy, L. (1983). How language structures space. In H. L. Pick, Jr. and L. P. Acredolo (Eds.), *Spatial orientation: Theory, research and application* (pp. 225–282). New York: Plenum.

Zhan, F. B. (1998). Approximate analysis of topological relations between geographic regions with indeterminate boundaries. *Soft Computing, 2*, 28–34.